MIKE ADAMS' GREATEST HITS

100 Chart-Topping Columns

COMPILED AND NARRATED
BY
DAVID ADAMS

Ballast Books, LLC
www.ballastbooks.com

Copyright © 2024 by David Adams

First Edition

All rights reserved. No part of this book may be reproduced in any form or by any electronic or mechanical means, including information storage and retrieval systems, without permission in writing from the publisher, except by reviewers, who may quote brief passages in a review.

ISBN: 979-8-8692-2841-3

Printed in the United States of America

Published by Ballast Books
www.ballastbooks.com

For more information, bulk orders, appearances, or speaking requests, please email: info@ballastbooks.com

CONTENTS

Introduction..1
1 – UNC-Wilmington Feminists Abort Free Speech..........5
2 – With Liberty and Comfort for All...................8
3 – Of Holt and Hypocrisy.............................13
4 – The Abolition of Tenure...........................17
5 – My Last Lecture...................................21
6 – How to Talk to an Atheist (and You Must)..........25
7 – An Anti-Communist Reading List....................28
8 – My Presidential Acceptance Speech.................37
9 – Academic Insanity, Part 184.......................41
10 – Light in August..................................46
11 – Life and How to Live It, Part V..................50
12 – I Had a Dream....................................54
13 – I Don't Have Enough Faith to Be an Atheist.......57
14 – Unconscious Racism...............................62
15 – Philippians 4:13.................................66

16 – The End of Affirmative Action 70
17 – The Ten Commandments of Charity 74
18 – How to Read the New Testament 78
19 – Why Johnny's Sociology Professor Will Die in Obscurity . . 82
20 – Life and How to Live It, Part IX. .87
21 – Life and How to Live It, Part X 92
22 – Understanding Atheism 97
23 – Feminism Means Never Having to Say You're Sorry . . .102
24 – If I Ran the Zoo. 108
25 – How I Bombed an Abortion Clinic and Still Got Tenure . . 112
26 – Sea of Faces 116
27 – The Shadow Proves the Sunshine 120
28 – Primary and Secondary Racism 124
29 – Anarchy in UNC 129
30 – The Nature of Conservatism. 133
31 – Mike's Peak 137
32 – Does Fort Worth Ever Cross Your Mind? 142
33 – Two Kinds of Atheists 145
34 – Your Unsolicited Letter of Recommendation 149
35 – I Think; Therefore, We Should. 155
36 – Gibson Guitars. 159
37 – Life and How to Live It, Part XI. 163
38 – For the Love of Marx 167

39 – The Price Is Wrong........................171
40 – Life Chose Me............................175
41 – Arguments Do Not Have Testicles..........182
42 – How Obama Earned My Doctorate............186
43 – When Students Cheat, Liberals Retreat....190
44 – Unlearning Liberty.......................194
45 – Stand For Life...........................199
46 – The Enemy Within.........................204
47 – An Embarrassment to Higher Education.....208
48 – Teaching to the Ten......................212
49 – Defining Life............................217
50 – Standing at the Summit...................221
51 – Do Something.............................224
52 – Hello, Stranger..........................228
53 – Hands Up, Don't Abort....................233
54 – This Is Providence.......................237
55 – Pharisees and Pharaohs...................240
56 – Prayer and Preparation...................244
57 – Pride and Perjury........................248
58 – To Speak the Truth.......................251
59 – Our People...............................255
60 – Fifty....................................259
61 – Fat, Ugly, and Morally Inconsistent......266

62 – ESPN: The Enlightened Socialist Progressive Network..270
63 – Don't Blame Simpson Release on "Broken System" 274
64 – Get Out of My Class and Leave America 279
65 – Stuck on Hating Whitey 284
66 – Life and How to Live It, Part XII..................287
67 – You Are Not Alone 292
68 – Dead Things Don't Grow 296
69 – Imagine Heaven..............................300
70 – Onward Christian Pansies 306
71 – Silencing Whitey 310
72 – The Ferguson Effect 314
73 – Fascists & Theocrats..........................318
74 – Ministers of Multiculturalism....................322
75 – Academic Elites and Ignoble Duchesses 326
76 – Choose My Words Carefully 331
77 – The Last Birthday Card 335
78 – How to Kill Everyone on Welfare................338
79 – Professor Hypocrite, Tear Down This Door!.........342
80 – Life Lines...................................346
81 – My New Victim-Centered Tuition Proposal 350
82 – Never Underestimate a Father's Love 354
83 – Letter to an Aging Communist...................358
84 – Cowards in the Academic Trenches 362

85 – The Buck Stops Here 366
86 – Bold About What. 369
87 – Starkville Pride. 373
88 – Liberal Ideology Is an Incapable Guardian 377
89 – My Preferred Pronouns. 381
90 – How to Deal with Transgendered Students. 385
91 – Toxic White Heteronormative Femininity 389
92 – Cultural Appropriation 101 .393
93 – Bob and the Burning Research Lab 397
94 – Victoria's Secret 401
95 – Life and How to Live It, Part XIII 405
96 – My New Spread the Wealth Grading Policy 409
97 – Everlasting Life on Death Row. 412
98 – Two Kinds of Pro-Choice Advocates. 417
99 – The Third Stage of Academic Lunacy 422
100 – White Man Can't Breathe. .426
Bonus Chapter – The Last Communion. 430
Afterword. 435
Acknowledgments 437
Index 438

Introduction

Welcome to Mike Adams' Greatest Hits. *This is Mike's older brother and only sibling, David. In 2023, I published a book called* Life and How to Live It, *which was a selection of mostly autobiographical columns by Mike, into which I infused my narrative (which is italicized like it is in this book). The focus was on his life—specifically, his academic, spiritual, political, moral, and social transformations and how he inspired countless individuals throughout his lifetime.*

This book, as the title implies, is simply a collection of the best columns, regardless of the topic, presented in the order in which they were written. Thus, there is some overlap between the two books and among the ideas included within. Life and How to Live It *contains some material that is not in this book, but most of the columns in this book are not in the other.*

Also in 2023, I published his unfinished manuscript Aborting Free Speech, *which is what he was working on when he passed. As the title implies, it is about the intersection of the abortion issue and freedom of speech. More specifically, it addresses the efforts of abortion activists to shut down debate by suppressing the speech of those who dissent.*

In 2013, Mike published Letters to a Young Progressive. *In his words:* The book is written to a former student of mine. He was an angry, obnoxious, arrogant kid who hated his country. His father was a farmer in the Piedmont who never went to college.

He plowed fields for decades to afford to send his kids to college. What happened? This student wasn't the same person. He rebelled against his family and his values. He was not happy. He was angry about things that weren't even true. He had an outburst in my class one day in the spring of 2010. I told him, "Man, I wish I could have a talk with you about the crazy nonsense that you're fuming about." And I told him I would hate it if he were lost for seventeen years like I was. I told him it was inappropriate for me to have a political or religious or worldview conversation with him while he's in my class, but I asked him if he would mind if I wrote him a letter afterwards. In May, I wrote a letter to him, and I sent it. Then, I said, "That's not a letter—that's a book," and called my book agent. So the book is to him. In a sense, it's me writing to myself, sharing what I wish I would have known. But it's also for parents, a guide for what to do when your kid goes off to college in August and comes home for Thanksgiving and you can't have a conversation because he's defensive and angry. Well, here's the book. I wrote it for that purpose.

In 2008, Mike published Feminists Say the Darndest Things, *and in 2004, he published his first book,* Welcome to the Ivory Tower of Babel. *Both of these are largely exposés of his experiences in academia.*

Disclaimer: Some columns herein are edited for brevity.

Follow Mike's legacy on Facebook:

https://www.facebook.com/mike.s.adams.904

https://www.facebook.com/profile.php?id=100044217140167

CHAPTER 1

UNC-Wilmington Feminists Abort Free Speech

June 28, 2002

This also appears in the books Life and How to Live It *(2023) and* Welcome to the Ivory Tower of Babel *(2004).*

When a new women's resource center was established at my university (UNC-Wilmington) *[UNCW]*, I was concerned that it would serve as more of a resource for feminist professors than for female students. I also suspected that the center would try to advance a "pro-choice" agenda with little tolerance for the views of pro-life advocates.

Those suspicions were confirmed during my recent visit to the center's website. I noticed that the center claimed a dedication to education and advocacy on a variety of issues facing women of "all backgrounds, beliefs, and orientations." It also claimed an interest in working with many community-based organizations and in maintaining "clear lines of communication" between the students and "any organizations involved." Despite all that, the site gives contact information for the "pro-choice" Planned

Parenthood, while Life Line, a "pro-life" center, is conspicuously not mentioned.

I contacted the site's manager with a simple request for the center to add Life Line's contact information near that of Planned Parenthood, and I was directed to Dr. Kathleen Berkeley. Berkeley had pushed for the establishment of the women's resource center and is in charge of the center until its first official director assumes her duties in July. After a few days of deliberation and meeting with the dean, Berkeley denied my request, stating "the addition of Life Line Pregnancy Center would duplicate information provided by Planned Parenthood."

Of course, there is no "non-duplication requirement" for organizations posting information on the center's website. For example, the site features two community organizations offering rape crisis counseling—and no reasonable person could object to that kind of "duplication." Surely, if someone built a second domestic violence shelter in town, the center wouldn't deny a request to list it for "duplication." Not only is this supposed "non-duplication" standard nonexistent and unworkable, but it is also utterly inapplicable to the case at hand.

The differences between Life Line and Planned Parenthood are far greater than their similarities. The decision to keep Life Line's information away from students is yet another silly episode revealing the fundamental dishonesty of the university's so-called commitment to diversity. It is no accident that the university library has Planned Parenthood's response to Bernard Nathanson's film *The Silent Scream* and a book by Berkeley referring to *The Silent Scream* as "grisly sensationalism"—but not *The Silent Scream* itself. The university appears to prefer students reading reviews offered from one perspective than looking at the original—there's a risk the students might come up with a different opinion.

The problem with higher education today is not that people are unaware that the diversity movement is dishonest. It's that among those people with reasonable objections to the diversity agenda, there are too few willing to do something about it. Administrators at public universities simply have no right to take money from taxpayers and use it to advance their own political causes while systematically suppressing the views of their opponents.

I hope everyone reading this article will "duplicate" my efforts to expand the marketplace of ideas at their local university. If your tax dollars are being used to support a one-sided view on the issue of abortion, respectfully ask for information on the other side to be included. If you are denied, take your case before the court of public opinion or, if necessary, a court of law. After all, the right to free speech is older than the "right to choose." And censorship is decidedly "anti-choice."

In his twenty-seven years as a UNCW professor, Mike taught several thousand students in the classroom. In his twelve summers at Summit Ministries, it is estimated that he spoke to 15,000 students. In his seventeen years as a columnist, he extended his reach beyond the classroom to hundreds of thousands of readers.

This early column was not his first, but it is significant because it was so well-received that it helped him get hired by Townhall *in 2003 and later by* Daily Wire. *He would write up to one hundred columns a year until he passed away in 2020.*

The UNCW administration's hatred of Mike's columns ultimately resulted in the federal court case you will read about in Chapter 54 through Chapter 59.

CHAPTER 2

With Liberty and Comfort for All

March 29, 2004

Well, I suppose it had to happen. After eleven years of teaching at a public university *[UNCW]*, I finally got a call from one of my superiors informing me that I had made one of my coworkers feel "uncomfortable" in the workplace. For those who may not know, the right to feel "comfortable" at all times trumps the First Amendment at most public universities.

Naturally, when I found out that I had made a coworker feel "uncomfortable," I wanted to know what I had said or done to produce such an unthinkable result. That was when I learned that the "discomfort" occurred because I had been discussing some of my weekly columns here in the workplace (*i.e.*, at the public university). The penalty for that transgression was simple: a ban on discussing my columns in the office in front of those who might be offended by my opinions. This was accompanied by the shocking revelation that "not everyone sees things the way you do, Mike."

When it first hit me that while in the office I could no longer talk about gay rights, feminism, religion, Darwinism, affirmative action, or any issue I discuss in my columns, I was outraged. In fact, I got so mad that I raised my voice before storming out of my superior's office. I never thought that the right of each university employee to feel comfortable at all times would ever actually be enforced against me here in the workplace (aka the public university).

But after I thought about it for a while, my anger turned to elation. Surely, the power to trump the First Amendment rights of others in response to "discomfort" is available to all employees, not just a select few. Since that must be the case (because our public university is committed to equality), I decided to make a list of every situation I had encountered at UNC-Wilmington where I felt "uncomfortable."

Armed with such a list, university administrators can now identify and silence the responsible parties, and I can enjoy the right to life, liberty, and the pursuit of unmitigated comfort. The following list isn't yet complete, but I thought that I would share some highlights since I'm not allowed to talk to anyone in the office (here at the public university) about these issues:

- My first year at UNCW, a faculty member in our department objected to a job candidate because he was "a little too white male." Such comments make me feel really uncomfortable, being a white guy and all that.
- My second year at UNCW, we removed a white woman from our interview pool in order to make room for a black woman. When the university forced me to discriminate on the basis of race, I felt really uncomfortable.
- My third year at UNCW, someone suggested that we should reject a job candidate because he was "too

religious." It sure makes me feel uncomfortable when people say things like that.

- My fourth year at UNCW, someone objected to a job candidate because she felt that the husband played too dominant a role in the candidate's marriage. It also makes me feel uncomfortable when people say things like that.

- Then, there are all the times that the name Jesus Christ has been used as a form of profanity in the office. That makes me feel uncomfortable. By the way, I am especially offended by the phrase "Jesus f***ing Christ!" I mean, no one ever says "Mu-f***ing-hammad!" or "f***ing Buddha!," do they?

- Then, there was the time that a gay activist in our department suggested that I switch to bisexuality in order to double my chances of finding a suitable "partner." That made me feel uncomfortable, and she knew it. After I started to blush, she asked, "What's the matter? Are you a little homophobic?" So what if I don't think you can change your sexual orientation as easily as your underwear? Is that so wrong? Do I really have a phobia?

- And how about the time that a faculty member called another faculty member a "mother-f***er" in one of our meetings? That was before he said that he should have climbed over the desk and "slapped the s*** out of him." These sociologists need to start getting along with one another if they plan to build a utopian society. Plus, it makes me feel really uncomfortable to hear about these threats of violence in the workplace.

- Then, there's the professor in our department who thinks that I am trying to poison her with tear gas. A few years ago, the police questioned me about breaking into her office and spraying chemicals. That was a pretty uncomfortable situation. I think it even qualifies as a Maalox moment. By the way, how long do I have to work with this woman? She makes me feel very uncomfortable. *[Mike elaborates on this in Chapter 9, "Academic Insanity, Part 184."]*

- And then there was the time that the university attorney read two of my personal emails against my objections. Do you have any idea how uncomfortable that made me feel? That's a long story that you can read about in my new book [Welcome to the Ivory Tower of Babel], which I am not trying shamelessly to promote. I know that capitalism makes a lot of my colleagues feel uncomfortable.

- A member of the UNCW board of trustees has been heard calling people "white trash" and making other racist statements in public. She has to vote on my next promotion as well as the promotion of every other professor at the university. That makes me feel a little uncomfortable, still being a white guy and all that. Maybe my race makes her feel uncomfortable, but some of us can't afford to change the color of our skin.

Well, that covers the first ten items on my list. I have over two hundred more to go, but I'm getting a crick in my neck from writing all of this down. It's only 10:51 a.m. (EST), but I think I'll call it a day. I can't work unless I feel perfectly comfortable, both physically and emotionally, at all times.

I'll be back in the morning. In the meantime, the university needs to start rounding up all of the people who are interfering with my life, liberty, and pursuit of absolute comfort. I hope that no one will feel uncomfortable when they are reprimanded for making me feel uncomfortable.

I know that if everyone follows my lead, free speech will die here at our local university. But at least everyone will feel comfortable at all times. I guess that's all that really matters.

Mike's first two books, Welcome to the Ivory Tower of Babel *and* Feminists Say the Darndest Things, *are filled with stories like these.*

Mike would have to endure another sixteen years of this before he passed away in 2020. In fact, it would only get worse, and in future columns, he would write more about this hostile work environment. This would be one of several convergent issues that caused him to give up on life.

Chapter 3

Of Holt and Hypocrisy

December 13, 2004

Wythe Holt, a law professor at the University of Alabama, is a self-proclaimed defender of the First Amendment. In 2002, Professor Holt came to the aid of a young black female, who had been censored by officials at her high school in Huntsville, Alabama.

The student, Kohl Fallin, had written a poem comparing blacks and whites with the following line: "We are worth more than your pale white skin. Not a penny less but a thousand billion pennies more." She also described the way she felt when racist remarks were directed towards her by whites: "When I hear these words come out of your mouth it makes me want to slap the white off you and leave you with some sense."

After using this highly charged language, Fallin ended her poem on a more positive note: "If you spent your time focusing on ways we are alike instead of ways you think we are inferior to you, then you would see what we are really about, and you may then define us with words because you will know just how precious and priceless we really are."

After officials at Huntsville's Lee High School banned the poem from publication in a student magazine, Professor Holt wrote a letter to the board of education. In his letter, he suggested that the poem should be published and that the school should apologize to Fallin for stifling her right to express her frustrations with perceived white racism.

And Professor Holt was right.

I thought that the poem contained good and bad speech and, thus, served as a reminder of the two principal dangers of censorship. The first danger is the suppression of good speech. The second is the suppression of an appreciation for good speech, fostered by exposure to bad speech. But judging between good and bad speech is the role of individuals, not governments.

To the best of my knowledge, the Kohl Fallin case represents the last time that Professor Holt has been right on a First Amendment issue. Since then, he has not only been wrong but dangerously irresponsible in his approach to free expression.

In 2002, when a group of professors at the University of Alabama opposed a mandatory sensitivity training program, Professor Holt was incensed. After dissenting faculty contacted state representatives to oppose funding for the Orwellian initiative, Holt decided to launch an investigation of them. Launching an investigation of citizens for "petition(ing) the Government for a redress of grievances" would be foolish for anyone to consider. The idea that such an investigation would be launched by a law professor is more than foolish. It is cause for serious concern.

In 2003, Professor Holt declined to oppose a campus ban on flags because he viewed the Confederate flag to be inflammatory and offensive. This was despite the fact that the ban applied to other flags such as the American flag. It took an uprising among students to teach the administration that the ban was unconstitutional. They won a victory for the First Amendment without the support of Wythe Holt, the self-proclaimed defender of free speech.

If passive aggression towards free expression were Professor Holt's only error, this column would not be necessary. But now, Holt is actively involved in an attempt to systematically ban ideas he finds offensive at Alabama's flagship institution. The attempt takes the form of a new ban on "any behavior which demeans or reduces an individual based on group affiliation or personal characteristics or which promotes hate or discrimination."

Professor Holt's new campus speech code is so overly broad and vague that it stands no chance of passing constitutional muster if fully implemented and challenged. I am one of many who will not rest until a war against this initiative is fully engaged in both the court of public opinion and in a court of law. When clearly unnecessary and illegal speech codes are drafted for purposes of intimidation, justice demands no less.

Wythe Holt, like so many others in academia, fails to understand that free expression is a process, not a result. Public discourse cannot be rigged to guarantee certain results for certain groups contingent upon their present popularity with the powers that be.

Our Constitution demands that the government remain uninvolved in the marketplace of ideas whenever possible. Whenever government involvement in matters of free expression is necessary, it must take the form of facilitation that is viewpoint neutral. It cannot take the form of manipulation that is ideologically motivated.

Put simply, our commitment to the First Amendment is best shown when we reluctantly support those who contradict our views, not when we enthusiastically support those who share them.

It appeared for a time that Wythe Holt understood that principle. But now the public knows better. Because of his actions, precious freedoms are in danger at Alabama's flagship institution. Come to think of it, this isn't the first time.

Mike was a defender of free speech. Period. Right or left. This was not the first or last time he defended the free speech of someone he disagreed with. It is tragic that his adversaries did not acknowledge this and ironic that the left wanted to silence someone who was committed to defending their own freedom of speech—a value once shared.

Chapter 4

The Abolition of Tenure

December 27, 2004

After every article I write lamenting the deplorable state of higher education, I get letters from readers that say, "Thank God for tenure." I guess that many have concluded that tenure is solely responsible for my continued employment at the institution I so frequently criticize. I don't see it that way.

Over the last couple of years, my columns have been read by millions of people. Fortunately, many of my readers are among the finest lawyers in the United States of America. Some of those lawyers have now become my good friends. Put simply, I buy my ink by the barrel, and I have far better lawyers than those employed in the UNC system. That's why I don't have to feign respect for the people that employ me just to keep my job.

However, my opposition to tenure isn't based solely upon my belief that it does nothing for me. It is based instead on the problems I believe that it causes for me and for others on a daily basis.

Sometimes the problems caused by tenure are minor. For example, some untenured professors incessantly brown-nose me before they have gotten my vote for tenure. After they find out they have achieved tenure, the same professors will hardly smile or say "hello" when they pass me in the hallway. They become rude and withdrawn almost overnight. And suddenly, they show up late for every department meeting, they answer cell phones in the middle of committee meetings, and so on.

Worse than the way the newly tenured treat their colleagues is the way they become suddenly inaccessible to students. I will grant that few ever worked a forty-hour week before tenure, but some will never work a twenty-hour week after tenure. There are tenured professors I know who never come to work before noon. In one extreme case, a professor down the hall from me is so absent that I have considered putting a sign on my door saying, "No, I have NOT seen your professor today!" It wouldn't have much of an impact on our relationship since I only see that professor about twice a semester.

Then, there are the really extreme cases of incivility, which are produced by tenure. Recently, a tenured professor publicly accused me of creating a "hostile work environment" for writing an article exposing her for making a false accusation of sexual harassment against another professor. In her mind, a false accusation of sexual harassment is only false if no one talks about it. When they do, the false harassment becomes real because it is difficult to work in a place where people stigmatize you for filing false sexual harassment charges.

Idiocy of this magnitude is difficult to discover unless you spend time with tenured professors. Usually, untenured professors are capable of the same degree of idiocy but manage to keep it hidden until there is no chance that it will get them fired.

Of course, there is a "moral turpitude" clause that can technically be used to fire a tenured professor. A UNC professor was once fired under this clause after he was caught having sex with a male prostitute in a downtown alley. The second time he was arrested, the officer was a student. It was a real Maalox moment for everyone involved.

If the same incident happened today, the student/police officer would be expelled for sexually harassing (arresting) the gay professor. The gay activists who run the campus diversity movement have successfully put the notion of "moral turpitude" to rest. One result is that tenured professors can now file numerous false accusations of sexual harassment with impunity.

While these reasons are all good enough to abolish tenure, the best one is called (if only by me) the "McCarthy Effect." Put simply, this effect explains how the abolition of tenure would do a better job of rooting communists out of government work than Senator Joe McCarthy did in his entire career. Better still, it would do so without a single false accusation against an innocent party.

In order to understand the "McCarthy Effect," one needs to understand the concept of sample selection bias. One must also understand that communists are inherently needy. They are not drawn to communism because of the part of the doctrine that says, "from each according to his ability." They are attracted, instead, by the part that says, "to each according to his need." In other words, they are lazy people who do not want to compete in order to get ahead in society. Instead, they want to do as little as possible without any prospect of ending up with nothing. They believe that communism will afford them this opportunity.

But since the fall of the Berlin Wall, many have had to seek an alternative to the communist ideal. And many have found that alternative at the American university. Of course, when Marxists become professors, they do have to work for several years to get tenure. While it may not be perfect, they know that things will be better after tenure. Paychecks, pensions, and health benefits will be provided, regardless of productivity.

Many of those who are unfit for any job besides that of a tenured professor would be unemployed and homeless if we abolished tenure tomorrow. Without tenure, these people would not be such an irritation at work, although they would probably be just as irritating as panhandlers once their unemployment checks ran out.

Tenure is supposed to foster academic freedom on our nation's campuses. Instead, it fosters socialism, laziness, and incivility. I would enjoy my job a lot more without it. And more importantly, our children would get a much better education.

I suspect the title is in reference to The Abolition of Man *by C.S. Lewis.*

The next column, Chapter 5, "My Last Lecture," is a follow-up to this column.

Chapter 5

My Last Lecture

January 3, 2005

May 2, 2023, 2:00 p.m., EST:

I am so glad that all—well, nearly all—of my students showed up today for my last lecture as a college professor. I can hardly believe that it has been thirty years since I started teaching at the university level. It seems like just yesterday that I walked into my first lecture and a student named Patrick Boykin asked if my name was "Doogie Howser, MD." I was just twenty-eight then and too young to consider it a compliment. Although I still talk to Patrick from time to time, he doesn't call me that anymore.

As you know, things were rough for me for a few years before the revolution really took hold on our nation's campuses. After I turned away from atheism and liberalism, I began fighting the war on ideological bigotry and intolerance with a small number of supporters. It was a war that no one thought we could win. It was a war that I might not have joined if I had to go it alone.

Now that we have accomplished nearly all that we set out to accomplish, I find myself looking back in search of a turning point in the revolution. While several points were pivotal, the most crucial turning point came in the fall of 2007. That is when the first state decided, through legislative action, to abolish tenure. When it first happened, I could hardly believe it. Even more shocking was the snowball effect that would follow. Who would have ever thought that in just six short years, tenure would become a thing of the past in America? As you will recall, California was the last state to abolish tenure in 2013.

The most profound effects of the abolition of tenure occurred indirectly. There were not many professors fired in the wake of that historical national movement. Scores of professors predictably quit, or retired early, in protest. Others simply became more productive overnight. But more than anything, the number of people seeking jobs in public higher education declined. And that ended up becoming the principal benefit of the abolition of tenure.

When the size of the professoriate shrank, it was not an even reduction across disciplines. In our nation's schools of business and engineering, for example, there was a small reduction in the size of most departments. But those departments universally reported increases in productivity, despite their smaller size. Within the colleges of arts and sciences, there was a similar effect in some departments like chemistry and physics.

Disciplines like English were hit harder. For years before the movement, English professors were teaching just about everything but English. Many of them were recruited to direct the women's centers, gay and lesbian centers, and other branches of the office of campus diversity. That is why "creative writing" had to be established as a separate major in the 1990s. The English professors were too interested in tolerance to teach students how to write. They were also unwilling to impose their own standards upon others.

But after the abolition of tenure, English and "creative writing" had to be merged to handle the shortage of faculty. That is also when many of the diversity offices began to shut down.

A similar thing happened in the so-called social sciences. People stopped majoring in sociology and anthropology because those disciplines were previously set up solely to produce tenured professors. That is about the time that all of the so-called social sciences merged into one department. They were called "social sciences" until the real sciences of chemistry and physics teamed up to have them renamed "social philosophy."

Of course, both the school of social work and the school of education had to be eliminated altogether. That was cause for concern at first because each had its own multimillion-dollar facility built with bond money approved by voters during the 1990s. But then, we hired our first chancellor with a business background in the year 2012. Fortunately, he had no previous employment in education. His idea for converting the space was controversial but, ultimately, brilliant.

As many of you know, the old school of education building is now a parking garage. The school of social work building is home to Starbucks and a number of other profitable businesses. Trading the salaries of those unproductive liberal ideologues for the leases of those businesses is one reason we no longer have to solicit funds from alumni. We have been in the black for several years.

And finally, the problems of anti-conservative and anti-Christian discrimination are now a thing of the past. Put simply, we have now learned that over 90 percent of those problems were being produced by less than 10 percent of the faculty. Almost all of those "bad apples" have been rooted out by the abolition of tenure.

Today, we are no longer hearing reports that nearly all of the required student fees are being spent on liberal speakers and "co-sponsored initiatives" between gay student groups and the office of diversity. In addition to the abolition of the office of diversity, we are seeing more cautious behavior on behalf of our faculty. People can no longer blindly discriminate for fear of actually being fired. And of course, we are hiring fewer bigots in the first place.

This is the follow-up to the previous column, Chapter 4, "The Abolition of Tenure."

For additional discussion of tenure, see also Chapter 84, "Cowards in the Academic Trenches."

CHAPTER 6

How to Talk to an Atheist (and You Must)

January 24, 2005

When I pulled into the parking lot this morning, I saw a car covered with sacrilegious bumper stickers. It seemed obvious to me that the owner was craving attention. I'm sure he was also seeking to elicit anger from people of faith. The anger helps the atheist to justify his atheism. And all too often, the atheist gets exactly what he is looking for.

In fact, just the other day, I heard a Christian refer to an atheist as an "attention-craving SOB." It reminded me of the time I heard someone refer to another atheist as a "b**ch." I don't have the same reaction towards atheists, even when I see them attacking my basic religious freedoms. When I look into their eyes, I see an emptiness that evokes pity. Maybe that's because I was once one of them.

I still remember the night I publicly declared my atheism. It was April 3rd, 1992. I was a long-haired musician, playing guitar at a bar called The Gin in Oxford, Mississippi. The subject of religion came up in a conversation during one of my breaks. An

Ole Miss law student, who had been an undergraduate with me at Mississippi State years before, asked me whether I was still dating my girlfriend. Then, he asked why I had broken up with my previous girlfriend two years before.

After I explained that my former girlfriend was too much of a fundamentalist while I was an atheist, his jaw nearly hit the ground. "Are you really an atheist?" he asked. He assured me he didn't mean to pry and that he was merely concerned. He didn't have to tell me that. His reaction gave him away. It was a reaction he could not have possibly faked.

That law student, whose name I have forgotten, made no effort to convert me on the spot. But he did plead with me to pick up a copy of *Mere Christianity*. "I've heard it all before," I said. He told me I was wrong. He said that C.S. Lewis was the best apologist of the twentieth century, but he didn't push the matter. The conversation ended abruptly. I never saw him again.

Years later, I read *Mere Christianity*, and it did have a great effect upon me. But recently, I was thinking about what really drove me to read the book. How could I have remembered the title of a book I heard only once? After all, it was many years before at the end of a long night of drinking in a bar in Mississippi.

The answer is simple. The advice was given to me by someone who sincerely considered the matter to be urgent. And that sense of urgency was conveyed without a trace of anger. It was just a matter of one human being communicating his concern for another without being pushy and holier than thou.

If a Christian really believes the things he professes to believe, he will go to great lengths to share it with others. He would even crawl on his belly across a desert of broken glass if he thought he could reach an atheist. He would certainly do more than utter profanity and show contempt for the atheist.

I don't think about those days as often as I should. But the next time I see an atheist, I will try to remember. And when I feel some sadness, I will try to keep the faith that there is always hope.

I am glad that law student remembered. I plan to thank him when I see him again.

I assume the title is in reference to How to Talk to a Liberal (If You Must) *by Ann Coulter (2004).*

Later, Mike would describe his dramatic escape from atheism, as detailed in Chapter 27, "The Shadow Proves the Sunshine."

Chapter 7

An Anti-Communist Reading List

April 11, 2005

It seems like just yesterday that I was riding back from the Piggly Wiggly after grocery shopping with my mother. *[It is now an Aldi, by the way.]* Of course, it wasn't yesterday. It was more like the summer of 1970. If memory serves me correctly, I was five years old.

While we were riding in our 1965 Pontiac Catalina, I heard a reporter on the radio say something about a war in Vietnam. I didn't know we were in a war until I asked my mom if we were fighting the Germans again. That's when I first heard that terrible word. "No, son, we are fighting the communists." I asked her who these communists were and where they came from. She paused and said, "No one really knows."

Today, things are different. We know who the communists are and where they come from. Most of them teach at American universities. We work hard every day to pay the taxes that, in turn, pay their salaries. Meanwhile, they work hard to subvert everything we do, everything we value, and everything we love.

Of course, they don't call themselves communists. They prefer the term "socialist."

The modern socialists also attack our Christian heritage with a zeal inspired by Marx's mordent declaration that "religion is the opiate of the masses." They know that capitalism can never fall as long as our nation retains that Christian heritage. As long as the socialist attack upon our economic system is rooted in social and moral upheaval, there can be no meaningful distinction between the economic and the social conservative. The two components of our conservative heritage simply cannot be divorced.

Hardly a day goes by without parents asking me for advice on how to protect their children from the harmful secular and socialist influences they will encounter in college. Today, I present a reading list, which should help any high school student understand the reality of socialism long before setting foot on a college campus. It will help abort any professor's attempt to advance his agenda by rewriting socialism's disgraceful history.

We the Living (1936) – This is the first and most autobiographical of all of Ayn Rand's novels. It is also a good book for teenagers. So many young lives are destroyed before they have really begun in this gut-wrenching novel. For those who consider Rand to be arrogant and caustic, it is necessary to understand what she witnessed as a young woman in communist Russia. This book will make you appreciate all of the blessings we enjoy in this great country.

Anthem (1938) – I have recommended this book before (see last year's summer reading list). It is a good starting place for teens who have an aversion to reading. At around one hundred pages, it has a fast-moving plot. As a professor at a university dominated by identity politics, I see this novel as something more than grim prophecy. Rand captures *1984* ten years before Orwell. She explains the campus diversity movement fifty years before its onset.

The Road to Serfdom (1944) – After I published last year's summer reading list, I was criticized for two omissions. One was *Orthodoxy* by G.K. Chesterton. The other was *The Road to Serfdom* by F.A. Hayek. Complaints regarding the latter exceeded complaints regarding the former by about two to one. Nothing more need be said.

Animal Farm (1946) – Maybe your high school student is having trouble in his English classes. Maybe that is, in part, due to his inability to pick up on symbolism. I flunked English four years in a row in high school, partly because of my inability to pick up on obvious literary symbols. Nonetheless, I picked up on everything in this great little novel. While this list is presented in chronological order, *Animal Farm* might be the best starting place among these ten books.

1984 (1948) – Over the next few years, how many students will get a daily dosage of "the two minutes hate" by professors who are still seething with anger after the defeat of John Kerry? And how many times will the office of diversity remind us of the opening pages of *1984* as it seeks to do exactly the opposite of what its name implies?

Witness (1952) – This is one of the most important books of the twentieth century. Before and after reading this book, parents should encourage their children to visit www.biography.com and search for the name "Alger Hiss." What they read will demonstrate just how far in denial this nation still is regarding the Soviet infiltration of our government during the Cold War.

The Gulag Archipelago (1956) – If you did not think that *We the Living* painted a realistic portrait of Soviet Russia during the Stalinist purges, this great work of non-fiction by Aleksandr I. Solzhenitsyn will set matters straight. Some call it the greatest non-fiction book of the twentieth century. I can't argue.

Atlas Shrugged (1957) – This is my favorite American novel. It is my second favorite novel behind *The Brothers Karamazov*. Based on her other writings, Ayn Rand seems to have considered John Galt's speech to be the highlight of the novel. Francisco d'Anconia's speech at Jim Taggart's wedding was my favorite part of the novel. At over one thousand pages, this one is going to take time for your high schooler to read. If they refuse, you can always teach them a lesson about capitalism by paying them to read it. The results will be well worth the investment.

Enjoy the reading, my fellow capitalists!

Mike was a voracious reader. His office was wall-to-wall, floor-to-ceiling bookcases. And he actually did read those books. I can tell because he made notes in the books as he read them. I kept just a portion, but that was still enough to fill a bookcase in my home. A small sample of his library is on display in the Mike Adams Recording Studio at Summit Ministries in Manitou Springs, Colorado. To learn more about the studio and Summit, please see Chapter 31, "Mike's Peak," and Chapter 50, "Standing at the Summit."

Later, Mike would publish more reading lists. I don't have space to include them all, but here are some notable recommendations:

More Than a Carpenter by Josh McDowell. This is a very fast-reading apologetic that helps to refute some of the common arguments against the deity of Christ. Frequently, even avowed atheists will acknowledge that Christ was the most important person to walk the face of the Earth. Nonetheless, they will argue that more books have been written about Christ than anyone else simply because He was a "great moral leader." McDowell walks the reader through all of the different options a person has when deciding "what to do" with Christ. For me, only one of those options makes sense.

The Vision of the Anointed by Thomas Sowell. This book explains the real difference between conservatives and liberals. I offer this book as a partial response to those who ask, "How can you be so conservative and still call yourself a Christian?" *[He expounds upon this in Chapter 30, "The Nature of Conservatism." Mike was a big fan of Sowell in general and had many Sowell titles in his library.]*

Shadow University by Alan Kors and Harvey Silverglate. This book changed the direction of my career. After I finished this one, I realized that the problems on my campus concerning both free speech and due process were not unique. The success of this book also served as a springboard for the indispensable Foundation for Individual Rights in Education (FIRE).

Anna Karenina by Leo Tolstoy. Thinking about committing adultery? Think again. This book is the ultimate tragic novel. It illustrates the consequences that bad choices have upon those who make them. It also shows how those choices affect innocent parties. Our country needs to examine the important moral lessons of this book more than ever. Although it's about 900 pages long, I read this book in eight days. I simply could not put it down. In my opinion, it is Tolstoy's greatest work. Here is my favorite quote: "In former days the free-thinker was a man who had been brought up in ideas of religion, law, and morality, and only through conflict and struggle came to free-thought; but now there has sprung up a new type of born free-thinkers who grow up without even having heard of principles of morality or of religion, of the existence of authorities, who grow up directly in ideas of negation in everything, that is to say, savages." That was written in 1877. It could just as well have been written today.

The Brothers Karamazov by Fyodor Dostoevsky. I read this novel for the first time at age nineteen. I read it again nineteen years later. This may be the greatest novel ever written. Its themes are timeless. From "The Grand Inquisitor" to Father Zosima's "Of hell and hell fire, a mystic reflection," this is profound reading. Not a bad little murder mystery either.

The Count of Monte Cristo by Alexandre Dumas. This is the longest "page-turner" I have ever read. Its unforgettable lead character is almost as intriguing as the complex themes of revenge and forgiveness that run through this great novel. This book inspired me to read *The Three Musketeers* shortly thereafter. While also a page-turner, the musketeers could not quite match the count, in my opinion. Dumas moved far up my list of all-time favorite writers after I tackled these two classics last winter. I will certainly be reading both of these novels again.

Crime and Punishment by Fyodor Dostoevsky. This is another one I read at age nineteen and reread at thirty-eight. Raskolnikov's behavior contradicts much of what we know about human behavior in general, particularly the relationship between attitudes and behavior. Nonetheless, it is realism that strikes me as this novel's greatest strength. Dostoevsky wrote this novel in a way that made me believe that I was there in the room with the main character during his greatest time of suffering. The book's closing pages dealing with the relationship between the young murderer and the prostitute, Sonia, are among the greatest pages in the annals of literature. This tale of fall and redemption captures the essence of the human experience like no novel written before or since.

Robinson Crusoe by Daniel Defoe. This is a much more serious novel than I remember reading as a child. Crusoe's independence and self-reliance make him an unforgettable hero. The religious themes of repentance and perseverance resonated more for me on the second reading. Like *Crime and Punishment*, the ordeal of the lead character is so vividly portrayed that it is difficult to climb out of this novel after only a few minutes of reading. Like the main character, the reader can achieve a good measure of self-awareness by spending time with this great novel.

New Living Translation Life Application Study Bible. There is little question that one cannot be called an "educated person" unless he has taken the time to read the Bible at least once. The only question is "which Bible?" This is the eighth translation I've tackled, and it ranks as one of my favorites. I tend to like literal translations (like the New American Standard Bible) or paraphrases (like The Living Bible). The only versions of the Bible I have not enjoyed are those (like the New International Version) that try to split the difference. The NLT is like The Living Bible but slightly more literal. It is an especially good first choice for teenagers and college students.

Tactics by Greg Koukl. You can talk substance all you want, but if you don't know how to argue, you're in trouble. Greg teaches you to be careful instead of jumping in and making assertions and arguments immediately. You need to stop, and you need to get in the driver's seat and first of all expose the weaknesses of the other person's argument. Koukl does a better job of teaching Christians how to do that than anyone who has ever put the pen to paper. Of all the books that I recommend, *Tactic*s is the only one that I recommend reading two or three times because it will help you when you're overwhelmed. It'll teach you to structure your arguments well, to stay calm, and not to panic when under fire. *[I have heard or read Mike recommending this book many times.]*

The Case for Life by Scott Klusendorf. Being victorious in the pro-life movement means you have to do two things. First of all, you have to use science to establish that the unborn are human. Secondly, you need to use philosophy to establish that there's no difference between the unborn embryo you once were and the adult you are today that would justify killing you at that earlier stage of development. Scott sets the moral framework, and for that reason, I always recommend this first on the issue of life. *[As I write this, a revised second edition is scheduled to be published on November 14, 2023. See also Chapter 45, "Stand For Life."]*

Mere Christianity by C.S. Lewis. The part I found to be the most persuasive was the part about the moral law because stage one of my conversion occurred in 1996 when I was visiting that prison in Quito, Ecuador, and there was something that awakened within me *[as described in Chapter 27, "The Shadow Proves the Sunshine."]* When I finally got around to taking that guy's advice from that drunken bar conversation *[previous chapter, "How to*

Talk to an Atheist"], and I finally sat down and read *Mere Christianity*, it strongly resonated with me. There are so many different parts of the book that are persuasive. The part about the moral law being written on our hearts—well, I knew that to be the case. And it was also very well-written and coming from a person who was a former atheist, someone I could identify with. *[This is another of Mike's top picks. I also refer to this in the postscript to Chapter 97, "Everlasting Life on Death Row."]*

I Don't Have Enough Faith to Be an Atheist, which Norm Geisler co-wrote with my good friend Frank Turek. *[Mike references this in the column with the same title on July 20, 2006, and it is included here as Chapter 13.]*

Scaling the Secular City by J.P. Moreland. I read this book in just a couple of days and loved every page of it. Since then, I have met J.P. and have heard him lecture several times. On the basis of those lectures, I decided to read another of his books called *Love God with All Your Mind*. I liked it even more.

CHAPTER 8

My Presidential Acceptance Speech

April 28, 2005

When I first heard there was an organized effort to expel Rosemary DePaolo as UNC-Wilmington's chancellor, I was taken aback. I thought the student group (called "I hate my chancellor") was way too harsh in their criticism of Dr. DePaolo. But later, when I found out there was a group called "Mike Adams for chancellor," I got over it.

Tonight, I am pleased to accept your offer to lead UNC-Wilmington for the next three years.

My first act in office will be to change the name of my position. I will be called President Adams, not Chancellor Adams. I don't even know what the term "chancellor" means. It sounds like an overpaid, pompous ass to me.

Next, I will take a 50 percent salary cut. At over a quarter of a million dollars per year, our previous chancellor was grossly overpaid. Since I get royalties and honoraria as a professional author and speaker, I really could cut my salary even further. But then again, I really enjoy buying guns I don't need. Therefore, we'll keep the salary cut at 50 percent.

My next act in office will be to stop stealing money from the students of UNC-Wilmington. That's what the previous administration has been doing. For example, they have been charging you a hefty computer use fee without granting you full access to the computers. In fact, the university ran out of paper and toner and had to start shutting down labs on just the second day of school last year.

Of course, you never got a refund of your computer fees. That is called theft. I believe theft is absolutely wrong despite the claims of the moral relativists in the office of diversity. Incidentally, I will pay for your new paper and toner by shutting down the office of diversity. They can't claim that shutting them down is wrong because they don't recognize a distinction between right and wrong. Everything is relative, remember?

The university is also stealing your money by charging you $175 for parking every year and not providing you all with a parking space. Currently, there are four students for every parking space. Pardon my language, but that really sucks. Expect to immediately receive a 75 percent reduction in your parking fees. Next, I will build a parking deck on campus. When I am finished, you will be able to park there for free.

The new parking deck will be in the place of the cultural arts center, which is currently being built on the edge of campus. Let's face it, that center will probably be filled with sculptures of vaginas and African warlords within a year. Since no one cares about that artsy-fartsy crap, I plan to tear it down even before it is even finished.

Remember that administrators just fund these diversity projects to pad their vitae in order to get the next administrative job that pays more money. And let's face the facts: no other school is going to hire me after I'm done with this place.

In order to fund the parking deck, I plan to cut back on the number of administrators at UNC-Wilmington. When I came here twelve years ago, this school was run by only a fraction of the administrators we have now. Even then, they managed to get bored enough to think of stupid ideas like sensitivity training sessions for transgendered employees. Now, since most of them will be fired, the rest are going to have to work a little harder.

But I won't cut the total number of jobs at UNC-Wilmington. For every administrator I fire, there will be a university policeman added to the force. That has something to do with the murders of two UNCW students last year. It also has something to do with the fact that I intend to start selling beer on campus.

I have to be honest. I am going to allow beer to be sold in the student union only because I am sick and tired of students coming to me for help after a drunk driving charge. If you're going to get drunk, I want you to do it within walking distance of your dorm. Speaking of self-interest, I will only allow Sam Adams to be sold on campus because that's my favorite beer. If you don't like it, that's tough. I'm the president.

I want to address the issue of dorms right now. Earlier this year, the administration kicked the juniors and seniors off campus because they claimed there is not enough room for you—especially in light of our many new building projects. I am hereby reversing that decision. Starting next year, there will be a giant new upper-class dorm on campus.

The new upper-class dorm is currently referred to as the "school of education." If you've ever had an education class, you know what a joke that school is. By the way, the education professors were already fired this morning. It will probably take a few months for them to clean out their offices. It takes education professors at least ten times as long as the average person to accomplish any simple task. Sorry for the delay.

I also plan to close the university bookstore. If you don't know why, see my previous remarks about theft. You can now buy your books on Amazon.com or anywhere else you see fit.

Those stupid Seahawk paw prints that were recently painted all over campus will also be removed. They just look too much like giant rat paws to stay. I was beginning to think the psychologists forgot to lock up one of their Skinner boxes after another ground-breaking experiment. But now I know that the administration was behind it, I am going to make them clean up their own mess. The administrators who just got fired will have to remove them before they pick up their final paychecks.

And finally, I want you to know that the women's resource center, the leadership lecture series, and all of the Democratic Party's campus slush funds will be shut down. After all, the name of this school is UNC-Wilmington, not DNC-Wilmington. Since we won't be funding the Democrats anymore, you can forget about the 11 percent tuition increase previously scheduled for next year.

This concludes my inaugural address. Since it was given via email and was not a part of a week-long installation (like the one given for my predecessor, Rosemary DePaolo), I have just saved you about $100,000.

Now, go out and buy yourself a beer. Make it a Sam Adams. And make a toast to Mike Adams. That's President Adams to you.

Another example of Mike being ahead of his time. Since this was written, university expenditures have continued to rise, driving up tuition and, in turn, student debt.

CHAPTER 9

Academic Insanity, Part 184

July 13, 2005

Author's Note: My present department chair (who began that position on July 1, 2005) was not involved in any of the events documented below.

> You shall not circulate a false report. Do not put your hand with the wicked to be an unrighteous witness. —Exodus 23:1
>
> Whoever secretly slanders his neighbor, Him I will destroy. —Psalm 101:5

Dear President Broad:

In December of 2001, I experienced the second most anxiety-evoking event of my professional career. It came in the form of a stern (but friendly) warning from the UNC-Wilmington police to avoid all contact with another professor in my department. I was advised not to be caught in the same room with this woman because she was, in the opinion of (numerous) school officials, both delusional and potentially dangerous. That informal order resulted in my resignation from the position of coordinator of the criminal justice program. I had volunteered for that position just three months prior to these events.

My resignation took place a few weeks after the aforementioned professor filed a false police report accusing me of conduct, which, if duly proven to have taken place, would constitute a felonious criminal act. More specifically, it was claimed that I was trying to poison my accuser with tear gas. Her report to the police suggested that I was breaking into her office with the help of the department chair in order to spray these toxic fumes. There was no indication as to how we obtained the tear gas or where we kept our canisters and gas masks hidden during the course of the day. I assume these attacks were supposed to have been carried out in the dead of night.

Because the UNCW police (and other administrators) intimated that this professor was suffering from paranoid delusions and was potentially dangerous, I followed their advice and cooperated fully. That included participating in the most anxiety-evoking event of my career—a taped interrogation with a sworn police officer at police headquarters.

As you may guess, the command to avoid all contact with the professor resulted in more than my resignation from the role of coordinator of the criminal justice program. It has also resulted in numerous absences from department meetings and faculty gatherings since December of 2001. I have also obeyed the police and exited the room every time the delusional faculty member and I have ended up together in the main office of the department. In other words, I have been a good employee and have done all that university officials have asked me to do.

But now we have a problem that has put a damper on my cooperative spirit.

This year, in my annual performance evaluation, I have been "written up," so to speak, by my immediate supervisor. This first negative evaluation that I have received in twelve years at UNCW mentions, among other things, my failure to attend most departmental meetings. I am sure you see why this is a problem, given that the warning to avoid contact with my accuser has never been rescinded.

It has now been three and one-half years since the state bureau of investigation concluded that there were no actual break-ins by tear-gas-wielding professors. It has been over three years since the university attorney asked me not to "go public" with this information. It is now time for the university administration to answer some questions:

1. Why did the university attorney assure me (in May of 2002) that UNCW was working on a solution that would remove this delusional and potentially dangerous faculty member from the department? Was the university lying to me? If not, did someone simply drop the ball?

2. Is it morally acceptable for UNCW to a) not punish a faculty member for making a false criminal accusation but instead b) punish the falsely accused (on his annual performance evaluation) for merely following police orders and avoiding all contact with the accuser?

3. Has the inaction of the UNCW administration created a hostile working environment for me and for the other falsely accused professor?

4. The accuser in this case also made a false accusation of sexual harassment against a professor in 1999. Did the university fail to investigate that claim? If so, did they violate federal law?

5. Now that the taxpayers of North Carolina have paid for a criminal investigation for a crime that did not take place, who will pay them back? Should it be the false accuser? If not, who should it be?

6. How many false accusations of sexual harassment and office terrorism are feminist professors allowed to make with impunity? Three? Six? A dozen? Is the number unlimited?

7. Is my accuser really fit to teach our department's only class in counterterrorism? For that matter, is she really fit to teach any class within the field of criminal justice? What kind of message does it send when criminal justice professors file false police reports?

In addition to these questions, I have a few requests:

- I would like to know whether my accuser has received any treatment or counseling for her delusions. I must have the answer in writing before I resume full participation in departmental activities.

- If my accuser has not been treated and no other action has been taken, I want UNCW to apologize for putting me through this ordeal. I also want the university to acknowledge unequivocally that I have been falsely implicated in a crime that never actually took place. I also want the university to apologize to the North Carolina taxpayers for wasting their hard-earned money.

- I want all references to the decrease in my participation in departmental activities from 2002 to 2005 to be purged from my personnel records.

I expect to hear back from you soon. If you do otherwise, you underestimate my resolve.

Mike S. Adams

See also Chapter 2, "With Liberty and Comfort for All," and Chapter 99, "The Third Stage of Academic Lunacy."

Chapter 10

Light in August

August 1, 2005

I write a lot of articles criticizing my administration for a simple reason: they deserve it. Our administrators make a lot of bad decisions, too many of which are born of unmitigated ideological bigotry. But occasionally, you have to praise them for making a good decision. I just wish moments like this would come more often.

On August 18th, when classes resume at UNC-Wilmington, Susan Bullers, an associate professor of sociology, will begin her duties as the new director of our university's women's resource center (WRC). This will mark the end of a four-year reign of ideological terror, which has crippled the WRC since it was established in 2001.

When examining the last four years, it is difficult to decide which WRC incident (often discussed in my weekly column) was the greatest source of embarrassment for the university or which provided the greatest evidence of feminist fanaticism run amok.

Maybe it was the time the WRC decided to hang cartoon pictures of Condoleezza Rice (featured standing in a cage holding a bunch of bananas) all over the university library. The feminists who produced the picture claimed to be opponents of racism.

Or maybe it was the time the WRC decided to hang cartoon pictures of a woman kicking a man in the face while hurling obscenities (including the f-word).

Perhaps it was the time they advertised *The Vagina Monologues* with a large sign featuring the p-word displayed right in front of the university cafeteria. The sign was in full view of parents and their small children.

Of course, the most distasteful WRC ad could have been the flashing vagina sign positioned right in front of the university and directly across from the Greek Orthodox Church.

And let's not forget the anonymous feminists who dressed as apes and threw bananas at a UNCW audience in 2004. They were hired by the WRC for $6,000.

And how about the time the WRC website posted a link to a "Jesus on a Rainbow" essay after refusing to post a Crisis Pregnancy Center link because the organization was "explicitly Christian."

Then, there were those vagina-shaped lollipops sold by the women's resource center on campus.

And before we move on, let's not forget the queer Muslim speaker and the "How Bush's Attack on the International Family Hurts Us All" speech funded by the mostly Bush-supporting Christian heterosexual taxpayers of North Carolina.

I mention all of these embarrassing episodes for a reason: I think Susan Bullers is far too smart, too reasonable, and too levelheaded to allow WRC facilities and funds to be abused like this in the future.

This is not to say that Bullers is some sort of a conservative or even a moderate. I consider her to be a liberal (and know she is a Democrat). But she is well-qualified to hold an administrative position in the diversity movement by virtue of the fact that she is not an extremist. That is, of course, good news. Reasonable people know that where extremists rule, there can be no diversity of ideas.

And that is why the diversity movement should be handed over to people more like Bullers and less like her WRC predecessors. Some examples follow:

There is a professor in communications who actually organized a high-profile campus debate between a liberal and a conservative last year.

There is also a professor in philosophy who is so fair and balanced in class that students constantly argue about his true political orientation. He keeps them guessing at all times.

And finally, there is a professor, a liberal who teaches African American studies and communications, who actually seeks out people with different ideas to provide them with moral support when they have been targets of censorship.

None of the professors I just mentioned are conservative Republicans, but all have unique qualities and can play an important role in restoring dignity to our university in a time of unprecedented constitutional chaos.

Maybe some leftists who read this article will finally understand what the booming campus conservative movement is all about. We are not demanding affirmative-action-style quotas for Republicans. We don't want to start firing extreme leftist professors. We don't want to ban fanatics like Eve Ensler from appearing on campus.

What we are demanding is a reasonable attempt to restore intellectually honest debate on our campuses. And we are demanding that it take place in an environment where administrators refrain from endorsing the ideas they love and suppressing the ideas they despise.

With this latest administrative appointment, my university can now begin to slowly crawl back towards the realm of academic sanity where ideas may be freely exchanged without fear of government-imposed retribution.

Nonetheless, we are still a long, long way from home.

Mike was an outspoken critic of academia, but he also gave the devil his due. Additionally, he was an optimist. He once believed our failing system of higher education could and would be saved in his lifetime—and that he would play a part in that. Unfortunately and obviously, things have only gotten worse, and I believe that weighed heavily on him at the end of his life. In our final conversations, I sensed hopelessness, discouragement, and despair.

Chapter 11

Life and How to Live It, Part V

March 13, 2006

This also appears in the book Life and How to Live It *(2023).*

Recently, a conservative atheist wrote a very angry yet moving letter about the passing of his wife. She suffered from cancer for a prolonged period of time. Apparently, she was in terrible pain for months before she finally passed. After decades of marriage, he found himself alone in a house full of memories. That's when he wrote me, insisting there isn't a God and urging me to "get off of religion" and stick to my "bread-and-butter" topic of campus censorship.

The letter reminds me of another great woman who died of cancer. The year was 1962. The woman's name was Nell Myers Rester. She was my maternal grandmother.

Nell's death at the age of forty-eight was probably the result of an error by the physician who removed a cancerous organ during a prior surgery. Later, when another organ was consumed by cancer, the doctor was consumed by guilt. He concluded that he could have also removed the other organ and, thus, saved her life.

After it was too late, he tearfully apologized to her at her bedside. That was back in the days when doctors spoke honestly to their patients instead of worrying about future litigation.

When my grandmother passed, that doctor drove from New Orleans to Gulfport *[Mississippi]* to attend her funeral. There, he told my mother that for years he had to console patients, but that Nell Myers was the only patient he ever had who tried to console him. That story was corroborated by several black nurses who had asked to come along to Nell's funeral. That was rare in the segregated Mississippi of 1962.

The consensus was that Nell didn't care that the doctor probably made a mistake that prematurely ended her life. She only wanted to make sure that he was all right and that he knew he was forgiven. During the advanced stages of her illness, she even wrote him an uplifting letter that he kept in his office desk for the rest of his career.

And the doctor wasn't the only one changed forever by the way my grandmother handled her bout with cancer. My mother—upon hearing the doctor's tearful account of Nell's loving treatment of him—decided that her faith in the face of adversity was conclusive proof of the power of an Almighty. So she set about proving an important point regarding life and how to live it:

Whether a tragedy remains a tragedy or becomes a catalyst for good is entirely a function of individual free will.

And so my mother was soon collecting money door to door for the American Cancer Society. When I was a young boy, I remember cigarette smokers slamming the door in her face. But she just kept on going for years after her mother's death.

And then there were the trips to the worst slums in Houston. Mom would buy a bag of groceries and just knock on someone's door in the ghetto to deliver them unannounced. I remember the way the recipient's face would light up when she just walked away without asking for anything in return. She didn't even need to open her mouth to witness to them.

Then, there were the prisoners she began writing to in the 1970s. I never saw their faces until twenty years later when I began visiting prisoners myself. That was when I was thirty-two—about thirty-four years after Nell died. About that time, I realized I really had known my maternal grandmother after all.

Of course, it doesn't take a tragic death to transform a life from one of complacency to one of great works. In fact, it is a dual tragedy when we wait for a tragedy to take hold of our lives and force us to choose a life of gratitude over a life of self-pity.

Rather than praying to God the same way you talk to your store-bound spouse—merely listing the things you want Him to get you—you should confine yourself to enumerating the blessings you already have. In fact, you could do it in alphabetical order—picking one blessing for every letter. If you follow my advice, your only problem will be choosing between the many blessings you have but rarely even think about.

And that proves another point about life and how to live it:

Self-pity and gratitude are mortal enemies. Where one exists, the other cannot.

By the way, "Life and How to Live It" is the name of a song by R.E.M. from their 1985 album Fables of the Reconstruction. *R.E.M. was Mike's favorite band in college.*

In another column, we learned that Dad was the architect of Mike's academic and vocational transformation. So where was Mom when this was going on? Right there beside them, of course. But her influence, albeit more subtle, was more profound, building a foundation for her son's future spiritual transformation. To understand why Mike was so principled, one must understand our mother, Marilyn Rester Adams.

Mom was heavily influenced by her mother, Nell Myers Rester, and her grandmother, Julia Lee Myers ("Big Mama"). Three generations of solid, humble, loving, Christian women. I cannot overstate the influence of these amazing women on their friends and families. This article is one of my favorites.

There was not enough space for the above article to make it clear that Mom was very different when she was young and that her mother's death didn't just inspire her to do good works. It transformed her—and for the better. Mike would explain this very eloquently in his powerful eulogy at Mom's memorial service in 2019. I delve deeper into this in my previous book Life and How to Live It *(2023).*

Chapter 12

I Had a Dream

July 20, 2006

Author's Note: Pseudonyms are used in today's column. Other minor facts are altered to protect the identity of former students.

Last night, I had a dream that I was sitting in a diner not far from the beach. A girl with a suntan walked into the diner and sat down next to me. She had beautiful green eyes, sun-bleached hair, and the face of a cover girl. We knew each other through a mutual friend who teaches in the public schools.

When I asked her how she was, she said that she was having trouble finding her place in the world. She had just changed careers twice in the last month. She had no college degree, so she decided it was time to go back to school. But for the time being, she had to raise some money. She had no savings at age twenty-five.

Immediately after she told me that she planned to work in one of the local topless bars to save some money, she saw my stunned reaction. So she tried to overwhelm me with the numbers. "The girls make $500 a night, tax free," she said. Then, she started to add up the numbers for a whole year of dancing and otherwise living modestly. My expression didn't change, and she got frustrated. She reminded me that some topless dancers make more money than professors.

And I dreamed that I resisted the temptation to respond sarcastically by reminding her that drug dealers make more money than doctors. Instead, I told her about Carolyn.

Carolyn was from Massachusetts. She was a bright student—at least she was about ten years previously. Her father was a lawyer. It was her dream to become a lawyer too. She took a job in a topless bar. Before long, she was spending her cash on the cocaine that freely flows within the walls of that bar—the cocaine the police seem to overlook. Carolyn ended up sleeping with her boss and getting pregnant. When she had misgivings about an abortion, she was fired. She dropped out of college, and she isn't a lawyer today. She isn't even a stripper.

And then I told her about Meghan. She was from a small town near the Virginia border. She went to work in the topless bar as a cocktail waitress, promising she would never actually become a stripper. But she did become a stripper.

I told her how I saw Meghan in the store the other day and hardly recognized her. And I recalled when she enrolled at my university and looked like she was twelve years old. Nine years later, she could pass for forty-five. A single year in a topless bar can put a decade on a young woman's face.

Then, I told her about Angie. She was a gorgeous young girl who prided herself on her athletic ability. She, too, started out as a cocktail waitress. Then, she became a stripper. After she gained a few pounds, the manager fired her. Now, she works behind a makeup counter in the mall.

Angie's friend is a graduate of the university with a good career. She keeps in touch with me from time to time. She says that somewhere between the cocaine parties and the group sex,

Angie lost her self-esteem and the desire to do anything with her life. She wears a lot of makeup that hides the lines written on her face and reveals the shame written on her heart.

Finally, I told her about Scarlet. She was a stripper for years, hoping to save enough money to get a doctorate. She came by my office the other day to drop off an application. Every six months or so, she changes jobs. She is never happy in any of them because she never got her doctorate. She never could seem to hold on to the money. One look at her once-pretty face—a face that now looks like a worn-out baseball glove—tells the tale of how she lost her money. And on top of it all, she deeply resents every man with whom she works.

Like Scarlet, most young women who decide to strip are already equipped with low self-esteem the first night they walk into that strip bar. When they finally decide to leave, they often walk out with STDs, drug addictions, a string of unwanted pregnancies, and even lower self-esteem. But they never seem to walk out with the money.

But I have a dream that someday the so-called men who frequent these establishments will realize that that they are helping fund the destruction of these young women one dollar bill at a time. And I dream that they will come to see these women as someone's lost sister or perhaps the estranged daughter of a friend.

I have a dream that someday we will judge them by the content of their character, not the revelation of their skin.

Hopefully, it is obvious that the title and punch line are a nod to the famous MLK speech. However, I have learned that it is dangerous to assume anything.

Chapter 13

I Don't Have Enough Faith to Be an Atheist

July 20, 2006

Jimmy Duke was my pitching coach in 1976, the year we won the Little League championship. I first met him at Clear Lake Baptist Church (CLBC) in 1973. That was just a year after I met his son, Jim, in Mrs. Ogden's second grade class. Thirty-one years after we were first classmates, Jim would be one of the groomsmen at my wedding. I've been friends with him for thirty-four years now.

Jimmy stopped taking his family to CLBC after a tragic car accident killed the two little girls of a good friend. For him, God just couldn't allow such a thing and still be worthy of worship and praise. The girls' deaths were violent, and the fatal accident seemed to take Jimmy's faith with it to the grave.

Jimmy and his wife, Sandy, would divorce in the late 1980s, and I would seldom see him afterwards. Glimpses of Jimmy's life in recent years would come to me in little bits and pieces via the funny stories I would hear about him from family and friends.

Jimmy's sense of humor was a foundation for his great success as a businessman.

When his daughter Gwen married in the late 1990s, he struck up a friendship with Pastor Roger of the local Hope Community Church. Roger would have lunch with Jimmy several times before he asked him, "Jimmy, what are your thoughts on the Lord these days?" Jimmy's answer to Roger was an instant classic: "As I understand it, you have to be Mother Teresa to get into heaven, and I'm not giving up my private airplane." Roger laughed when he later told me that story.

However, there was nothing funny last summer when his ex-wife, Sandy, died suddenly and painfully of lung cancer. It would remind him, probably, of the car accident that killed two little girls and drove him from the church decades earlier.

After Sandy passed, I would have some long, tough phone calls with Jimmy's son. How does one make the argument that a tragedy—especially one like the painful death of one's mother—may someday be revealed as a blessing? How can such an argument be anything but offensive while the wounds of a loved one's death are still fresh?

I tried unsuccessfully to compare my friend's loss of his mother to the loss of my grandmother forty years before *[Chapter 11, "Life and How to Live It, Part V"]*. The latter brought about the conversion of others, though her life was cut short after forty-eight years. Could Sandy's life bring about a similar change in others too? Thankfully, his father, Jimmy, kept in touch with Pastor Roger.

Because Jimmy and his second wife, Linda, kept in touch with Sandy too, it was possible for him to be influenced by her passing in a real and meaningful way. After Pastor Roger led the memorial for Sandy, he would speak to Jimmy again. When asked about his thoughts on the Lord, this time, Jimmy said, "It seems God in the Old Testament is a whole lot different from God in the New Testament." Roger told him he wouldn't live long enough to get answers to all his questions. But that one death reminded him of his mortality. And that is when his spiritual journey began.

Jimmy took a day off work to roam the aisles of Barnes & Noble to search out the perfect Christian apologetic. That day turned into two weeks, as he couldn't find the right book. Jimmy was looking for a book with numbers and charts. He wanted science and logic and archeological evidence all rolled into one package.

Finally, he decided upon a book by Geisler and Turek called *I Don't Have Enough Faith to Be an Atheist*. He read that book, followed by another by Josh McDowell. Then, he topped it off with a reading of the Old Testament. *[For more book recommendations, see Chapter 7, "An Anti-Communist Reading List."]*

Around that time, I got a note from Texas written by a reader named Bob, who attended Pastor Roger's church. He told me he'd just met a man who knows me too. "Jimmy Duke and his lovely wife, Linda, joined my Bible class recently," he said. Linda was a long-time Christian, and Jimmy was coming around fast.

While still in the process of conversion, Jimmy bought thirty copies of Geisler and Turek's book. He passed them out to anyone who would take a copy. Jimmy's thirty plus years as an agnostic were coming to an end. His former wife's painful death was becoming a catalyst for his conversion to full-time believer and part-time witness.

Just last week, Frank Turek—the man who co-wrote the book that launched Jimmy's spiritual journey and subsequent conversion—contacted me out of the blue. Over the phone, I told Frank—whom I had never spoken to before that day—the powerful story of Jimmy the agnostic turned witness. I told Frank that he and Norm Geisler should be overjoyed that they played a big role in Jimmy's conversion.

Later that day—after I got off the phone with Turek—Jimmy Duke checked into a hospital in Clear Lake City. He died unexpectedly the next day, surrounded by his loved ones.

Today, I'm just going to sit here writing the story of Jimmy's conversion with one hand while the other is holding a couple of painkillers I'll have to take after I finish this column. As soon as I recover from a shoulder injury, I'm going to celebrate the last year conversion of Jimmy Duke. To carry out that celebration (literally), I'm going to need two good arms to carry thirty copies of Geisler and Turek's book out of Barnes & Noble.

Giving those books out to anyone who will take them will be a nice way to celebrate the life of Jimmy Duke. Some people believe in a world generated by chance, governed by natural causes, and devoid of miracles. I don't have that much faith anymore. And none of us has that much time.

"A tragedy...may someday be revealed as a blessing..."

This is a recurring theme in Mike's writings and also in my own life. For example, I remember being laid off just days before Christmas in 1996. The whole department was axed, so it was nothing personal. Still, that was little consolation to a man who had a wife and kids and cats and dogs to feed and almost no money in the bank. That put a bit of a damper on the holiday spirit. But just a few weeks later, God did not merely replace my lost job—He gave me a much better one. I am forever grateful for losing that job.

Mike also once wrote this:

When a loved one dies, it is understandably viewed as an unmitigated tragedy. But it is also a reminder that someday we, too, will be called home. And that is no tragedy. We were made for another world.

Jim Duke remained one of Mike's lifelong friends, along with another elementary school friend, Scott Maxson. You can read more about them in the book Life and How to Live It (2023).

Chapter 14

Unconscious Racism

September 27, 2006

The other day, a student asked me the meaning of the term "unconscious racism." As a conservative Christian, he was tired of all the expanded definitions and examples of racism proffered by the left in order to obscure the decline of real racism in America. He saw this as a lame attempt to market socialistic solutions by exaggerating social problems.

But he was wrong. Just like individual racism—and institutional racism and subtle racism—unconscious racism really does exist. And my boss, Rosemary DePaolo *[at UNCW]*, provides a good example of what it means to be an "unconscious racist."

My discovery of Rosemary's unconscious racism would never have been made had a young black staff member not complained to me about one of her policies—a policy born of her false belief that she is an anointed queen, not a university president. It seems the young black man was required to enter by the back door when he made a service call to Rosemary's mansion where she lives free of charge (the free mansion is one example of welfare reform that was overlooked in the 1990s). He was told that had he been a professor, the chancellor would consent to an entrance through the front door. But unfortunately for him, staffers must enter through the back door.

Since the staffers entering through the back door are disproportionately black and the professors entering through the front door are disproportionately white, there is a clear pattern of racial discrimination. And since Rosemary is a liberal, she can't argue the nonexistence of unconscious racism. And if unconscious racism exists, the argument that she "did mean to" implement a discriminatory system is irrelevant.

Even more compelling examples of unconscious racism can be found within the halls of academia. And there is no better place to look for them than in a department of sociology where the people who pledge their lives to the eradication of bigotry are perhaps the most intolerant and bigoted segment of our society. And unlike the Klansmen, they cannot claim a lack of education as a defense.

Some years ago, one of my so-called colleagues heard me tell the story of a drug raid I went on in a working-class neighborhood in Wilmington. I approached a crack house with a law enforcement officer who had instructed me to purchase one crack rock from a man in a wheelchair who was on parole. Just before we got inside, someone drove up to buy some drugs. We circled the block until the transaction was completed.

Halfway around the block, we decided to cut through two houses and watch the place for a few moments before entering. When we did so, we were able to see two lookouts jumping out of a tree that we had been standing under just a few minutes before. They were young and did their jobs poorly. The second they realized there was about to be a bust, they ran towards their homes in the nearby projects.

When the coast was clear, we went inside. Before long, the drug agent was given consent to search the parolee's room. Needless to say, he was in possession of numerous crack pipes, some used recently. And so the agent cut a deal.

In order to be spared from a trip back to prison, the parolee had to provide information leading to a bigger catch before the evening ended. Because of the constant influx of prostitutes, users, and other dealers, that wasn't hard to do. In fact, it was a small-time heroin dealer—a friend of the parolee's—that intervened and led the agent to an amount of heroin sufficient to divert his attention from the handicapped felon.

I had hoped it would only be a few minutes that I was left there in the crack house while the agent went to check out the lead. But I sat through an entire HBO movie while the crackheads drank and smoked everything in sight—but not any crack as they assumed I was an agent. I couldn't figure out how they managed to pay the cable bill while the doors were falling off the hinges and the cockroaches crawled up the walls.

By the time the evening ended, the drug agent had what he wanted. And by the time I finished telling the story to the "colleague," he had what he wanted—namely, grounds to accuse me of racism. "Why didn't you just burn a cross in his yard, Adams?" the enlightened professor quipped.

But the suggestion that we were racists wrongly targeting the crack addict suffered a fatal flaw—namely, that the addict was white. At no point in the story did I mention the man's race. But my "colleague" heard the word "crack" and assumed—incorrectly assumed—that all crack addicts are black.

So it seems that unconscious racism is not just real but thriving on the campus of UNCW. Whether you're talking about the chancellor or just a tenured professor, the roots of racism run deep. And its occasional revelation does nothing to diminish the arrogance of the unconscious racist. It only increases his guilt and his zeal to engage in racial scapegoating.

And once the cat is out of the bag, the rest is done with full and conscious awareness.

CHAPTER 15

Philippians 4:13

October 30, 2006

Don't let the biting sarcasm and all the talk about firearms fool you. There are times when I am wholly lacking in courage and simply afraid I have bitten off more than I can chew. In fact, I was feeling that way just last week when I arrived at the University of Minnesota-Morris (UMM) to give a speech called "How to Win Friends and Irritate Feminists."

When I walked into the room—which initially had only 100 seats—they were bringing in extra chairs for the overflow crowd. That helped eventually squeeze 168 people into the room. With the crowd running out the door and down the hall, well over 200 people were able to hear my speech. The vast majority were there to protest by walking out or by simply peppering me with hostile questions. Among those hostile individuals was Dr. P.Z. Myers, an associate professor of biology at UMM. Here's how he described me on his website the day before my visit:

"Mike S. Adams, columnist for Townhall, Horowitzian shill, anti-feminist, creationist clown, homophobic bigot, warrior for free speech, professional racist, gun kook, academic-by-accident, beauty contest judge, and just generally contemptible far, far right-wing nutcase."

Myers also took a few shots at UMM conservatives while he was insulting the school's next guest speaker:

"I'm very disappointed in our students. We're far off the beaten track and we don't get that many speakers passing through our area, and they had to go exhibit the poor taste to invite this sorry sack of rethuglican excreta to our campus. Couldn't they have at least tried to find an intelligent conservative to bring out here? Why'd they have to scrape the bottom of the barrel for this guy? At least we're seeing our rather dismal right-wing campus rag's fading credibility implode with their sponsorship of such a low-wattage guest speaker."

So given the atmosphere, it might not surprise my readers that this was the one time I walked into a campus auditorium and drew a complete blank before I started to deliver an important speech. So I did what I always do when I am lost. I said a prayer, recited a verse, and asked for guidance.

When the speech began, all the words came out to my satisfaction. In fact, the event went so well that students from both sides (politically) peppered me with compliments afterwards. One said that he had never in his life seen a man turn such a hostile audience in his favor so quickly and so effortlessly.

But of course, such compliments are misplaced. I didn't do anything impressive or praiseworthy Thursday night in Minnesota. I simply took a situation I could not handle and turned it over to a higher power. If I were not such a faithless and flawed character, the request for guidance would hardly have been necessary.

Contrast what happened to me that evening with what happened to Professor Myers. He had stated on his website that the university "paid good money to ferry this stiff here," saying "let's at least have him put on a show and argue with him." And he speculated about what he might ask me if he could make my talk: "I'm tempted to ask him to simply expound on the distinction between micro- and macro-evolution, so that he can scuttle himself with his own words…"

Dr. P.Z. Myers did, in fact, make my talk Thursday night, and something very strange happened: He, too, experienced a sudden and dramatic change in his level of courage during the course of the speech.

During the question-and-answer session, Professor Myers simply leaned against a door post with his arms crossed and said nothing. He just stared at me blankly and stood motionless in the same place where he was standing for the last twenty minutes of the speech. During the "Q&A," I looked directly at him and asked, "Are there any other questions?"

There was nothing but silence from Dr. Myers. But here's how he described the scene on his website:

> "…a fellow with a darker complexion and a long ponytail raised his hand to ask a good question, one that was actually very close to what I was going to ask as I was working my way up towards the room. He pointed out the fundamental inconsistency in Adams' conversion story—it didn't make sense that a good liberal would, in anger at feminism, abandon all liberal principles to so whole-heartedly embrace all of the completely contrary principles of conservative extremism (his answer: it was complicated, and there was more to the story than he'd been able to tell—I bet). The questions were just starting to warm up and drill down into Adams' hypocrisy, when one of our local ringleaders, who had

jumped up out of his seat when Mr. Radical Ponytail had raised his hand, abruptly cut off the questions."

The problem for Professor Myers is that—perhaps unbeknownst to him—the speech was videotaped. The videotape—taken by the school newspaper—will clearly show two things:

The man who asked the question about my conversion was white.

After I answered the white man's question, the darker man in the ponytail asked a question about civil liberties, which I answered. He was not prevented from asking a question by a "local ringleader."

More important than what the video will show is what it will not show. Specifically, there will be no image of Dr. Myers mustering the courage to ask a question of Dr. Adams. Instead, he simply cowered away and then ran back to his home computer in order to blog a fictitious account of a wonderful event—probably while sitting in his pajamas.

But it is a shame that Dr. Myers lacked the courage to ask me a single question. I certainly had a couple to ask of him. And I'll bet the audience would have liked to hear him explain how an evolutionist who deems the universe to be accidental can be so full of moral superiority. Or perhaps how the accidental moralist can be an atheist and yet so angry at God.

It takes courage for a man to admit that he is sometimes afraid. But that courage is not a gift of random mutation. It is a gift from a God who loves even the most hardened atheist.

Mike was actually one of the most courageous people I have ever known. Read more about his life in the book Life and How to Live It *(2023).*

CHAPTER 16

The End of Affirmative Action

November 14, 2006

This also appears in the book Life and How to Live It *(2023).*

For years, people have asked me why I switched from being a left-wing Democrat to a right-wing Republican. When I'm not in the mood to talk, I give a one-word response: reality. When I'm feeling more verbose, I give a two-word response: affirmative action.

Affirmative action in theory bears no resemblance to affirmative action in reality. The theory part was taught to me as a doctoral student in a sociology department in the late 1980s and early 1990s. Most of the academic rhetoric focused on what affirmative action isn't.

But sometimes, my professors would calm lingering doubts by saying what affirmative action is—namely, that it is both temporary and a tiebreaker. Those are really the only affirmative statements I've ever heard about affirmative action.

But then I graduated from college and finally had an opportunity to experience affirmative action in reality. Those early experiences, like the later ones, were uniformly negative.

As a young Ph.D. student, I was told by a department chair at Memphis State (now the University of Memphis) that, due to race, I had no chance in a head-to-head contest with the only other interviewee, a black male. He was honest enough to say that they were under too much pressure from human resources to give me a fair shake.

So I withdrew from that interview only to learn a year later that I couldn't fully escape the overt racial discrimination of affirmative action. In my first informal recruitment meeting as a professor in the University of North Carolina system, I listened to a social worker object to an applicant on the grounds that he was a "little too white male."

Of course, it should come as no surprise that people engage in racial discrimination in hiring when they are specifically asked to do so by human resources. But what is surprising about affirmative action is the extent to which it encourages discrimination along the lines of other variables not classified as "allowable" under official policies.

I have simply lost count of the number of times over the years that my colleagues have brought factors such as political affiliation and religion into discussions of job applicants.

Objections such as "He's too religious" or "He's too much of a family man" or "Her husband plays too dominant a role in their marriage" are simply indefensible. And it is worth asking whether such criteria would be so casually considered if human resources did not open a Pandora's box by deeming some discrimination to be an "acceptable" means to a desirable end.

But the discussion of affirmative action should by no means focus on the bad results it produces for white males like me. The real tragedy is its negative impact on the groups it purports to help. The effect is one I describe with a phrase called the "Reverse Roger Bannister Effect."

When Roger Bannister broke the four-minute mile in 1954, a whole class of people—not a race but those who run them—realized for the first time that a seemingly insurmountable goal could be achieved. So naturally, others started breaking the four-minute barrier left and right just as soon as the bar of achievement was raised by Bannister.

That is precisely the opposite of what is happening with affirmative action. By lowering the bar and (in the short term) making things easier for minorities, we guarantee persistent gaps in achievement. President Bush calls this the "soft bigotry" of low expectations. I prefer to call it the "hard reality" of low expectations.

Affirmative action is also an embarrassment for minorities who do not need or want to be measured by a lower standard. A black female student I taught in 1993 summed it up best by saying that although she had been admitted to college on the basis of outstanding grades and test scores, no one believed her. Whites just assumed she was there because of affirmative action. Once a class of people is given credit for something its members did not achieve, individuals in that class forfeit credit for the things they actually did.

I also look back on certain experiences and realize that affirmative action degrades whole institutions, not just individuals.

Twice, our department has flown in a white candidate under the mistaken belief that he or she was black. But we cannot accuse these candidates of lying about their race just to get an interview. In fact, we lie to them when we print "The UNC system does not discriminate on the basis of race" on every application. And I wonder how we still have the moral authority to punish students who plagiarize or cheat.

But maybe widespread lying is the best solution to the problem of affirmative action. If our students would all wake up one day and decide to start checking the box for "African American" on every university form, our affirmative action programs would break down altogether. Then, maybe we could replace "race consciousness" with the colorblindness Martin Luther King envisioned.

Mike elaborates on his political transformation in an earlier article (that is not included in this book):
My political transformation was perhaps even more gradual than my religious transformation. It was more of an issue-by-issue conversion. Some examples follow:

After a fellow fraternity member and his girlfriend were abducted by an armed assailant and murdered during my last year in college, I decided to abandon my support of gun control.

After learning in graduate school that affirmative action did not involve quotas and reverse discrimination—that it was merely a tiebreaker for equally qualified applicants (and a temporary program to boot)—I went to work in the academy and saw how it really worked. Confronted with the truth of affirmative action, I had to abandon my support of what was clearly a permanent and discriminatory policy.

After seeing a film of an unborn child yawning, rubbing his eyes, and playfully rolling around in his mother's womb, I realized that the fetus becomes a person long before birth and long after the Supreme Court allows it to be aborted. Therefore, I had to abandon my support of abortion rights.

Eventually, I woke up and realized that I had more in common with the Republicans than I did with the Democrats. I was also beginning to develop a new appreciation for moral absolutism, which would help to revive me spiritually.

Chapter 17

The Ten Commandments of Charity

January 18, 2007

Yesterday, I ran a column on panhandlers, which pretty clearly summarizes my feelings about giving money to beggars on the street. Those who wrote to tell me they are superior Christians because they don't judge people (like I do) are unworthy of a rebuttal. They are free to continue to purchase alcohol and crack for the unemployed and to do it all in the name of Jesus.

But those who wrote complaining that I opined on what not to do while omitting advice on what to do are deserving of a follow-up. For them, I supply the following Ten Commandments of Charity. All of them are brilliant because they are not original. They are all based on the conduct and advice of those I respect deeply. I hope they are helpful:

1. Never disclose the amount of money you give to charity. One evening, I was watching a speech by Bill O'Reilly. He was addressing an audience at Harvard University. One very belligerent student demanded to know the exact amount Bill gives to charity every year. He very forcefully

told the kid it was none of his business. Remember what the Sermon on the Mount says about charity. The moment you broadcast your good deeds, you start to lose focus on their true meaning. If you cannot follow rule #1, please skip #2 through #10 and give all your money to panhandlers.

2. Small charitable organizations are better than large ones. Years ago, the Sigma Chi fraternity (at Mississippi State) was debating where to send its Derby Week contributions. The decision was important, as we ended up raising over $50,000. Just as we were about to go with The United Way or some standard national organization, a member named Hamp Bryan told us about a hospice in his hometown that was in danger of being shut down. We ended up going with the smaller charity and helping it keep its doors open. The United Way did just fine without us.

3. Individual charities are often better than organizations. What happens if you can't find a satisfactory charity? Is there any reason why you should not target a person or family? Some years ago, my mother helped a former heroin addict (and convicted felon) get on his feet. When he got a job, he needed money for gas and other miscellaneous expenses. His family was invited into our home for nice home-cooked meals. When he went astray (and back into a life of drugs), she knew it immediately. It's easier to know when to stop giving to an individual, but it's harder with an organization that goes astray.

4. Conduct a thorough investigation of every charity. Speaking of organizations gone astray, I used to contribute money to The United Way (not knowing that they sometimes give money to Planned Parenthood). That is tough

to live with but no one's fault other than mine. Do your homework so you don't have such a thing hanging on your conscience. Trust me, I've been there.

5. The Fair Tax is our nation's best potential engine for charity growth. Those who make wisecracks about compassionate conservatism being an oxymoron generally believe in "compelled charity," which is the true oxymoron. Nancy Pelosi and her followers are the most uncompassionate and uncharitable people in America. They want the IRS to collect our "charity" at the point of a gun. But charity, once compelled, ceases to be charity. If we want to see an explosion of charitable giving in America, we must abolish the IRS. The Fair Tax is our only realistic hope.

6. Volunteer first, contribute second. It is always better to give to a charity with which you are familiar. There is no better way to learn about an organization than by volunteering for that organization. Give your time first and your money second.

7. Don't settle for the existing charity. Yesterday, I was talking to one of the best (if not the best) First Amendment attorneys in America. He mentioned that his church has a fund for those seeking to adopt children. The fund, which was started by a couple at the church, probably has close to zero overhead. I thought to myself, "Why didn't I think of that?" The real question is: How many people reading this column will be inspired to duplicate it?

8. Use charity to defeat prejudice. Once, there was a woman who overheard her youngest son making fun of a handicapped child. She made him help her do volunteer work

with handicapped children. She kept giving him his weekly allowance but made him give it to a charity helping handicapped kids. Later, as an adult, he gave to the same charity—but this time of his own free will.

9. Practice spontaneous charity. Did you hear the one about the lady who was driving through a slum and saw a poor woman walking home from her job as a cook in a cafeteria? She was about to have to cook again for her own family when she heard the knock on the door. As she was handed a bag of groceries and a hot meal, all she heard was, "Don't thank me—thank Jesus."

10. Use charity as therapy. Sometimes, we have bad days. We wake up angry at the world. I had an excellent education professor (one of three in America) who said that the best cure for a bad mood was just to greet everyone we saw with a smile and a few polite words. He said it would soon be contagious. Imagine what would happen if we took that $150 for our next therapy session—the one we go to for reasons of status ("well, MY analyst says")—and bought clothes for the homeless instead.

After Mike passed, I ended up with his car, a nice 2019 Accord that he had purchased just the previous summer. My old car was still in excellent condition, so I gave it to a single mother in our church who had no car. I mention this only because I was just following the good example that Mike set: When he bought this car, his old car was still in great shape, but he didn't trade it in; he gave it to a student who needed a car. That's the kind of guy he was. He practiced what he preached.

Chapter 18

How to Read the New Testament

May 21, 2007

Everyone I know seems to be reading the Bible these days in search of answers. That is usually a good thing, but not always. In fact, too many of the biblical discussions I get into with friends and family members relate to the "end times" and whether they are upon us. That is a shame because reading the Bible can enrich one's daily life provided one is not obsessed with using it as a device to decipher the future.

Because of one relatively simple error in dating one book of the New Testament, author Tim LaHaye has misled tens of millions of people into thinking that a great time of tribulation is near. He has Christians everywhere looking for signs of an emerging anti-Christ and, ultimately, in a cowardly fashion, looking forward to a time when Christ will rapture his church away from earthly troubles.

If Christians would simply study the New Testament themselves—instead of relying upon twenty-first century "prophets" writing fictional books for twenty-first-century profits—they would arrive at a few very simple conclusions:

1. The Revelation to John was written around 65 AD, not 95 AD.
2. The anti-Christ was Nero, not some world figure yet to emerge in the twenty-first century.
3. The tribulation occurred in the first century around the time of the destruction of the temple in Jerusalem in 70 AD.
4. The "rapture" never happened, and it never will.
5. The words of Jesus in Matthew 24 plainly reveal that most of the discourse in The Revelation to John is based on events in the first century.

Once an individual realizes he is stuck here on Earth and will not be raptured away from all of his troubles, he can begin to read the Bible the way it was intended to be read. I have a word of advice for those who have never really thought about reading the Bible as an end in itself rather than as a means to some goal, such as predicting the future. My advice is actually borrowed from a friend who received a moving card from his wife just a few months ago.

After receiving the cherished card from his wife, my friend would sneak into their bedroom late at night (she always fell asleep while he was finishing his last TV show). After giving her a kiss while she was sleeping, he would take the card off his dresser and go into the spare room to read it by the light of a small lamp.

There were certain lines he would read three or four times over: "It is a privilege to know you, to share myself with you," "I never knew such a person could exist until I met you," and "You lift my spirits to places where my troubles seem so much farther away."

It was wonderful to hear that a dear friend had found his "soulmate" and all of the joy that comes from lifelong companionship. But at the same time, I could not listen to his story without thinking of all the other friends I know who have suffered through a painful divorce or, in some cases, never even met someone with whom they share a special bond of love. And some are growing older and lonelier by the day.

But recently, I received a new insight into what seems to be an unfair distribution of soulmates among God's children. It came as I was listening to a pastor named "Mike" whose last name I do not even know. His message was broadcast from Port City Church in Wilmington to a theater rented out to handle the overflow of his growing congregation.

He urged each member of his church to read the First Letter of John during the coming week. He also urged them to read it as if it were written just for them by someone who is madly in love with them.

I was so intrigued by this take on the proper approach to reading the New Testament epistle that I immediately bought a copy of the English Standard Version—a version I've been meaning to read for quite some time. Later that night, I opened it and started reading by the light of a small lamp:

> "…Whoever says he is in the light and hates his brother is still in darkness. Whoever loves his brother abides in the light, and in him there is no cause for stumbling… I am writing to you, little children, because your sins are forgiven for his name's sake … Beloved, we are God's children now, and what we will be has not yet appeared; but we know that when he appears we shall be like him, because we shall see him as he is.

And everyone who thus hopes in him purifies himself as he is pure... We know that everyone who has been born of God does not keep on sinning, but he who was born of God protects him, and the evil one does not touch him..."

After reading those lines, it occurred to me that I had only been skimming through this great epistle on my last several runs through the New Testament. My zeal to get to The Revelation to John has been such that I have hardly noticed those great words in the years following the attacks of 9/11.

We all need to learn to read the Word as if it were written for us personally by someone who could not love us more. When we cannot get enough of it in the here and now, the future seems so much less important. And a little uncertainty is hardly the end of the world.

Ironically, Mike was inspired to read the Bible by a death row inmate, as told in Chapter 97, "Everlasting Life on Death Row."
Speaking of Bibles, Mike also once wrote this:
Last week, I picked up a copy of one of my mother's old Bibles. I just started reading through it. Fortunately, it contains extensive highlighting and numerous post-it notes summarizing her reactions to various scriptures. I am grateful to have the chance to do this. Too few people have such an opportunity, and I will cherish it daily. The commandment to honor our parents does not end with their death.

CHAPTER 19

Why Johnny's Sociology Professor Will Die in Obscurity

June 25, 2007

Just a few years ago, a sociologist I know got really depressed—even more so than the average sociologist. His depression stemmed from the fact that the most famous sociologist in the world had just passed away, and hardly anyone noticed. Indeed, one of America's foremost liberal publications had dedicated no more than a few sentences to the man's life, despite his many accomplishments in the field of sociology.

Naturally, the depressed sociologist was disheartened by the lack of attention paid to his idol's passing. It even prompted him to ask me a serious question: "What do sociologists have to do to get a little respect in this world?" Today, I'm finally getting around to answering his question.

If one wants to identify steps that can be taken to increase the standing of sociologists—relative to academics that are taken more seriously—one first has to identify what they are doing wrong. A comment by a recently retired sociologist at

UNC-Wilmington is illustrative of what ails the pseudoscience of sociology. The comment came in response to an attack on the work of my friend David Horowitz.

As many readers know, Horowitz has been spending a lot of time speaking on the issue of academic freedom and indoctrination in higher education. In many of his speeches, David quotes studies from major universities showing that at some schools Democrats outnumber Republicans by ratios as high as nine to one (sometimes even higher) in various "social science" and humanities departments.

But recently, a respected political science journal published a study asserting that there really is no liberal hegemony in American higher education. The study says there is also a recent trend toward greater political moderation among professors at American universities. Why does the study contradict what Horowitz has been saying? The answer is simple: It relies on a survey of the professors' subjective evaluations of their political leanings relative to others rather than objective data regarding their partisan political affiliations. ("I'm not really an extremist. In fact, I feel that I'm middle of the road. Just ask me and I'll tell you!")

When the study of the subjective feelings of American professors was published, a Democrat in the political science department forwarded it to a Democrat in the sociology department. The Democrat sociologist then forwarded it to another Democrat sociologist. (But he wasn't engaging in political discrimination because there are no Republicans in the department of sociology to whom he could forward it in order to ensure a more balanced critique of the study.)

Next, one of the Democrat sociologists forwarded the study to a Marxist sociologist who sent it around to the whole department. Then, a Democrat sociologist hit "reply all" in order to tell the whole department that he agreed with the results of the study, which claimed that there is no liberal hegemony in American higher education. That's when the soon-to-be-retired Democrat sociologist Gary Faulkner responded.

Faulkner's response was very simple. He said that there was nothing like "the cool hand of the empiricist" to quiet the "ravings" of the "ranters." It is not surprising that Faulkner dismisses people like David Horowitz and Mike Adams as "ranters" for asserting that there is a leftist bias in higher education. This is because a) sociologists are well below the professorial average in IQ—that is, if you buy into the use of objective indicators—and b) those below the average in workplace IQ are prone to resort to name-calling when their culturally acquired beliefs are challenged.

The significance of Dr. Gary Faulkner's remark can be best understood by restating his main thesis without resorting to name-calling. That thesis follows: "Emotion can best be removed from a debate by employing subjective, rather than objective, measurements."

Sociologist Gary Faulkner feigns an interest in rationality. But critics of the discipline know that sociologists are not objective scientists committed to rationality. They are simply contrarians committed to the obfuscation of fairly simple problems.

If the average person believes that homosexuality is chosen, the sociologist rails against the ex-gay movement. If the average person believes that transgendered people are mentally ill, the sociologist shows a film in class of the transgendered doing everyday things. If the average person believes that objective data help to make debate more civilized, the sociologist argues that this occurs better through the use of subjective data.

Faulkner's remarks remind me of a time when I interviewed for a job in Florida. Everything was going well until I presented the results of a longitudinal study on the causes of juvenile delinquency. I argued that longitudinal studies—measuring independent variables at one point in time and dependent variables later—were necessary to make cause-and-effect statements when studying juvenile delinquency. But one sociologist thought otherwise.

With a straight face, the sociologist actually argued that by using longitudinal data, I was "forcing" a cause-and-effect relationship that might not exist. Unsurprisingly, when I went home and reviewed some of his published research, I discovered that in the past he had only done cross-sectional research (i.e., research conducted at a single point in time).

The sociologist's best-known cross-sectional study claimed to measure the effects of "blocked opportunities" on juvenile delinquency. In other words, juveniles don't engage in delinquency because they choose delinquency. They engage in delinquency because they perceive that they cannot get good jobs and a good education.

In order to measure the independent variable, or cause (blocked opportunities), the sociologist naturally asked youths about their feelings. "Do you feel you will be able to get a good job?" "Do you feel you will be able to get a good education?" The sociologist also asked the youths how much delinquency they had engaged in during the previous year.

Having found a strong correlation between blocked opportunities and delinquency, the sociologist reported that the former is the cause of the latter. But many of my readers noticed the sociologist's sleight of hand—namely, that he measured the effects of present perceptions of blocked opportunities on past delinquency. In other words, he put the purported cause after the purported effect, which, again, shows why we need longitudinal, not cross-sectional, data.

So there is a lesson to be learned in all this. When a sociologist tells you that blocked opportunities lead to crime, you know that he really means that the choice to commit crime will lead to fewer opportunities. When he says that labeling people as delinquent causes the youth to be delinquent (the so-called "self-fulfilling prophecy"), you know he really means that youths who choose to be delinquent will later be labeled as delinquent. And when the sociologist says that associating with delinquents causes delinquency, he really means that if you chose to engage in delinquency, conformists will no longer seek your company.

And needless to say, when the sociologist says that subjective data show that the American academy is not a liberal stronghold, he is really saying that objective scientific data has shown time and time again that it is.

Although most sociologists will die in obscurity, it shouldn't be that way. We should all have our children sign up for their classes, take copious notes, and believe precisely the opposite of what these ideologues tell them.

If we do, we'll all live long and happy lives. And best of all, we'll all be remembered long after we're gone.

I love how he makes fun of his own profession! Chapter 43, "When Students Cheat, Liberals Retreat," and Chapter 28, "Primary and Secondary Racism," are also good examples.

Chapter 20

Life and How to Live It, Part IX

July 23, 2007

This also appears in the book Life and How to Live It *(2023).*

It's no secret that I wasn't the best student ever to attend Clear Lake High School. I failed English all four years. I failed to reach the 2.0 GPA mark. I finished in the bottom 1 percent of my graduating class. There was a distinct reason why I performed so poorly: I attempted to get a "D" in every class and to fail English every year so I did not have to get a summer job. The fact that I got above a 1.0 GPA was due to a bunch of accidental grades of "C" from some overly generous teachers.

My total lack of effort in high school was largely due to my success on the soccer field. At the age of fifteen, I won a state soccer championship together with some magnificently talented players—most notably, Joey Gunderson, Sam Hinson, and Peter Royster. After Mike Olmedo and Steve Zobel joined our team, we would soon be headed for another state championship game. This time, we were heavy favorites, with several players who had won a state title previously as underdogs. I was certain that I was one of several players on the team who were headed for the pros. In fact, I thought I was a lock.

But then something strange started happening at the end of my junior year. In April, I was averaging about sixty miles a week on the jogging trail as I was gearing up for a crack at the Houston Marathon. As I was training, I began to hear and feel a small clicking noise around my left ankle. Over the next few months, it began to actually hurt, so I went to see a doctor. The news wasn't good. A bone spur was starting to slice my Achilles tendon, which, according to the doctor, would surely rupture without corrective surgery.

So I did what you would expect me to do. I told the doctor to kiss my (backside) and kept on running through the injury. Needless to say, I eventually had to stop running completely. I was so hopelessly out of shape at the beginning of the next season that I could not even make the team.

I finally had the surgery in November. And it was unsuccessful. In fact, I would be unable to run even a single mile for over three years. Needless to say, my dream (the only one I ever had) of becoming a professional soccer player was over. I started smoking, drinking, and occasionally using drugs in preparation for a two-year sentence to junior college. There wasn't a university in America pathetic enough to take me. Not even Ole Miss. [*That's an inside joke—"Ole Miss" (the University of Mississippi) is the savage rival of Mississippi State University, which was Mike's and our father's alma mater.*]

But nonetheless, I had to take the fall from being a star athlete at a great high school to an absolute nobody at a junior college in the pathetic little town of Pasadena, TX [*another rivalry, by the way*]. It was either that or work as a mechanic. Having rebuilt the engine on my 1970 GTO (together with my father),

I could have gotten employment as a grease monkey somewhere in the Clear Lake area. But that was even worse than junior college in Pasadena. Needless to say, I was one miserable and angry eighteen-year-old.

Miserable as I was, I buckled down, and after two years of misery, I was in a position to get into a four-year university. I applied and was accepted to Mississippi State University. It wasn't prestigious, but at least it wasn't Ole Miss. And my dad was so happy that I had started to turn things around that he rewarded me with an invitation to join a fraternity at his expense.

After I was initiated into the Sigma Chi fraternity, I did something very rare among Southeastern Conference Greeks: I managed to actually raise my GPA in my first full semester living in the fraternity house. In fact, it was now nearly double my high school GPA. Through a little perseverance, the GPA continued to climb despite my dwelling place in Room 13 of the Sigma Chi house. I was easily accepted to graduate school and started working on my M.S. degree right after finishing my B.A.

At the end of my M.S. program, I turned down an offer to pursue a doctorate in psychology at the University of Georgia. Instead, I finished my four-year doctoral program in just three years at Mississippi State. It wasn't the most prestigious place to get a Ph.D., but at least it wasn't Ole Miss.

I spent the week of graduation—my last week at Mississippi State—driving my friend Jerry's old Jeep Wrangler. He was borrowing my truck to move his things back to Vicksburg. Every night that week, I would go out driving my friends Dana, Stephanie, and Becky around town while they drank beer, and I enjoyed the company of three very pretty former members of the Phi Mu sorority—one of whom was also finishing grad school that week.

When Jerry got back in town, I offered to buy that old Jeep Wrangler from him. He laughed and said he would never sell the vehicle to a good friend. Jerry said it was so prone to breaking down that you would almost have to be a professional mechanic to keep it on the road.

At just that moment, I was struck with a profound realization: Had I not been unexpectedly injured, I would have been a former professional soccer player by then. And I would have been a professional mechanic without a single college degree by then too. Instead, I was a twenty-eight-year-old Ph.D. who had just landed a good job in North Carolina.

There is no tragedy or setback so great that it cannot be turned into a blessing with the help of a little persistence and hard work.

First, Mike was not against being a mechanic—if that is your calling. Obviously, it was not his, so it would have been the wrong choice for him. In fact, Mike once said to me something to the effect that we, as a nation, have made it too cheap and easy to attend college and pushed kids into college who weren't really interested and qualified to be there. This caused the student loan bubble and a general degradation of the college experience.

Second, I tried to convince Mike that the setback of his early retirement could well be a blessing in disguise. I reminded him that the three greatest tragedies of my life—being laid off unexpectedly the week before Christmas in 1996, my bitter divorce in 2005, and my near-fatal motorcycle accident in 2010—all turned out for the best, in time. I also reminded him that, just a few years ago, someone else close to us was also devastated by an unexpected early retirement—and that turned out to be a good thing after all.

As hard as I tried, I failed in my attempt to assure Mike that things would work out for the best. At the time, I sensed that maybe he was just politely letting me talk and that I wasn't really getting through to him. But I wasn't too worried about that, as I thought we would continue to have those talks over the coming months. I also hoped that the encouragement he was receiving from me and from his other close friends would ultimately help him to see that things weren't as bleak as he believed them to be. Unfortunately, I did not realize the actual depth of his discouragement until after the fact.

When discouraged by a tragedy or setback, please remember this story—and don't give up!

Chapter 21

Life and How to Live It, Part X

July 30, 2007

This also appears in the book Life and How to Live It *(2023).*

You may recall that I had a less-than-stellar record as a high school student. It took a while for me to get things going but, as soon as I gathered momentum, I had a hard time slowing down.

My first year as a college professor *[1993]* demanded a lot of hard work. I had to prepare for several classes I hadn't taught previously. But by plugging away nightly, I was able to get through the year with flying colors. I somehow registered the highest teaching evaluations in my department after only one semester.

During my second year as a professor, I had to focus on research. I knew that if I spun a couple of articles off my dissertation and wrote or co-wrote a couple of "new" articles, I would be a lock to get tenure. Things worked out well. My department voted unanimously to grant me tenure after just four years and two months on the job.

Instead of taking a rest after getting tenure, I started to study for the LSAT. The following month, I took the test and scored high enough to get into all three of the schools I had been considering seriously. Then, in one of the most foolish moves of my life, I turned down a scholarship offer from the University of Georgia School of Law. I later accepted an offer from UNC School of Law and enrolled in the fall of 1998.

For the first few months, I studied diligently—an average of about five hours a night. But for some reason, I started to have serious attention problems in class by the time November rolled around. The Clinton impeachment scandal was dominating the political shows on both radio and television. But unfortunately, I didn't have enough time to weigh in on the serious issues that confronted our nation during that time.

As Thanksgiving approached, my problems staying awake in class were getting worse. I was becoming very bored with law school in general. I also found it hard to take UNC law seriously, as the school seemed to offer more seminars dealing with transgendered rights than seminars dealing with serious legal issues. So I decided to take a weekend off and head out of town to catch up on some shopping.

As I was looking through some books at the mall, I came across *Sexual McCarthyism* by Alan Dershowitz. As I was holding the book, I had an immediate realization about my life and where it was headed. I knew I did not ever want to practice law. I knew I wanted to teach college and become an irreverent columnist and author, much like Alan Dershowitz. I knew I had taken a wrong turn in my career by pursuing a law degree I would never put to use.

As you can imagine, the months that followed my decision to return to academia were depressing. After all, I had wasted a year's salary in order to find out what I did not want to do with my life. I had sold an awesome row house built in 1912, which was the coolest place I'd ever lived. And to make matters worse, I was forced to end a relationship with a girl I was falling in love with over the summer preceding my enrollment in law school.

For months on end, I sat up late at night, staring at the ceiling and asking myself why I had not just slowed down after getting tenure so I could just enjoy life for a few years. After falling asleep, I would often wake up in a pool of sweat thinking about all that I had lost in the preceding months. Sometimes, it was the money. Sometimes, it was the house. Sometimes, it was the girl.

I didn't realize just how far I had been set back financially until I went back to Wilmington to look for another house. I could not find anything I liked as much as my old 1912 row house. So I settled for an overpriced, cheaply built, and utterly boring townhome near the beach.

When I moved in during the summer of 1999, I was feeling pretty sorry for myself. I was a wannabe pundit with no book deal, no column, and no radio or television show. I simply did not have a platform. I only had debt.

Seven years (to the day) after I moved back to Wilmington, I got a very surprising phone call from my agent, D.J. Snell. He told me that Penguin U.S.A. was offering me a contract for my book *Feminists Say the Darndest Things*—the advance and bonuses totaling $10,000 more than the salary I had lost that year I was in law school. So after I got off the phone, I bought a six-pack and headed to my back deck to do some serious thinking. Naturally, this was done while I watched the bug zapper.

As I was sitting on the back deck, I thought about the 1912 row house I had sold in 1998. It had not appreciated that much since I moved away. But the townhouse I bought to replace it ended up doing quite well. In fact, after someone decided to build the shopping center next door, its value went up enough in just six months to recoup that year's loss of salary that once had me feeling so depressed.

And the story gets even better. I took the money I made on that townhome and rolled it over into a house twice as big. That investment paid off to the tune of an appreciation over the next two years that was three times the salary I lost by taking the year off. Oddly, I ended up making a lot of money I never would have made had I not taken the year off to head to UNC School of Law.

I guess that, unlike my other "Life and How to Live It" articles, this one needs no bold letters to highlight the main point. Just read it again the next time you think God has abandoned you. And realize that your best days may be ahead of you still.

For further reading: Romans 8:18-28

In case you don't have a Bible handy:

> [18] I consider that our present sufferings are not worth comparing with the glory that will be revealed in us. [19] For the creation waits in eager expectation for the children of God to be revealed. [20] For the creation was subjected to frustration, not by its own choice, but by the will of the one who subjected it, in hope [21] that the creation itself will be liberated from its bondage to decay and brought into the freedom and glory of the children of God.
>
> [22] We know that the whole creation has been groaning as in the pains of childbirth right up to the present time. [23] Not only so, but we ourselves, who have

the first fruits of the Spirit, groan inwardly as we wait eagerly for our adoption to sonship, the redemption of our bodies. ²⁴ For in this hope we were saved. But hope that is seen is no hope at all. Who hopes for what they already have? ²⁵ But if we hope for what we do not yet have, we wait for it patiently.

²⁶ In the same way, the Spirit helps us in our weakness. We do not know what we ought to pray for, but the Spirit himself intercedes for us through wordless groans. ²⁷ And he who searches our hearts knows the mind of the Spirit, because the Spirit intercedes for God's people in accordance with the will of God.

²⁸ And we know that in all things God works for the good of those who love him, who have been called according to his purpose.

Romans 8:18 – "I consider that our present sufferings are not worth comparing with the glory that will be revealed in us."
   Mike is now in that glory. Not long after he passed, I was shown a brief but moving vision of my brother and our parents. They were simply smiling at each other. There were no words, but I felt the emotion. All anxiety, fear, worries, sadness, etc., were gone and replaced with peace and contentment. I know that God was telling me that I don't have to worry about them and letting me know that is what I can look forward to.

CHAPTER 22

Understanding Atheism

October 29, 2007

Author's Note: Special thanks to Amy, Brad, Mike, and the Freethought Society at Clemson University.

I declared myself an agnostic in 1983 and stayed that way until I declared myself an atheist in 1992. The road from Christianity to atheism and back to Christianity was—with my apologies to Beatles fans—long and winding. It took many years to travel.

The decision to major in psychology was one of many factors that led to my decision to leave the church. Not many psychology departments have more atheists than the nearest philosophy department. But many come close. And the way the discipline of psychology approaches religion is likely to lead some students astray.

I recall quite well my first exposure to Freud and his ideas about the Oedipus complex. I became well-schooled in his ideas about man's compelling psychological need to create a God in his own image—to resolve various feelings of guilt flowing from childhood trauma. I was so captivated by these ideas that I read *Moses and Monotheism*, *Totem and Taboo*, and *The Future of an Illusion* in my spare time. Each took me further away from God.

B.F. Skinner had a similar impact on my thinking. The principles of operant conditioning were not always used to explain religion away. Strict behaviorists seldom have a compelling need to "look inside the black box" or, in other words, analyze unobservable thoughts. But these principles do provide a ready explanation for those convinced that man created God, not vice versa. I was so captivated by Skinner that I read *Walden Two* and *Beyond Freedom and Dignity* in my spare time. These books pushed me further in the direction of atheism.

The notion that psychology might provide an explanation for atheism—rather than theism—never really occurred to me during my years as a psychology student (from 1983 until 1989 when I received my M.S. in psychology). But in March of 1989, a woman named Martha Hamilton—the mother of my "second mother," Lisa Chambers *[one of Mike's greatest influences, as described in Chapter 60, "Fifty"]*—responded to my praise of B.F. Skinner and the behaviorists with the following comment: "It just sounds like a bunch of people trying to get out of serving God."

I must confess that I thought Mrs. Hamilton was just a simple-minded fundamentalist. Now, I realize that she was right, and I was wrong.

If psychologists were really interested in the fair and balanced treatment of religion, they would see the obvious connection between cognitive dissonance theory and atheism. And of course, they would discuss it in their classes in conjunction with the application of Freudian and Skinnerian theories seeking to explain religion away.

In the 1950s and 1960s, psychologists like Elliot Aronson began to suggest that behavior sometimes causes attitudes rather than vice versa. In the wake of this discussion, cognitive dissonance became a popular psychological theory. Put simply, it spoke to the issue of how beliefs sometimes emerge from a tension between certain cognitive elements.

For example, if a person is cognizant of the fact that smoking causes cancer, he will experience dissonance when he thinks about the fact that he is a smoker. He may be inclined to adopt other beliefs like "They will probably find a cure for cancer before I get it." He may develop powerful, even silly, rationalizations like "I'll quit next year" or "It does not matter because the world could end tomorrow in a nuclear holocaust" or "I could be hit by a car tomorrow, so I might as well smoke today."

Because Christianity is sometimes a demanding religion, it, too, may create a good deal of cognitive dissonance. For example, the declaration "I am a Christian" can sometimes clash with the awareness that "Christians are supposed to tithe" or "Christians are supposed to love their enemies."

I have seen people who began tithing to the church and loving their enemies upon converting to Christianity. But that is not how it always ends for the converted Christian. Like me, many other Christians have resolved the tension by, at least temporarily, deciding to abandon the Way. Sometimes it is simply easier to say, "I am not a Christian."

Those who become agnostic or atheist often say that it was due to an intellectual journey or an intellectually honest appraisal of childhood faith. But as my mentor David L. McMillen *[Chapter 60, "Fifty"]* used to say, "People rarely understand their own motivations."

I believe that cognitive dissonance theory helps people better understand their own motivations. I believe it has helped me to understand my fall from Christianity, which, thankfully, ended with a return to the church.

But the theory might also explain why it took me so long to get back to church. I abandoned atheism on March 7th of 1996 *[as told in Chapter 27, "The Shadow Proves the Sunshine"]*. But I did not return to the church until October of 2000. The reason for the delay was simple: I was ashamed.

As I imagined myself walking back into a church, I also imagined people thinking and perhaps even saying, "What is Mike Adams doing here at church?" But I made it back, and my life continues to be blessed as I walk further with Jesus every day.

I can understand the dissonance that is felt by the young woman who wrote to me last week telling of her multiple suicide attempts in the wake of a battle with manic depression. She says she cannot seem to get out of bed on Sundays because of the shame she feels for the harm she has tried to inflict upon herself. She needs to hear from confessing and humble Christians who say they desperately want her back regardless of what she's done.

I often wonder why we speak of atheists as if they are our enemies. And I wonder whether that should matter if we call ourselves Christians. I hope this column will inspire some cognitive dissonance for the writer and the reader alike. And I hope the tension will be resolved with love, which is the best cure for dissonance or, for that matter, anything else.

Mike wrote about deeply serious topics, but he was a very funny person. He was just fun to be around, and his social media feed was peppered with humor, such as:

> My next book will be called "Your Mother Just Sent Me a Friend Request: And Other Things You Never Say in a Biker Bar."
>
> My next book will be called "Your Daughter Is Going to Be Just as Hot as Your Wife: And Other Things You Never Tell Your Best Friend."
>
> My next book will be called "Your Mother Is Good-Looking: And Other Things You Can Tell a Girl Once But Not Twice."
>
> I'm writing a self-help book for dolphins. It's called the porpoise driven life.

CHAPTER 23

Feminism Means Never Having to Say You're Sorry

January 1, 2008

Two years ago, during our annual peer evaluation, a feminist professor suggested (via email) that I may have falsified information in my annual productivity report. She claimed I had listed an article as "in print" without placing any reprints in my "supporting documents" folder. A few minutes later, she wrote back admitting she had misread my report. I had listed the article as "in press," which meant that the absence of reprints was simply a function of the fact that the article had not yet been printed.

The incident did not surprise me. Feminists are generally more confrontational in emails than they are in person—unless, of course, they are with a large group of feminists. They also approach orgasm every time they think they have caught a man doing something wrong. But although it was unsurprising, the incident was certainly enlightening.

I say the incident was enlightening because, seven years before that, another feminist listed a first-edition book as "in print" in her annual report without providing any supporting documentation. Then, three years later, she listed the same first-edition book as "in print," thus twice receiving credit for the same publication. I brought this to the attention of the department chairman, but to my knowledge, nothing ever happened.

More recently, feminist Rosemary DePaolo appears in an ad misrepresenting her accomplishments as UNC-Wilmington chancellor. The ad, appearing in "The Black Pages" phone book, which advertises black-owned businesses, used this bold heading:

New Black Faculty 2006 – 2007.

Among the fifteen pictures of "new black faculty," there were several of black professors who have been at UNC-Wilmington for many years. There was also at least one picture of a black professor who has been gone from the university for several years. It was a triple blow to the university because she was (and still is, I suppose) a black lesbian.

But the university solved the problem of losing a black, a woman, and a homosexual—all rolled into one person—by simply lying with taxpayer money in an ad meant to a) appease the black community and b) cover up the failures of the chancellor with regard to improving diversity. It is a strong accusation, but there were simply too many "errors" in the ad to attribute to the administration's generally high level of incompetence.

Of course, despite the obvious deception, nothing has happened to the chancellor, and nothing ever will because she is a feminist. And we all know that feminists are held to a lower standard than men because, curiously, we think that is a good way to end sexism.

But there really is more to these cases than "society" simply holding women to a lower standard of ethical conduct. I think such cases really have a lot to do with the current goals of the feminist movement. This revelation came to me when I heard two feminists talking the other day about an alleged relationship between Ashley Olsen, twenty-one, and Lance Armstrong, thirty-six.

I don't have to tell my readers that both feminists were offended by the relationship. Nor do I have to explain that they were offended because they thought Armstrong was taking advantage of the younger Olsen and that he was somehow perverted for taking interest in one so young.

But perhaps I should at this point remind the reader that feminists are staunchly opposed to parental notification requirements for minors seeking abortions. Feminists will almost always defend a teenager's right to make such a decision on her own. They are even reluctant to require parental notification in cases where the girl is not yet a teenager.

So why is a twelve-year-old mature enough to have an abortion, while a twenty-one-year-old is too immature to date Lance Armstrong? The answer lies in what I think feminism has come to mean now that a woman has the same opportunities as a man:

Feminism is a political movement that seeks unlimited rights for women without corresponding responsibilities by exempting women from all criticism.

The arrogance of modern-day feminism is best illustrated by the case of a feminist atheist who was mad at God after several people were killed in a natural disaster. "How could a God who is good and just decide arbitrarily who should live and who should die?" she asked indignantly.

Of course, the feminist is pro-choice on the issue of abortion. She feels entitled to as many abortions as she deems necessary. She can abort every other pregnancy, every third pregnancy, every odd-numbered pregnancy, every even-numbered pregnancy, or, for that matter, every one of them if she so chooses.

But no one will ever confront the angry feminist with her hypocrisy. It shows more than that the modern feminist believes she is above God. It shows that the modern feminist movement is succeeding wildly in achieving its current political objectives.

Shortly after publishing this column, Mike published his second book, Feminists Say the Darndest Things.

I think Mike enjoyed coming up with the titles for his columns as much as he enjoyed writing them! But some of his cultural references may be a bit obscure, especially for younger readers. "Love means never having to say you're sorry" was an iconic quote from Love Story, *a book by Erich Segal and then a hit movie in 1970. Here are some more amusing examples from columns not included in this book:*

> "Alexander the Mediocre" (12/17/2007)
> *The title refers to Alexander the Great.*
> *The column is Mike's response to criticism from Alexander Tristan Riley, a sociology professor at Bucknell.*
>
> "Full Metal Yellow Jacket" (12/26/2010)
> *The title refers to "full metal jacket" ammunition, which is commonly used in handguns and rifles.*

The column is about crime and gun control on the campus of Georgia Tech, whose mascot is the Yellow Jacket.

"Hannibal's Lecture" (5/25/2016)
The title refers to Hannibal Lecter, a fictional character in The Silence of the Lambs.
The column is about professor Bryce Hannibal of Texas A&M University.

"Horton Hears the Who" (6/1/2014)
The title references the popular children's book Horton Hears a Who! *by Dr. Seuss.*
The column is about UNCW activist Brice Horton and the song "My Generation" by The Who.

"Me and Julio Down by the Schoolyard" (2/28/2007)
The title is the name of a song by Paul Simon from his eponymous 1972 album.
The column is one of several about (now former) Associate Professor Julio Pino of Kent State University.

"PETA Principles" (7/30/2004)
The title references the 1969 book The Peter Principle *by Laurence Peter, which is about incompetence in organizations.*
The column mocks PETA.

"The Merchant of Venison" (3/9/2005)
The title refers to The Merchant of Venice, *a play by William Shakespeare.*

The column is a response to someone who criticized Mike for posting a picture of a deer he killed. The critic asked Mike how he could eat such a beautiful creature, and Mike replied with recipes.

"The Old Rugged Cross-Dresser" (5/4/2006)

The title refers to "The Old Rugged Cross," a popular hymn written in 1912 by American evangelist George Bennard.

The column is Mike's response to criticism from a transsexual at UNC-Chapel Hill.

"The Passion of the Censor" (1/31/2005)

The title refers to Mel Gibson's The Passion of the Christ.

The column is about how a college prevented a Christian student group from showing the film.

"The University of Nude Copulating Asians" (8/15/2005)

The title refers to the University of North Carolina at Asheville.

The column is about the university's view of the "American porn industry as racist, in that it has excluded Asian-American men."

Chapter 24

If I Ran the Zoo

June 16, 2008

The good folks at the National Association of Scholars have asked me to write a short piece modeled after the Dr. Seuss book *If I Ran the Zoo*. Specifically, they want me to enumerate the changes I would make in higher education if I ran the system.

Of course, I've never really imagined being in charge of the zoo because, you see, I am an endangered species. I am a Christian, a Caucasian, a Conservative, and a Capitalist. But these four "Cs" were not something the liberals could foresee. When I was hired, I was an Atheist, an America hater, an Abortion supporter, and a bit of an Alcoholic. The changes in these four "As" are now the cause of my forays.

Since I am now an endangered species, the liberals like to come by my cage and stare at me while I work. They've never really seen the likes of an animal such as me in the zoo in which they work. But I am used to them now. And so I will write about what it would be like to be on the other side—as silly as the proposition might be.

In the zoo in which I work, students applying for the position of resident's assistant are asked whether they would have any religious objections to providing RU 486 (upon request) to the pregnant young women living in their dorms. Student applicants are disqualified from the job if, for religious reasons, they would refuse to do so.

If I ran the zoo, I would make employees in the division of student activities go deer hunting with the Second Amendment Club. These employees would have to provide ammunition to the hunters if they ran out. They would be fired if they refused to do so.

In the zoo in which I work, students are not allowed to post signs on their dorm room doors if those signs might "incite" people. They can find themselves in front of a disciplinary committee for violations of this or one of our many other speech codes.

If I ran the zoo, university administrators would be required to read Supreme Court decisions, which have stated that "Every idea is an incitement" (See *Gitlow v. People of New York*, 1925). Every dormitory student would be required to post materials that are meant to incite on his door. No student would be given a degree unless he could prove that he incited his fellow students and that he did so with regularity.

In the zoo in which I work, female students are provided with a women's resource center. But male students are not provided with a men's resource center.

If I ran the zoo, I would interpret Title IX as prohibiting the building of a center for one sex but not the other. But I would raze the WRC, not build an MRC. This would be symbolic of the fact that Title IX is almost always used to destroy opportunities for some and provide opportunities for none. Afterward, I would put a nursery in the place of the WRC to care for the children of female students who choose not to abort their children. I would reward these brave pro-life students with free tuition—paid for by doubling the tuition of male students who get women pregnant out of wedlock.

In the zoo in which I work, a pro-life group was recently denied official status by the school. The reason was the injection of a "faith statement" in the club's constitution—one the university saw as too exclusive.

If I ran the zoo, the people who rejected this pro-life group would have to do community service. I would make them do it all for groups with whom they do not voluntarily associate. They would clean up beer cans at NASCAR races, spent shells at gun ranges, and diapers at Christian day care centers. And after they were through, I would have them write "Diversity Is Our Greatest Strength" 100 times. Or they could just admit that they don't really believe in diversity.

In the zoo in which I work, feminists ban words they deem offensive. For example, they ban the use of words like "mankind" and phrases like "year of our Lord." They are always losing control of their emotions—usually in the midst of asserting their equality, emotional and otherwise.

If I ran the zoo, the feminists would be sentenced to mandatory "de-sensitivity" training. In order to make them less sensitive, they would be strapped down and tranquilized while hearing disagreeable terms repeated in a soft and soothing (preferably female) voice. After hearing words like "adoption" and phrases like "innate gender differences" and "stay-at-home moms," they would eventually learn to tolerate ideas they don't necessarily endorse.

That is really all I can think of at this time. So let me end with a little rhyme:

I guess that if I ran the zoo,
this is what I'd choose to do.
But since my name is not McGrew,
I guess I'll never run the zoo,
and so I'll sue and sue and sue.

This was one of the six Seuss books that were canceled in 2021.

CHAPTER 25

How I Bombed an Abortion Clinic and Still Got Tenure

October 27, 2008

Ann Potts, an assistant professor in the Watson School of Education, has disgraced the University of North Carolina at Wilmington by signing a petition in support of unrepentant terrorist Bill Ayers—himself an education professor at the University of Illinois at Chicago. The real disgrace is actually twofold: First, there is her willingness to support Ayers. Second, there is her unwillingness to support me for engaging in similar actions years ago in pursuit of a very different political agenda.

Some years ago, I was involved with a radical anti-abortion group that was frustrated with efforts to overturn *Roe v. Wade*. We targeted two abortion clinics—one in Birmingham and the other in Atlanta—for bombings. We successfully carried out both of those bombings without killing anyone on the premises. We wanted to send our message—at least initially—without any unnecessary bloodshed.

After we carried out the bombings in Birmingham and Atlanta, we gathered together in Charlotte, North Carolina, for the express purpose of making a number of bombs that would be used in additional attacks on abortion clinics throughout the southeast. Regrettably, an accident occurred during the construction of those additional bombs. Several members of our group died during the unexpected blast. Shortly thereafter, I left the group and decided to enter the field of higher education.

I want to make one thing perfectly clear: I do not regret my decision to engage in the bombings of those abortion clinics. In fact, I regret that we did not do more.

Some people on the far left in America are trying to hold the pro-life movement accountable for actions I engaged in before Sarah Palin was even involved in politics. And no one in academia is willing to offer me forgiveness for actions I've never said I regretted. Ann Potts's name is not on a petition of my academic supporters for one simple reason: I don't have any.

For those who are not Swift enough to grasp satire, let me explain something: You are presently reading satire.

Put simply, there is no chance that an unrepentant right-wing domestic terrorist could ever land a job in higher education in America. The "liberal" would prevent the white male abortion clinic bomber from teaching on the basis of identity politics. The conservative would arrive at the same conclusion on the basis of principle.

Lest you think that I am exaggerating, turn back the clock eighteen months to the last time I spoke out against an academic leftist who supports violence as a means of disseminating his political views. Some readers remember when Kent State professor Julio Pino publicly advocated the bombing of innocent Jews by Palestinian children.

I spoke out against Pino's advocacy of violence by writing a column called "How to Bomb a Gay Bathhouse." This was shortly after the controversy involving Ann Coulter's use of the term "fag" to describe John Edwards. In that column, I suggested that Kent State hire Ann Coulter and allow her to construct a website advocating violence against gays since they were silent on the issue of Pino's advocacy of violence against Jews.

When columnist Andrew Sullivan read my column, there was much lisping and gnashing of teeth. Too dense and emotionally unstable to understand the satire, Sullivan dubbed me an "ugly bigot" and ran excerpts of my column on his website. And even after having the satire explained to them, our student newspaper ran an editorial suggesting that I advocated domestic terrorism. The chancellor's assistant, Cindy Lawson, made the dim-witted remark that my column was deplorable, even if satire. Apparently, it was deplorable if advocating violence but still deplorable if doing the opposite.

The way people to my left reacted to my column showed a great desire to find a conservative who advocates domestic terrorism—even in the absence of any evidence he's engaged in terrorism—and to punish him for his advocacy of violence.

But in the case of Bill Ayers, we have a leftist who not only advocates domestic terrorism but has actually carried out acts of terror in his own country. And those who accused me of advocating violence are now either a) unwilling to talk about Ayers or b) actually willing to sign a petition supporting him.

Ann Potts, who taught at Virginia Tech when a student opened fire and killed nearly three dozen, is a reminder of just how intellectually and morally challenged one can be and still survive in the field of education. Her unrepentant idiocy is a call for the overthrow of the government-run education system—by non-violent means, of course.

For a follow-up on Pino, see Chapter 46, "The Enemy Within."

Chapter 26

Sea of Faces

December 15, 2008

Late one morning in May of 1996, I stuck my head out of the window of James and Stephanie's Manhattan apartment to get some not-so-fresh air while I drank my morning coffee. We were just getting up before noon after a long night of talking God and politics at an Irish pub called Peter McManus's located somewhere around 20th Street. I looked down at the droves of people flooding the streets for the noon lunch break, wondering whether it was possible for God to have a plan for each one of their lives as well as a concern for each one's well-being.

Those questions may seem odd for one to ponder over morning coffee, but they aren't so strange for one who just weeks before had broken the chains of atheism that had bound him for so long. Just because I renounced atheism one day on the way out of a damp prison in Quito, Ecuador, *[as told in Chapter 27, "The Shadow Proves the Sunshine"]* did not mean I instantly became a Christian. That would not happen until years later when I recognized that a personal relationship with God was not only a possibility but an indispensable aspect of Christianity.

Since that time, I've had the opportunity to share my faith with a lot of people. In fact, many people who read this column tell me to stop doing it. My awareness that it gets under their skin is the principal reason I continue. Christianity is not always comforting, and those most annoyed with it are often the closest to conversion.

It should go without saying that I'm always pleased to hear when a reader turns to Christ. There's no greater joy than hearing the good news that someone has accepted the Good News. By the same token, there is nothing more devastating than hearing of a reader turning away from Christianity. That happened to me recently when a fellow I once witnessed to said, "I still believe in God, but I feel like he only intervenes in my life when he wants to (expletive) with me."

The fellow who told me that also said he was not a "conservative Christian" like me but instead a "more liberal Christian." He may or may not know that he's on the verge of no longer being a Christian at all.

Perhaps the most accurate thing my reader has recently said about Christianity is that I am a conservative Christian. That conservatism is reflected in two things I believe to be absolutely certain about the life of a Christian:

1. I believe that—because we live in a world broken by sin and occupied by fundamentally flawed individuals—storms are inevitable. If all hell has not yet broken loose in your life, it soon will. Chaos would not be so pervasive if people were as fundamentally good as the so-called liberal Christian deems them to be.

2. When all hell breaks loose in life, each individual is faced with the choice of moving toward the Cross or away from the Cross. Every person in every tumultuous situation

chooses one or the other of these two options. A man has no one but himself to blame for the consequences of making the wrong decision—though the so-called liberal Christian probably dislikes my emphasis on free will.

When one responds to tragedy by moving towards the Cross, it is impossible to believe that God only intervenes in men's lives when he wants to (expletive) with them. The closer one moves to the Cross, the more one understands that God really is willing to intervene in the lives of men. One also understands that God does it because he loves all of his children and wants to have a real and permanent relationship with them.

That is why I am so irritated with self-proclaimed liberal Christians like John Shelby Spong. Those like Spong who either deny the importance of the resurrection or deny its occurrence altogether share a transparent political motivation. If you get too close to the Cross, you get too close to the reality of sin and its consequences. And then you alienate valuable political allies.

Some may believe that the liberal Christian's willingness to cut out portions of the New Testament prohibiting sexual sin makes it easier for him to cut out portions dealing with the crucifixion and resurrection of Jesus. Maybe it is more accurate to say that the removal of the crucifixion and resurrection story makes it necessary to delete all of the commandments that make the liberal Christian feel uncomfortable.

Seldom has the so-called liberal Christian's discomfort with the Cross been as evident as in the aftermath of Mel Gibson's *Passion of the Christ*. Reviews in magazines like *The Nation* showed unbelievable hysteria from the so-called Christian left ending with a chorus of accusations of anti-Semitism directed towards Gibson and his movie.

Whatever anti-Semitic feelings Gibson may harbor, his movie was not anti-Semitic. I would like to personally thank the Jews. Because of their role in killing my Savior, they helped to secure my salvation.

But the so-called liberal Christian sees it differently. He is reminded of his sin when he sees the bloody torture of Jesus of Nazareth. So he asks why we don't just focus on all of Jesus's acts of kindness toward the poor.

And that is where my reader finds himself today. When he is not proclaiming that God only intervenes in his life occasionally to (expletive) with him, he is out building houses for Habitat for Humanity.

Jesus did posit as his second great commandment that we should love our neighbors as ourselves. But before we reach out to do good for our neighbors, the first great commandment says we must love the Lord with all our heart, mind, and soul. We can't do that without moving toward the Cross of Christ when things are stormy in our lives.

It is only when we focus on the horror of Jesus's death that we realize how much he loves us. And it is only when we believe the resurrection that we know Jesus stands outside of time and hears our cries above the thunder.

"Sea of Faces" is the title song from the 2004 album by the CCM band Kutless—Mike was a fan—and starts with:

> I see the city lights all around me.
> Everyone's obscure.
> Ten million people each with their problems.
> Oh, why should anyone care?

Chapter 27

The Shadow Proves the Sunshine

December 16, 2008

This also appears in the book Life and How to Live It *(2023).*

This morning, I received an email that was so touching and so important I had to respond with a full column rather than a short email. Actually, I could write a number of columns in response to the email. But for now, I'll just respond to these two important lines embedded in its first paragraph: "Right now I'm in doubt about the existence of a God at all. I'd like to know more about what you believe—how you look at tragedy and evil in relation to a loving God."

What the reader is asking, in effect, is how can one believe in God despite the existence of evil. In my case, abandoning atheism came about because of the existence of evil and a desire to see justice in its aftermath.

The very second the inner gates of that Ecuadorian prison opened up, I could smell the foul odor of rotten food, urine, and solid waste. I knew to the very core of my being that it was wrong of the government to have no maintenance budget for that

150-year-old prison. It was wrong to let prisoners walk around through puddles of their own urine mixed with fecal matter as they awaited trial for years—even for offenses carrying sentences of mere months.

When Pedro told me he had been acquitted weeks before but was still in prison, I again smelled something rotten. I knew it was pure evil that led the officials to force him to raise money for "processing fees" in order to set him free after four years of wrongful incarceration.

As I walked into the thirty-six-square-meter cell, I saw forty-five men staring back at me—some of them wearing the same rotting clothes they had worn the day they were arrested months or years before. When I saw a butcher knife sitting on top of a broken TV set, I knew why so many of the prisoners wore bandages. And I knew it was pure evil that kept the guards from seizing the weapons and from even caring that prisoners killed other prisoners every day.

When I saw a young man—he appeared to be a teenager—up against a wall being beaten with a club, I knew that I was witnessing pure evil. The guards quickly stopped the beating because they knew it too. As I heard the sound of that club whacking against his torso, I wasn't sure whether I heard the sound of bones breaking. But I knew I was witnessing evil.

It was that same sick feeling I had when I first went to the Holocaust Museum in Washington, D.C. The pictures of those bodies piled upon bodies at Auschwitz made me sick to my stomach immediately. No one had to teach me to feel sick. I just did. It was because of what God had written on my heart.

And I felt very sick again when I walked into that prison kitchen and peered down into the boiling vats. I asked the cook to explain why they were boiling everything—the fruit, the vegetables, and the meat. It was because it had all started to rot after no one would buy it in the old town market in Quito. So they sold it to the prison officials who tried to boil off the rot before serving it to the prisoners.

As I walked out of the prison doors, I thought of the guards telling me they did not need capital punishment. When they wanted to shoot someone, they just told them they were free to go, shot them in the back, and reported it as an attempted escape.

But no one was shooting at me as I looked up at the statue of the Virgin Mary. I was free to walk out of the prison and out of the shadows of evil and darkness that shook me to the core on that damp March afternoon.

It was at that very moment that I recognized the wrongfulness of my hardened atheism. I knew then that those dark shadows were conclusive proof of the existence of the sunshine. Without the sun, I would not know what darkness was. And without the Son, I could not escape it.

The reader who inspired this column asked how I look at tragedy and evil in relation to a loving God. That is simple: I look at tragedy and evil in relation to a loving God.

Mike's death was a tragedy, and the way he was treated was evil.

The title is also the title of a 2005 song by Switchfoot, one of Mike's favorite bands.

DAVID ADAMS

Mike's 1996 trip to Ecuador was a major life experience for him; it was key to his spiritual transformation, to his decision to turn away from his avowed atheism. Mike often spoke of this in his speeches and writings, as he does here. But you don't have to go to a foreign land to get closer to God; it can happen anywhere at the most unexpected times—as you will see in Chapter 97, "Everlasting Life on Death Row."

Chapter 28

Primary and Secondary Racism

December 22, 2008

Ann Coulter was right when she said the essence of being a liberal is having one set of rules for oneself and an entirely different set of rules for other people. Similarly, it could be asserted that the essence of liberal arts education is developing one set of theories that apply only to other people. Few better examples can be found than in the case of labeling theory, which derives from the pseudoscience of sociology.

Frank Tannenbaum had a number of valid points when, in the 1930s, he established some basic premises of labeling theory. He argued that, as a juvenile, everyone engages in some form of delinquent behavior. And he correctly pointed out that not everyone who engages in delinquency is caught and, therefore, labeled "delinquent."

Tannenbaum was also correct in saying that parents, teachers, and peers sometimes overreact to juveniles caught in an act of delinquency. He was again on firm ground in asserting that these occasional overreactions could actually produce more delinquency.

Surely, those who are labeled delinquent are less likely to be invited to associate with those who aren't. And ostracism from conformists can lead to delinquent associations where the strengthening of deviant tendencies can occur.

Writing just a few years after Tannenbaum, Edwin Lemert did a lot to shape labeling theory into its present form. It is a form popular with progressives everywhere.

Lemert argued that people can engage in delinquency for any number of biological, sociological, or psychological reasons. Delinquency produced by any of these broad (categories of) factors is called "primary deviance." But Lemert's real contribution to various progressive causes (and socialist policies) flows from his explanation of a form of delinquency known as "secondary deviance."

Lemert believed that if an individual was caught in an act of primary deviance, he was likely to be placed under greater subsequent scrutiny by parents, teachers, and various agents of social control. This, of course, meant the child was more likely to be caught engaging in delinquency again. Adopting Lemert's premises, it is easy to understand how a vicious cycle could develop.

At some point, of course, the child might internalize the notion that he is a "deviant," a "delinquent," or just generally "bad." This could lead to higher rates of delinquency. When it does, according to Lemert, "secondary deviance" has occurred. Many of us have come to dub this process, perhaps somewhat simplistically, as the "self-fulfilling prophecy."

Notions such as "secondary deviance" and "self-fulfilling prophecy" have done much to undermine the integrity of public education in this country. If you learned to read in first grade in the 1970s, you remember the "yellowbirds," "redbirds," and "bluebirds" reading groups. Labeling theorists thought it would be better to call a child a "yellowbird" than to call him "slow."

(Author's Note: I was a "yellowbird" in first grade, and we all knew we were slow. We just contented ourselves with beating up the "bluebirds" during recess. Fortunately, due to the kindness of my favorite teacher, Elsie Stephenson, I eventually became a "redbird.").

Regrettably, all of this emphasis on self-esteem and negative labeling has resulted in many schools doing away with letter grades altogether. And when the kids play games at recess, they are often forbidden from keeping score. They don't want anyone to suffer the emotional trauma that results from being labeled a "loser"—even if for a day.

Liberal progressives have spent years taking a theory from sociology and applying it increasingly to the field of education. These progressives have shown a clear interest in the question of whether negative labels (e.g., "criminal," "dumb") are more frequently applied to blacks and other historically victimized groups.

But curiously, one area of research remains unexplored: What impact does labeling someone a "racist" have on his self-image—and his propensity for future acts of racism?

Frank Tannenbaum, if he were alive today, might argue that everyone engages in some form of racist behavior. And he might point out that not everyone who engages in racism is caught and labeled "racist."

Tannenbaum might also say that parents, teachers, and peers sometimes overreact to juveniles caught in an act of racial insensitivity. He would be on firm ground in asserting that these occasional overreactions could actually produce more racial insensitivity.

Surely, those who are labeled "racist" are less likely to be invited to associate with those who aren't. And ostracism from non-racists can lead to racist associations where the strengthening of racist tendencies can occur.

Lemert might agree that people can engage in racism for any number of biological, sociological, or psychological reasons. Racism produced by any of these broad (categories of) factors could be called "primary racism."

Lemert might also agree that if an individual is caught in an act of primary racism, he is likely to be placed under greater subsequent scrutiny by parents, teachers, and various agents of social control. This, of course, means the child is more likely to be caught engaging in racial insensitivity again. Adopting Lemert's premises, it is easy to understand how a vicious cycle could develop.

At some point, of course, the child might internalize the notion that he is a "racist" or just generally "bigoted." This could lead to higher rates of bigotry. When it does, one might say that "secondary racism" has occurred. Many of us might call this a "self-fulfilling prophecy."

We all know that liberals often manufacture cases of racism in order to keep liberalism alive. But we need more research in the pseudoscience of sociology in order to determine how reckless accusations of racism are actually creating more real racism in America. The research can be used to test whether liberals really believe in labeling theory and whether they are willing to apply it to their own conduct.

If liberals really do believe in labeling theory, they should reconsider their own careless accusations of racism. If not, they should fess up, assign grades, and let children keep score during recess.

Good stuff. Now, let's take a short break for some of Mike's trademark humor:

> Reader: It must be nice going through your entire life knowing you're always right.
> Response: I wouldn't know. I used to be a Democrat.
>
> Q: Why is a laundromat a really bad place to pick up a woman?
> A: Because a woman who can't even afford a washing machine will probably never be able to support you.
>
> Hate mail of the day: "I don't look down on other people like you do."
> Response: "Well, I guess that makes you better than me."

CHAPTER 29

Anarchy in UNC

April 20, 2009

Last week, I was away speaking at Michigan State University. While I was gone, my inbox filled with requests that I write about the recent disruption of Tom Tancredo's speech at UNC-Chapel Hill. I am pleased to do so. As a professor in the UNC system, I'm also pleased to explain why this embarrassing incident occurred.

If one is to understand the Tancredo incident, one must be familiar with ten rules that apply to free speech and to other rights in the UNC system. One must also understand the origin of at least some of these ten rules. Once one is properly educated in these rules, it becomes obvious that Tom Tancredo is not a victim in any sense of the word. In fact, it is Tancredo, not the protestors, who should be embarrassed.

1. Groups, not individuals, possess rights. Many observers are confused into thinking that Tom Tancredo's constitutional rights were violated last week in Chapel Hill. This is based on the antiquated notion that free speech is an

individual right. Because our Founding Fathers owned slaves (read: violated individual rights), those rights have now been transferred from individuals to groups.

2. The rights of any given group are determined by the extent of historical oppression the group has suffered. Obviously, as a group, African Americans now have rights because of slavery. Illegal aliens also have rights, as a group, because the conditions that caused them to become "illegal" were oppressive.

3. Oppression need not have occurred in this country to produce rights in this country. Some will note that the oppression that produced illegal immigration occurred in another country, implying that this does not create any rights here in this country. This criticism assumes the legitimacy of the term "countries," which, like the term "laws," is suspect. It should also be noted that prior to any discussion of how to patrol our border, the term "border" is designated as oppressive. This helps us to think globally.

4. Jews are exempt from rule #3. Jews have suffered a lot throughout history. But most of that suffering occurred in other countries. Since the Jews now control so much of America and probably planned 9/11, there is no need to grant them unnecessary rights.

5. Rights do not compel responsibility. The notion of responsibility is antithetical to the notion of collectivism. Notions of responsibility help to advance capitalism, which helps to advance oppression. In other words, it is irresponsible to advance responsibility because it is responsible for a lot of group oppression.

6. Whites may establish rights temporarily by acting as spokespersons for oppressed groups. The fact that most of the people protesting Tancredo were, like Tancredo, whites in the country legally is irrelevant. They had free speech rights because they were speaking up for the oppressed. Tancredo did not because he was speaking out against the oppressed and, hence, advancing oppression.

7. Oppressed groups need not give consent to their spokespersons. White liberals always know what is best for minorities who do not always know what is best for them.

8. Vandalism is a permissible form of expression. Jonathan Curtis, a UNC administrator, aided and abetted the theft of the conservative *Carolina Review* in 1996. He went unpunished. Since then, the administration has been reluctant to suggest that lawlessness is illegal. Lawlessness can be a good way of showing how laws are oppressive. This includes pounding on windows and shattering glass while people are trying to speak.

9. An effect may precede its cause. The protestors claimed that the Tancredo incident was the fault of the police who sprayed pepper spray to disperse the crowd. It should not matter that the disruption happened first. These kids have taken sociology courses where they are taught that labeling someone "delinquent" causes delinquency. They have taken education courses where they are taught that labeling someone as "slow" causes bad grades. These assertions are not backed up by longitudinal studies that can separate cause and effect. That would constitute "evidence," and

evidence is oppressive. In fact, the videotape of the protestors smashing a window is oppressive.

10. The law is an instrument of oppression, and criminality is a form of expression. Tom Tancredo supports the enforcement of the law. He is an oppressor. The protestors were breaking the law as a form of expression. In the same way, illegal immigration is a form of expression protected by the First Amendment and unaffected by antiquated notions like "citizenship." Citizenship is oppressive.

Now that you have heard the rules and know something of their origin, you may decide to sympathize with the protestors. Or you may decide that I've been right about what I've been saying in this column for the last six years. And why I often feel like an alien in a strange land speaking a language no one understands.

This reminds me of something Mike wrote:
People often approach me in public and say, "Thanks for standing up." What they forget to say is "so I don't have to."

Chapter 30

The Nature of Conservatism

May 18, 2009

The terms "liberal" and "conservative" are bandied about by many who fail to understand the crucial difference between them. Many believe the difference lies in the liberal's willingness to support government spending. But that explanation falls short. Conservatives are always willing to spend more on defense. Liberals would rather spend money on social programs.

Others believe the liberal is the one who supports "change," while the conservative supports the "status quo." That explanation also falls short. Ronald Reagan was a conservative. When he came to Washington in 1981, he shook the establishment and brought about change the liberals could not believe in.

If there is one thing that separates the conservative from the liberal, it is his view of human nature. The conservative sees man as born in a broken state. This tragic view of human nature sees man as selfish and hedonistic by design. Given his nature, it is no wonder a man chooses crime. It is a wonder he ever chooses conformity.

This tragic view of human nature also explains why conservatives often speak of religion and family values. Given his selfish nature, man must internalize some reason to behave in pro-social ways. The fact that he falls short of these values does not mean he is a hypocrite. The one who does not even believe what he says is the hypocrite. The one who believes what he says and falls short is merely human.

The conservative knows in advance that he (and others) will fall short of what religion expects of him. But his solution is not to give up on religion. His solution is to implement a backup plan. In the context of crime, that backup plan takes the form of a criminal justice system focused on punishment.

According to the conservative, effective punishment is that which produces fear of transgression. Fear of transgression occurs when the punishment is swift, certain, and severe. In sum, the conservative believes we should first try to love people into conformity. If that does not work, we should scare people into conformity.

But the liberal sees things differently. Everyone is born "good" with a blank slate. To the extent that people become "bad," it is because "society" corrupted them. Nowhere does the liberal explain how combining many good people makes a bad society.

But this is what the liberal thinks. And it is why he sees the criminal justice system as one that should focus on rehabilitation. If people were taught to be bad, then, surely, they may be taught to be good again. There are two victims for every crime: the victim of the crime and the criminal himself.

These competing views of human nature produce very different views on how a nation should conduct foreign policy. The liberal, of course, sees the United Nations as a valuable tool. Since people are fundamentally good, war is often a product of misunderstanding. The UN provides a place where we can sit down and talk out these misunderstandings in order to preserve peace.

But the conservative sees the UN as a waste of prime real estate in Manhattan. We don't misunderstand each other at all. For example, Ronald Reagan understood that the communists sought total world domination. The communists understood that we didn't want that. And they understood exactly what we were saying when we built up our defenses and actively sought the means to shoot their missiles out of the sky.

The conservative Ronald Reagan understood what the liberal Barack Obama does not: When it comes to foreign policy, it is better to be feared than to be loved.

Barack Obama's incorrect assessment of human nature renders unnecessary any wishes that he will fail in his plans to move America toward a socialist economy. Regardless of whether we want him to fail or just want his policies to fail, both will. Human nature demands it.

I tried to illustrate the wrongfulness of Obama's economic policies a few weeks ago when I penned the satirical column "My New Spread the Wealth Grading Policy." *[Updated version published in 2019; see Chapter 96.]* First, I stated that I would take ten points from all students making "A" grades and give them to students with "F" grades. This would make a more equal grade distribution—one with only three grades of "B," "C," and "D."

The next part of my satirical policy was the total leveling of the grade distribution. Students with a grade of "B" would be forced to give ten points to students with a grade of "D." Thus, everyone would wind up with an average grade of "C."

This was to show that a system designed to promote equality will inevitably destroy the work product. No one will put forth his best effort if his outcome (mediocrity) has been determined in advance.

The point, for those who missed it, is twofold: 1) My "spread the wealth" grading policy would inevitably produce a lower standard of academic achievement. 2) Obama's "spread the wealth" economic policy will inevitably produce a lower standard of living.

Human nature dictates that I am right. People have an inborn desire to compete. When deprived of the chance to compete, they simply quit trying. I challenge my liberal readers to convince me that I'm wrong.

For further reading: *The Vision of the Anointed: Self-Congratulation as a Basis for Public Policy* by Thomas Sowell.

This was one of his favorite book recs, and Sowell was one of his favorite authors. For more recs, please see Chapter 7, "An Anti-Communist Reading List."

Chapter 31

Mike's Peak

May 28, 2009

I could not have been in a worse mood when I wrote the check. It was the biggest one I had ever written, but at least matters were settled. I could begin to put things back together again. Going back to work immediately afterward proved to be a huge mistake.

The letter that was sitting in my mailbox wasn't the first to make me question my commitment to teaching in the UNC system. It was more like the straw that broke the camel's back. Or, I should say, almost broke the camel's back—at risk of getting ahead of myself.

I called Frank and talked to him at length. He wanted me to resign and come to work at a school of journalism at a private Christian university. I thought maybe it was time. I decided not to write the letter of resignation until I got back from a three-day trip to Colorado. I was going there to teach at Summit Ministries. That was Frank's idea too.

I packed my bags with a nice blue suit, my favorite Carolina blue tie, and a bottle of pills my doctor gave me to help me sleep. I hadn't slept well for months as the turmoil in my life was being resolved slowly in the court system. So far, things were going well. But I still could not seem to sleep.

When I got off the plane in Colorado Springs, I was taken aback by the beauty of my surroundings. Then, I found out Delta had lost my baggage. At the time, I really needed to lose a little baggage.

I would later realize that God was sending me a message. I'd be lecturing in jeans and a polo shirt dressed like everyone else. God isn't impressed by Joseph A. Bank. And He's offended by insomnia. Insomnia is another form of worrying. All worrying (faithlessness) is offensive to God.

We ate dinner on picnic tables next to the old Summit hotel at the base of Pikes Peak. I was enjoying the cool breeze and the lack of mosquitoes when Judson told me it was time to speak. I had just met Judson a few hours before, but for some reason, he seemed like a son to me.

I spoke for about an hour, during which I felt the most awesome flow of energy from me to the audience and back. If it felt like the Holy Spirit was in the room, it was probably because the Holy Spirit was in the room. I met so many incredible kids there afterward and felt such excitement that I feared I would not get any sleep before giving two more speeches the following morning.

That night, I slept like a baby.

The next morning, I gave a speech called "Unequally Yoked." I discussed the lengths universities will go to in order to infringe upon the rights of Christians at public universities. During the speech, I referred to the Southworth case, which, theoretically, prevents public universities from collecting mandatory student activity fees and then refusing to fund Christian groups and activities.

After the speech, Doc Noebel, the president of Summit, introduced himself, saying, "Mr. Southworth is a Summit graduate." I already knew Summit was there to teach kids a Christian worldview—one that would help them survive a secular onslaught in college. Now, I knew that Summit gave young men and women the courage to fight back. Even to the Supreme Court, if necessary.

After Doc took me to lunch, we sat out on the front porch of that old hotel. I was enjoying the cool summer breeze that was flowing through the mountains. A man and his wife were there from Iowa spending the afternoon with their teenager who was enrolled in Summit. "How often do you hear from former students?" the man asked. Without hesitation, Doc replied, "Every day."

About ten minutes later, a fellow—I believe his name was Harris—came walking up the steps to shake Doc's hand. "You probably don't remember me," he said. "I was one of your students back in 1962. Summit Ministries changed my life."

That afternoon, I went with the kids to play sports—volleyball, tennis, etc. After a few minutes, I took a rest because I hadn't adjusted to the 7000 foot altitude. A few minutes later, someone—who knew I used to play for a living—shoved a guitar in my hand. I played a few tunes before we headed to the grill for supper.

I don't know exactly what heaven is going to be like, but I know it will involve perpetual worship—the type one experiences when admiring God's creation. And I know it will involve joyful fellowship with one's brothers and sisters in Christ. In that sense, Summit is the closest thing to heaven on Earth I've ever seen.

When my luggage finally arrived, I called Delta to change my flight arrangements. They assumed that losing my luggage prevented me from finishing my business in Colorado. The truth is that I was having too much fun to leave.

When I got back to North Carolina, I called one of my lawyers, Travis Barham, at the Alliance Defending Freedom. I told him that far from wanting to quit, I was ready to get back in the trenches and try to make things right in the UNC system. When he asked why I seemed so rejuvenated and full of fighting spirit, I told him about my week at Summit. That's when Travis told me he was a graduate of Summit Ministries.

"I should have known," I told him. And I really should have known.

See also Chapter 50, "Standing at the Summit."

For a brief look inside the new Mike Adams Memorial Studio at Summit Ministries:

https://www.youtube.com/watch?v=1nJ5ht1Ejt0&ab_channel=DaveAdams

Incidentally, the inability of Mike to teach at Summit Ministries in the summer of 2020 due to the shutdown was another contributing factor to the depression that claimed his life. Every year, after two stressful semesters of working in a hostile environment, Mike looked forward to spending his summer teaching in the loving, healthy environment of the campus at Summit. It was his way of relaxing and recharging.

Chapter 32

Does Fort Worth Ever Cross Your Mind?

December 31, 2010

American communities are not what they used to be. Today's college graduate changes jobs about a dozen times in his career. Since he changes jobs every few years, he usually finds himself moving every few years. And since he figures he won't be with his neighbors for long, he seldom takes the time to get to know them.

It wasn't that way when my family moved to Fort Worth in 1968. Four different welcoming committees came to visit from four different churches—all asking whether we had found a church home. Our first batch of mail was hand-delivered by the postman. When he rang the doorbell, he introduced himself and asked, "Have you found a church home yet?"

We eventually found a church, but it was not the home of any of the four groups that came to visit. They must have all written off their visits as losses. But that was far from the truth. In fact, my mother was so moved by their hospitality that she began regular church visitation as soon as she joined a church. She kept doing so after we moved to Houston.

Mom's welcoming visitations paid particularly good dividends, as she met her closest friend for life, Lisa Chambers. *[Mike was also close to her and called her his "second mother," which is remarkable because his first mother was so great, it wasn't like he needed another one. Mike has more to say about her in Chapter 60, "Fifty."]* Our whole family became friends with their whole family. In fact, the friendships endure to this day. There were many more friendships formed in the process. We still get Christmas cards from people who joined the church for whom Mom was visiting. Of course, there are untold numbers of people we never hear from but whose lives were affected nonetheless. My mother knew from experience to never write them off as losses. I hope by chance that one of them is reading these words today.

When my folks retired and moved to Huntsville *[Texas]*, there were fewer opportunities for visitation. There weren't many people moving into the small neighborhood in which they retired, so Mom stopped doing these visitations regularly. But one day, a different kind of welcoming took place in their little neighborhood.

Mrs. Bishop was a very nice lady with a very ill husband. She also had a son with a criminal record. So the two police officers who lived in our neighborhood decided to pay the Bishops a visit right after they moved into their new home. The officer knocked on Mrs. Bishop's door and boldly stated that for years there had been no crime in the little neighborhood. And they promised that if anything happened, they would come looking for Mrs. Bishop's son in a heartbeat.

One of the officers came over to our house after going to the Bishops'. He reassured my mother that Mrs. Bishop had been warned and that, therefore, there would probably be no trouble in the neighborhood. The officer was proud of himself, but my mother was horrified.

Next thing we knew, my mother went into the kitchen and found her favorite apple cake recipe. She didn't always bring a cake when she went on a visitation. But she figured Mrs. Bishop really needed one after her rude reception in the neighborhood. Naturally, when my mother knocked on her door and gave Mrs. Bishop the cake, she was thrilled.

Mom got a "thank you" card from Mrs. Bishop, which was a rare occurrence. She later got a request for the recipe for that apple cake, which she gladly passed along. She also got a renewed interest in doing church visitations. I guess you could say she decided to come out of retirement.

When the next family moved into their little neighborhood, Mom cooked an apple cake and took it down to them. But this time, something happened that had never happened before. The woman of the house looked at the cake and laughed and said, "We don't need another apple cake, Mrs. Adams." She saw my mother's puzzled look and then explained, "Mrs. Bishop brought us one this morning."

We can't change the world overnight. But we can change our neighborhoods today. The recipe has been around for ages. We just have to keep sharing it with others.

Does Fort Worth Ever Cross Your Mind *is the fourth studio album by country music artist George Strait.*

CHAPTER 33

Two Kinds of Atheists

February 4, 2011

An atheist reader has asked that I devote a column to explaining what he sees as my contempt for atheists. In past columns, I have exhibited a careless tendency to lump atheists together into a single homogeneous category. In my experience, there are two distinct categories of atheists—the unbelieving atheist and the evangelistic atheist. Only the latter category is deserving of contempt.

There are a number of reasons why a person might identify himself as an unbelieving atheist. I believe very firmly that one can be reasonably mistaken in one's unbelief. While I think atheists are uniformly wrong, I do not consider them to be uniformly unreasonable.

It may well be the case that the unbeliever was raised by atheist parents in a home without religious instruction. I know of atheists who were raised in homes without a copy of the Bible. Each had to rely upon secondhand accounts of what the Bible says on a variety of issues. Most of them never got around to reading it firsthand.

Those who lack religious influence in the home and religious instruction at an early age are at a disadvantage in twenty-first-century America. Long before President Obama declared that we are no longer a Christian nation, our courts and schools began to lay the foundation for post-Christian America.

There is no mistaking the fact that our public school system has become secularized to the point of relinquishing any claims of neutrality. Most schools have reached the point of being overtly anti-religious. Kids who have no firm foundation in Judeo-Christian ethics are likely to become highly resistant to conversion at a later age. You can thank our public schools for that. We all pay for public education in more ways than one.

The unbelieving atheist often sets a high standard of proof when confronted with Christian apologetics. That is what his culture teaches. He is also taught that religion and logic are incompatible. I recently heard someone say, "One can't put the words logic and religion in the same sentence." Of course, that statement contains a serious flaw: it uses the words logic and religion in the same sentence.

Regardless of what others say, we are commanded as Christians to provide a ready defense for our beliefs. And that calls for the use of logic and reason and evidence. We are obligated to polish our arguments. It is a part of our obligation to hold out a candle and light up the world.

But holding out a candle cannot help others to see the sun. If things have become dark enough for them, our candle might even obscure their view of the stars. At some point, they must be willing to look beyond isolated arguments. They must open their eyes and contemplate their surroundings. And they must look beyond concepts like "luck" and "random variation" to find a more complex and refined view of the universe.

I love my unbelieving atheist friends, and I enjoy the conversations we have on many weighty issues. Even when they seem stubborn, they seldom seem unreasonable. The fact that many of them are politically conservative gives me great hope.

But the evangelistic atheist is a different breed altogether. One evangelistic atheist sits in his office with piles of anti-religious books as he prepares his next lecture for his Sociology of Religion class. He curses more than he uses words like "a" and "the." And he posts the headlines of the latest church scandal on his office door. He takes more pride in the failure of others than in his own personal achievements.

Another evangelistic atheist writes books distorting the history of Christianity and the life and words of Jesus—all the while calling it scholarship. He develops courses on "atheism and unbelief." He even posts "Godless!" (complete with the exclamation point!) in the "religious views" portion of his Facebook profile. Yet he claims emotional detachment on issues of faith and religion.

In short, the evangelistic atheist is characterized less by the absence of belief than by a zeal for destroying the beliefs of others. He is seldom politically conservative and almost always "very liberal." Just take a few minutes to examine his Facebook profile.

The politically conservative unbelieving atheist must wake up and connect the dots between religion and politics and between social and fiscal conservatism. He must realize that the evangelistic atheist is on a political rather than religious crusade. His evangelism targets religion because he seeks to destroy the family. And he seeks to destroy the family because he seeks to replace it with the welfare state.

Our individual liberties are in jeopardy. But they may only be taken away by men if it is presumed that they are granted by men. We need fair-minded unbelieving atheists to reconsider the underpinnings of their beliefs. A godless conservatism is only one election away from extinction.

For more on this topic, please see Chapter 6, "How to Talk to an Atheist (and You Must)"; Chapter 22, "Understanding Atheism"; and Chapter 27, "The Shadow Proves the Sunshine."

CHAPTER 34

Your Unsolicited Letter of Recommendation

February 18, 2011

Dear Stan:

You may be wondering why I'm writing you a short email with a letter of recommendation attached to the bottom. After all, you have not requested such a letter. Nonetheless, I occasionally like to send letters of recommendation to students who have not requested them. The reason I do this is to let them know how they are doing and what kind of impression they are making on at least one of their professors. You are one of my advisees, and it is likely that in the future a prospective employer will specifically ask for a recommendation letter from me. If such a request were to be made of me today, this is what the letter would look like.

> To Whom It May Concern:
>
> Stanley is one of my advisees. He has informed me that you are considering hiring him for a full-time

position. He has also informed me that you require a letter from his academic advisor. I am pleased to provide such a letter.

Stanley is the rare student who takes a substantial portion of what he learns in the classroom and applies it to his everyday life. His professors are overwhelmingly liberal, and he seems to listen to them and apply their ideas on a regular basis. Let me provide a few examples.

- In addition to advising Stanley, I taught him once in an upper-level night class. The class was full when he tried to sign up, but I made extra room for him because he had missed his advising appointments and therefore needed to get into several classes lest his financial aid be canceled. I also agreed to serve as his new advisor after he upset his previous advisor by failing to keep advising appointments. She berated him and that upset him. I took him on because I thought he could learn from the experience of being advised by the only Republican in the department. Dealing with his liberal victim mindset has been a challenge, to say the least. To date, he has never kept one of his advising appointments. That is why he never gets the classes he desires. **In short, Stanley seems to believe that rules are mandatory in reference to others and discretionary in reference to Stanley.**

- Stanley had a tendency to come to class listening to an iPod, which he did not turn off once the lecture began. He just kept his earplugs in and swayed to the music while I lectured on light topics such as first-degree murder and aggravated rape (I teach criminology, by the way). The syllabus clearly stated that he was not to do this (and allowed me to deduct a point from his final average for every transgression). I also reminded him of this by sending numerous emails. But since he did not read the syllabus and did not check his email, he never figured out that he was risking failing the class until it was too late. **In short, Stanley's disregard for rules is exacerbated by his lack of common sense and his propensity to live in the moment without regard for the long-term consequences of his conduct.**

- Stanley seemed to get confused in many of my lectures. I know this because—once he took off his earplugs and started to listen to the lecture—he often made strange faces. When I saw these pained expressions, I always stopped and politely asked Stanley what was wrong. He then announced that he was "lost." I just suggested that he should bring a pen and notebook to class rather than his iPod. That usually made him even angrier. **In short, Stanley seems to be more interested in broadcasting his problems to others than he is in pursuing common-sense solutions. He clings to his status as a victim because he has attention deficit disorder—a pathological need to draw attention to himself, which, seemingly, can never be satisfied.**

Stanley will probably be graduating this semester. But it has been a close call. He began his final semester on five waiting lists (to get into the last five classes he needs to graduate). This happened because he missed his final advising appointment, and all the required courses were filled up by the time he came by my office. He had to personally track down all of these professors and beg to get into their classes. For two weeks, he called my office constantly (and consumed more of my time than all of my other advisees combined). I advised him patiently throughout the ordeal but, to date, I have received no thanks for doing so. **In short, Stanley sees government officials as servants obligated to insulate him from the consequences of his own actions. At no point does he consider the possibility that the system would break down if everyone behaved the way that he does.**

There is a chance that someday Stanley will grow up and stop living in accordance with the worldview espoused by his sociology professors. But I pity his first employer. If you hire Stanley, you can expect him to be late, inattentive, confused, angry, and in constant need of supervision.

Aside from these concerns, I have no other reservations.

Sincerely,
Mike S. Adams

Stan, I know you might never read this email because you rarely check your university email account. So my words will probably never benefit you personally. That is why I have published your letter of recommendation on the internet. When others read it, they can benefit from your ill-considered decision to incorporate liberal ideas into a liberal lifestyle. Someday, you might grow out of this and become a responsible and productive citizen. If that ever happens, and if you do eventually read this email, I ask only one thing: Please share the attached letter with someone who needs it.

Although this letter may sound harsh, the fact remains that he was one of the most popular professors at UNCW. Here's a sample of some of the condolences we received from former students:

> Professor Adams taught me life lessons that will never be forgotten. He was always quick to help his students and instilled a quest for justice that will stay with me forever. He was truly an incredible man who fought for change.
>
> Dr. Adams was the best professor I ever had. I thank him for all he taught me as well as his endless mentorship and guidance. I wish I could reach out to him now as I start law school—a goal he helped me achieve.
>
> Dr. Adams met me and gave me a mini speech that, in the moment, I found slightly offensive. After going home, I realized that his speech was to teach me to not let things hold me back from success, even though they are things that I can't control. He also spiked my interest in becoming a DEA agent in order to get drug dealers off the street. Before Dr. Adams, I didn't think I could become a DEA agent; I didn't think I was strong enough. After Dr. Adams, I know that as long as I push forward and view obstacles as opportunities, I can accomplish anything I can set my mind to. I'm going to get my DEA badge in honor of the legacy Mike Adams left in my life.

Dr. Adams was the only reason I continued in my major after my freshman year. I deeply admired his dedication to his students and his work.

I took Dr. Adams' class because I wanted to be exposed to ideas outside of the four walls I'd built for myself. Mike blew the whole house up. What started out as political intrigue turned into a deep mentorship. Dr. Adams took me under his wing and showed me the importance of tolerance, debate, and the search for truth. He was genuine, kind, and unearthly intelligent. While I will forever mourn the loss of a truly great man, I'm beyond grateful for the blessing of his mentorship. The world is a better place because of Mike Adams.

He helped me in college, in law school, and once I entered the working world.

I got to UNCW as a lazy college student just looking to skate through college while having fun. Then, I met Dr. Adams. We had long talks about the struggles I was having in college. He was always there to listen and talk.

He was my professor in a Criminal Law class, which was the most informative, most interesting, and greatest learning experience I have had.

I signed up for every class I could taught by Dr. Adams. He made a huge difference in my education and life.

I was instantly captivated by the enthusiasm and passion with which he gave his lectures. It was clear how deeply he cared about advocating for truth and justice.

Chapter 35

I Think; Therefore, We Should

August 21, 2011

The most dangerous ideas in contemporary political discourse are easily identified. While they often take hours to explain, they are usually introduced in a conversation beginning with these four words: "I think we should." If you do not yet know what I am talking about, then a brief example is warranted. The following comes from a recent conversation I had with a self-identified liberal:

> "I think we should provide all of our citizens with national health care. I think we should continue to provide financial security for the elderly. I think we should also have national day care. And I think we should provide a free college education for every American."

What I have come to refer to as "I think we should" morality is not a completely bad thing. But it is, quite literally, a half-bad thing, which means it is also a half-good thing. The good half of

"I think we should" morality is the "I think" part. Let me illustrate with a few examples:

- When a person says, "I think providing citizens with health care is a good idea," there really isn't anything wrong. The person can always find someone who needs health care. And he can take the needy to the doctor if he so desires. In fact, he can take as many of them as he wants as long as they are willing to go.

- When a person says, "I think providing financial security for the elderly is a good idea," there is no problem. The person who says this undoubtedly knows someone who is elderly. And he is certainly free to take out his checkbook and write a check to that elderly person. In fact, he can take care of as many elderly people as he wants as long as they are willing to accept his generosity.

- When a person says, "I think providing day care is a good idea," there is no problem at all. The person who says this undoubtedly knows someone who has children. And he is certainly free to take care of his friends' children whenever he perceives that they have other responsibilities to which they must attend. In fact, he can take care of as many of his friends' children as he wants as long as their parents are willing and have trust in his supervision.

- When a person says, "I think providing free college education is a good idea," there is no problem at all. The person who says this undoubtedly knows someone without a college degree. And he is certainly free to send that person to college if he would like. In fact, he can spend his life savings sending other people's kids to college if he has none of his own. I know of a woman in Mississippi who did just that. She lived modestly—largely because she scrubbed toilets for a living. But she found a way to give.

The problem with all of these wonderful sentiments is not that they begin with "I think." The initial thought is not the problem. It is that the initial thought is followed by the two words "we should." This is problematic because the word "we," in reality, means "you." In other words, the proponent of "I think we should" morality is less interested in doing charitable things than he is in forcing you to perform his charitable acts for him. And so it is appropriate to ask these two questions of anyone any time he begins to lecture you with a sentence beginning with the four words "I think we should":

1. What are you presently doing to alleviate the problem?
2. Why should the government force others to do things you are unwilling to do yourself?

It is unlikely that the person will be able to identify anything he is doing to alleviate the problem. And his answer to the other question will be that no one will do these things unless compelled by the government. In other words, he will have admitted that, in his view, government, not God, must redeem man and save him from his sins of omission.

Confronting "I think we should" morality is a good way of getting liberals to admit that they favor legislating morality. It is also a good way of getting them to admit that there is a crack in the "wall of separation" between church and state.

And it is just big enough to let the secular humanist creep through.

Speaking of liberals, here are a few more of Mike's thoughts about them:

According to liberals, rights are not given to individuals by God. They are given to groups by government.

Liberals tolerate bondage so men can be equal. Conservatives tolerate inequality so men can be free.

Is anyone surprised that conservatives want to go back to work and liberals want to stay at home?

Chapter 36

Gibson Guitars

September 9, 2011

On the mantle above my fireplace there sits an old picture of my grandfather, Joe Dee Adams, Sr. The picture was taken some time during the Great Depression when he was a professional musician. It was actually his promo picture for the radio show he hosted on WSGN in Birmingham, Alabama. In it, he is holding an old Gibson acoustic guitar.

No one in our family has any idea what happened to that old guitar. It was lost, along with his purple heart from World War I, some time before he passed away in the fall of 1978. His death was just a year or so after I bought my first guitar. After my grandfather passed away, I remember my father saying how unfortunate it was that he never had a chance to hear me play. He could have taught me a thing or two in his later years.

Just a few years later, Dan Fogelberg wrote a song called "Leader of the Band." It was a wonderful tribute to his father. Dan always felt that his father was a vastly superior musician, and he felt guilty over the fact that he (Dan) became richer and more famous than the older Fogelberg.

Less than ten years after Dan wrote that song, I found myself playing music for a living. I remember playing one night in a bar called the C&G in Greenville, Mississippi. Without really thinking about it beforehand, I started telling the audience the story of my grandfather's short career as a musician.

My grandfather used to play with the likes of a young Red Foley. He was that good. And then he quit playing because he needed steady work to support a family. Later, Red Foley would become a member of the Country Music Hall of Fame. He even got two stars on the Hollywood Walk of Fame—one for recording music and one for television. But my grandfather would die in an old run-down house in Tarrant City *[Birmingham]*.

The line that separates fame from obscurity is a thin one that is often drawn by the hand of fate. I suspect that most people already know that about life. And I think that is why some people were visibly shedding tears that night when I finished telling my grandfather's story and then started playing "Leader of the Band" in my grandfather's honor.

So many great musicians, both well-known and unknown, have played those great Gibson guitars over the years. From Chet Atkins to B.B. King to Roy Orbison to Jimmy Page to Slash— the list seems almost endless. How many greats have we never heard because they never caught a break in the industry? God only knows. And I mean that literally.

The number of great musicians playing Gibson guitars could soon be diminished thanks to the Obama administration. The Obama Department of Justice recently raided Gibson's Nashville plant seeking allegedly illegal rosewood that was used to make Gibson fingerboards. The problem was that the fingerboards were supposed to have been fitted with inlays in India before they were shipped to America. Gibson is now in trouble for doing the work here. And the government has seized massive quantities of Gibson's work materials.

Many have asked this pointed question: Is the Obama White House committed to shipping American jobs overseas to India?

The answer to the question is simply "no." The Obama administration does not oppose keeping jobs in America. Its conduct is simply a function of the fact that it opposes businesses that are run by Republicans that donate heavily to Republican candidates and causes. But the administration is not opposed to using the Department of Justice to wage political warfare on private businesses. The Republican Gibson CEO is simply the target of government conduct that is more in line with third-world practices than with enlightened democracy.

It would be tempting for Republicans to simply bash the Obama administration and Eric Holder for this most recent politically motivated transgression. But that is not enough. Gibson Guitars needs our help, and they need it now. And that help can only take the form of buying Gibson guitars.

Personally, I was on the verge of buying a maple-top Taylor t5 until the recent raid on the Gibson Nashville plant. But I am now going to take that money and buy a Gibson J-45 that looks a lot like the old guitar my grandfather used to play. I know many readers cannot afford to buy guitars that run between two and three thousand dollars. But most can afford to buy the fine Epiphone guitars that are also made by Gibson.

Veteran guitar players are not the only ones that should be buying these all-American-made guitars. Novices should be buying them too. Those who have long wanted to learn to play guitar should use this as an opportunity to end their procrastination. Others should be buying them for their children and grandchildren. Christmas is just around the corner.

Regardless of what model they choose, new Gibson owners should remember to take a picture of their new purchase. And they should display it prominently on the mantle above their fireplace. New pictures of new guitars eventually become old pictures of old guitars. They can only be distinguished by the stories they have told and the ones that they will tell.

CHAPTER 37

Life and How to Live It, Part XI

September 16, 2011

This also appears in the book Life and How to Live It *(2023).*

One night during the summer of 1989, I was over at my friend Del Rendon's house. We both lived in Starkville, Mississippi. We also both played guitar. After playing half the songs in the Led Zeppelin acoustic catalog, we started to talk. Del tried to convince me to start playing music for a living with my friend Shannon, who is an enormously talented vocalist. Shannon was also over at Del's house that night, so we both heard an earful of compliments from our kind and humble friend.

By the middle of the summer of 1990, Shannon and I were both making ends meet playing in the local bars. The bar we played in the most was the Bully III in Starkville, where Del waited tables working for our mutual friend David Lee Odom. It took a lot of convincing, but one night, Del got up on stage with David and sang an old Zeppelin song. The crowd went wild. Then, Del stayed on stage and sang a song he wrote called "Brainstorming." It was and still is my favorite Del Rendon original.

Eventually, it was my turn to encourage Del the way he had once encouraged me. In 1993, I had finally achieved my goal of getting a Ph.D. and landing a job as a professor. Before I left town, I told Del to pick up where we left off. Starkville has a long and proud tradition of great local music. It also has a tight community of musicians who really look out for each other. Jim Beaty, Bill Cooke, Jeff Cummings, Jeffrey Rupp, the list goes on. I'll never forget those guys who have dedicated their lives to making people smile with their talent, their love of music, and their love of the people they play for.

I'm not sure I can really describe the happiness I experienced when I came rolling into Starkville one weekend in 1996 as I drove past the old Bully III and saw Del's name on the marquee. After I turned the car around and found a parking space, I slipped into a seat at a table in the back of the bar. Within just a few minutes, Del recognized me. He called me up to the stage to play an old tune (Zeppelin, of course) called "Your Time Is Gonna Come." It was a great time, and it was great to see Del playing guitar and singing in front of a live audience without a hint of the old shyness that used to keep him offstage.

When I came back to Starkville in 2000, I met an old girlfriend in one of the old dives I used to play in. When Del's name came up, she started to rave about his new band called Del Rendon and the Puerto Rican Rum Drunks. Before she was finished, none other than Del Rendon came walking into the crowded bar. After we caught up for a few minutes, Del went out to his car to get me a present. It was a copy of *Chameleon*, his band's new CD. In typical Del Rendon fashion, he would not allow me to pay him for it. So I bought him a beer instead.

I didn't see Del again until 2004. I was doing a book signing in the Mississippi State bookstore after a home football game.

Del was playing at a local restaurant/bar called The Veranda. So I went to see him play. As usual, he called me up to the stage just a few minutes after I walked in the bar. We played a few songs and then ended where we began—with an old Zeppelin tune. "Your Time Is Gonna Come" was an appropriate finale. When we finished the song, he just turned to me and thanked me for playing with him. That was the last time I saw Del Rendon alive.

When I picked up the phone that afternoon in the late summer of 2005, I just knew something was wrong. It was Dave Odom. He called to tell me that Del had died just a few hours before. It was the kind of sudden death so many musicians had died before him. But Del was so much more than just another musician.

Del the art teacher would be missed by his students. Del the singer/songwriter would be missed by his fans. Del the friend would be missed by his friends. His family, especially his wife and soulmate, would all be left with big holes in their hearts. They would be more like craters that no one else could ever fill.

Not long after Del passed, I started thinking about God's first great commandment. He said we are supposed to love Him with all of our hearts and all of our souls and all our minds. And that means we have no right to keep the gifts He gave us to ourselves. And of course, His second great commandment says we are to love our neighbors as ourselves. And that means we must shower them with encouragement when they are doing less with God's gifts than they should be.

The arrow between God's two great commandments points in both directions. When we encourage others to use their God-given talents to make others happy, we do more than just pave the way for the happiness of others. We also pave the way for our own happiness. Those who show kindness and

humility are not only the ones most likely to give encouragement. They are also its most likely recipients.

Among the best lessons Del Rendon the teacher taught us is that there's no time to be discouraged. We have to dedicate our lives to encouraging others. Pretty soon, our time is coming, too.

What Mike wrote about Del could be said, almost verbatim, about himself: "Del [Mike] the art [criminal justice] teacher would be missed by his students. Del [Mike] the singer/songwriter [speaker/writer] would be missed by his fans. Del [Mike] the friend would be missed by his friends. His family, especially his wife [fiancée] and soulmate, would all be left with big holes in their hearts. They would be more like craters that no one else could ever fill." It was almost like he was writing his own eulogy.

In 2016, Mike wrote the following:

I stuck my head in The Veranda tonight in Starkville. While I was there, I remembered that the last set I ever played in a bar was with Del Rendon in 2004. The last song we played was "Your Time Is Gonna Come." Eleven months later, Del was dead. He was one of the most unforgettable people I have ever met. Everyone in town talks about him to this day. The reason is simple: Del cared about people, and they knew it while he was alive. Live well, people. Your time is gonna come too. If you care about people and they know it, you'll not soon be forgotten.

Mike cared about a lot of people, and we will never forget him.

CHAPTER 38

For the Love of Marx

April 1, 2012

There are more Marxists teaching in sociology departments in America than living in the former Soviet Union. These sociologists hold themselves out as scientists despite the fact that they fail consistently in their efforts to predict the future. In fact, most of them lack the competence to accurately predict the past. Among the least competent and most intellectually dishonest is Gary L. Faulkner, professor emeritus from the University of North Carolina.

Faulkner recently claimed that Marx predicted the events we are seeing in the Occupy Wall Street movement. He also claimed that events from the twentieth century bolster the credibility of Marx as both an economist and political prophet. He further castigates Republicans for their refusal to embrace Marxism. Faulkner states, "There is something really ironic about Republicans' hatred of Marxism. Years ago, Marx predicted capitalism would collapse. The reason—workers would rebel."

And they did. They rebelled in China, Russia, North Korea, Cambodia, Afghanistan, and Vietnam. Their rebellion produced

Marxist governments. And the governments killed millions. The numbers of murders are striking:

Marxist China	65 million
Marxist USSR	20 million
Marxist North Korea	2 million
Marxist Cambodia	2 million
Marxist Afghanistan	1.5 million
Marxist Vietnam	1 million

Marx predicated all of this, right? Wrong. But we could have seen it coming. Marx was a violent man who unleashed racist and anti-Semitic assaults on anyone who dared to oppose the use of violence as a means of creating change.

Ferdinand Lassalle was one labor leader Marx hated for his desire to come up with practical solutions rather than violent confrontation. Lassalle's opposition to violence caused Marx to dub him a "Jewish nigger" and a "greasy Jew." Marx also said of Lassalle "the shape of his head and the growth of his hair indicate(s) he is a descendent of the Negroes who joined in Moses's flight from Egypt unless his mother or grandmother on the father's side was crossed with a nigger."

There is little question that Marx would have carried out violence on a large scale. But his poor physical condition prevented him from doing so—instead leaving the work to followers such as Lenin, Stalin, and Mao. His heavy smoking and drinking zapped his energy. His refusal to bathe—a trait also shared by Mao—resulted in boils all over his body. They brought on nervous collapse and fits of rage—both of which would have prevented him from working and earning his own living had he decided to do so.

Marx had a passionate hatred of capitalism because he was simply unable to handle money and to organize his own financial affairs. His inability to stay out of debt explains why his theory of capital is so deeply rooted in anti-Semitism. It also explains why he stole many of his most deeply anti-Semitic passages from Martin Luther.

Because he refused to work, even his own family remained unsympathetic to his requests for handouts, which he began making in college and kept making throughout the duration of his life. His own mother was credited with saying that she wished Karl would start accumulating capital instead of just writing about it.

Although he wrote about the need for revolution, Marx had a strange hatred for those who came from the revolutionary class. His son-in-law Paul Lafargue was from Cuba and had some black blood. He tried to keep his daughter from marrying him and later resented him for refusing to honor his wishes. Consequently, Marx referred to him as "Negrillo" and "the Gorilla."

In short, Marx considered both work and the worker to be beneath him. He lived nearly his entire adult life off of handouts from Engels, the co-author of *The Communist Manifesto*. While he was living off of Engels's capital, Marx kept a peasant woman around the house and refused to pay her for her services. Later, he fathered an illegitimate child by her and refused to provide financial support or even to acknowledge that he was the father. In other words, he exploited her labor and then abandoned her after she went into labor. Marx was not a great man worthy of admiration.

Nor was Marx a great prophet. He understood that there would always be men incapable of taking care of themselves. He understood that they would resort to violence whenever they did not get what they wanted. He also understood that there would always be academics who admired gross incompetence and the propensity toward violence.

Marx did not need a crystal ball to arrive at these truths. All he needed was a mirror.

Source: Paul Johnson, *Intellectuals* (1988).

For more book recommendations, see Chapter 7, "An Anti-Communist Reading List."

Chapter 39

The Price Is Wrong

May 4, 2012

There is an enormous free speech controversy that is pitting an outspoken North Carolina faculty member against a public university administration. For once, it isn't me (so keep on reading, liberals)! This controversy involves Jammie Price, a tenured sociology professor at Appalachian State University (ASU), who previously taught at UNC-Wilmington (UNCW). The current controversy also involves porn, so it should be a stimulating topic for my weekly political column (the liberals will surely keep reading now)!

Price has been placed on paid leave from the classroom after several students complained that she showed (allegedly without warning) a documentary about porn that actually featured people having sex. There are also student complaints that she accused the school of showing favoritism toward athletes (less controversial, I would think). Those statements are alleged to have been made in connection with sexual assault accusations against a couple of ASU athletes. Regrettably, the complaints about the athletic controversy have now coalesced into accusations of racism against

Price. Jammie Price may be many things. But she certainly is no racist. I regret that race has become entangled in an otherwise interesting free speech controversy.

While I would defend Price against charges of racism, I would urge others to be cautious before they make Jammie Price a poster girl for academic freedom. Hundreds of professors have signed a petition on her behalf. But she has a history of showing poor judgment in the classroom. That history is certainly relevant to the current controversy. At times, she also has shown outward contempt for those who do not share her vision of utopia as involving limitless guilt-free sex for everyone.

Price arguably should have been suspended by UNCW back in March of 2003 when she cancelled all of her classes for an entire week in order to protest the Iraq War. Her unprofessionalism was compounded when she offered extra credit—but only to those who would join her in protesting the war. Predictably, a student complained, and Price was reprimanded. She responded by correcting the problem. She organized an event for those who supported the war and gave students credit for participating. But the question remains: why did it take a student complaint for Price to understand the gross impropriety of her conduct?

Price is once again accused of using her class as a political platform. This is one of the many charges bundled together with showing pornography without warning and showing "racism" against student athletes. But this is a boring accusation. Sociology is an inherently political discipline, which is why it is generally regarded as a joke of a discipline. It is like political science without the science. If we were to fire Price for espousing politics in the classroom, we would have to fire 99 percent of the sociologists in America. Hey, wait, that could be a good thing! Could we look into that?

The far more important issue is whether Price was respectful of those who did not want to be exposed to graphic sexual content in the classroom. It is extremely difficult to apply the presumption of innocence to someone with such a poor track record for respecting others who have more conventional views of sexuality.

Around the time of my return to the church, I experienced Price's arrogant judgmentalism firsthand. One of our few faculty members of faith was having relationship troubles when Price recommended to him—in public, mind you—that he "switch to bisexuality" in order to "double his chances" of finding a partner. I was sitting just to the left (physically, not ideologically) of the faculty member at the time. We both reacted visibly. When Price noticed I was taken aback by the remark, she responded predictably by calling me a "homophobe" in front of other professors.

One question in the current controversy is whether this is just another example of Price's tired old "shock and condemn" tactic with regard to sexual morality. In other words, did she willingly shock the students with porn so she could later condemn them for drawing a moral judgment? This is an ingrained pattern of behavior that Price uses both inside and outside the classroom. Keep reading.

Over a decade ago, I got a complaint from one of Jammie Price's students. It began with an off-campus incident that soon spilled over into Price's classroom. It was all predictably orchestrated by Price in order to pass judgment on those who would dare to pass judgment (against her).

About a month before I received the student complaint, Price had foolishly shared a hotel room with another married professor while at a conference in San Francisco. When the travel receipts were turned in, the department secretaries figured out they had shared a room. False rumors of an affair began spreading.

Price decided to turn the incident into a teachable moment by sharing it with students. And that is the reason our mutual student came to me with the complaint. He considered the discussion unworthy of academic attention. I agreed. Then, I explained her "shock and condemn" teaching philosophy to him in simple terms:

1. Shock – Price shocks people with inappropriate comments and behavior. In this case, her sleeping arrangements with another married faculty member were a) disrespectful to both absent spouses and b) inappropriate for classroom discussion.
2. Condemn – Price condemns people for their predictable negative reactions to her disrespectful and inappropriate behavior.

I fear that the current controversy is just more of the same. Price probably derived a strange pleasure from seeing students recoil at the imagery in the porn documentary. But the real climax of the film was when she got to judge them for being so judgmental.

Price is setting herself up as a poster girl for academic freedom. But in reality, she isn't standing up for anything. She's just trying to build a utopian society that is nothing more than one protracted porn film. But in the final scene, the taxpayers are the only ones getting screwed.

The title refers to the TV game show The Price Is Right.

Chapter 40

Life Chose Me

June 27, 2012

This also appears in the books Life and How to Live It *(2023) and* Aborting Free Speech *(2023).*

In the summer of 1993, I went home for my ten-year high school reunion. I was so excited, I could hardly sleep all week. The kid who finished 734th in a class of 740 had made quite a turnaround. Over a span of ten years, I had gone off to junior college and earned an associate degree in psychology. Next, I added a bachelor's degree in psychology. Then, I earned a master's in social psychology. Finally, I topped it off with a doctorate in criminology. I could hardly wait to see my old classmates and tell them that I had just been hired as a college professor. I could not wait to see their reaction as I told them that the guy who failed English four times in high school was now a published author. But those were not the only changes that had taken place over the course of ten years. I had also become an atheist and a strong proponent of abortion.

With all of that education, I should have known better. When my professors told me the object of abortion was "nothing more than a clump of cells," I should have known that there was a powerful incentive for me to believe them. I should have known there was a psychological motive to avoid examining all of the evidence in the debate. If psychology had taught me anything, it taught me that attitudes and beliefs do not always drive our behavior. Often, it is our behavior that drives our attitudes and beliefs.

My behavior in those days was reprehensible. But it did not become that way overnight. It was all part of a gradual decline that began during my senior year in high school. A torn Achilles tendon ended my dreams of becoming a professional soccer player. And that's when I started to smoke and drink heavily and run around with women whose affections assuaged my damaged self-esteem.

By the end of my first semester in junior college, I was calling myself an agnostic. And that helped accelerate the decline in my quality of life. As an undergraduate, I gradually increased my consumption of alcohol and my casual relationships with women. In 1989, I joined a musical duo. As a traveling musician, I further increased my consumption of alcohol. I not only abused alcohol but also used the women I met at the bars in which I played. It is true that many women who follow musicians are looking for the same thing. But that isn't true of all of them. I usually kept a steady girlfriend as well as a couple of extra women on the side. And because I did not behave responsibly with them, I needed a backup plan. That's how I came to convince myself that abortion was permissible. My beliefs about abortion had nothing to do with moral reasoning. It was all about rationalizing a lifestyle. It was about finding a way, psychologically speaking, of dealing with unpleasant thoughts about the risks I was taking.

I'm convinced that others were like me—they began studying psychology because of a desire to solve their own problems, not because they wanted to help other people. I learned about a lot of theories as a student of psychology, but I always seemed to lack the objectivity necessary to apply them to my own conduct.

Cognitive dissonance is a psychological theory that asserts that human beings desire consistency in their cognitive life. In other words, it teaches that our beliefs and values and awareness of our behavior must all mesh with one another. When we feel tension between inconsistent beliefs and values, we sometimes adopt a new belief to resolve that tension. As a student of psychology, I was a living example of that theory without even realizing it.

I knew that sleeping with numerous women created a real risk of an unplanned pregnancy. I also knew that as a musician/student, I was in no position to raise a child. But I was also raised to believe that abortion was wrong. So I experienced real tension between my values and the awareness of my risky behavior and the consequences it might bring. I took the easy way out: I adopted the bland assertions of pro-choice advocates who claimed that the unborn were not human.

The behavior drove the attitudes. That is how the vicious cycle began. Once I had convinced myself that abortion was permissible because the unborn were not human, I sought out women who believed the same thing. In 1990, I went to the extreme of actually breaking up with a girlfriend as soon as she told me she would never have an abortion. Over the course of the next several years, I only dated women who were pro-choice. In other words, I would only date a woman if she was committed to giving me sex without the prospect of parenthood.

But all of that began to change in 1993 when I came home for that ten-year high school reunion. By God's divine providence, there were a couple of guests staying at my parents' house in Houston. Their names were Steve and Lisa Chambers. They were old friends we had met in 1969 when my mother was doing visitation for Clear Lake Baptist Church. *[As told in Chapter 32, "Does Fort Worth Ever Cross Your Mind?"] [They would remain among our closest lifelong friends.]*

After I became an atheist and a liberal, Lisa Chambers refused to give up on me. Every time she would see me, she would try to plant a stone in my shoe in the hopes that I would rethink at least one of my political or religious positions. In 1993, when I sat down to eat breakfast with her at my parents' house, she decided to whittle away at my pro-choice position. After I admitted that I was pro-choice, she began telling me about a friend of one of her sons who had worked at a pregnancy center. That was when I first heard about the effects of ultrasound technology on a woman's likelihood of going through with an abortion.

After telling me a little bit about ultrasound technology, Lisa talked about a man named Bernard Nathanson, the co-founder of the National Abortion Rights Action League, or NARAL. She explained that Dr. Nathanson had performed hundreds of abortions, including one on his girlfriend. But after aborting his own child, Dr. Nathanson would eventually see an ultrasound of an actual abortion procedure. And it would change his life forever.

Bernard Nathanson would later convert to Roman Catholicism and join the pro-life movement. He also made a film called *The Silent Scream* (1984), which featured an ultrasound of an actual abortion as it was taking place. Lisa Chambers saw that film and recommended that I watch it too. She also took the time to describe to me the ultrasound image of the child as it attempted to escape from the medical instrument that was dismembering it methodically. She also described the image of the baby's mouth opening and trying to scream—although no one could hear it from within the mother's womb. Lisa spent no more than a few minutes describing that imagery, but I could not seem to get it out of my mind.

So I eventually watched *The Silent Scream*. And I also listened to what critics said about the movie. I was unimpressed with virtually all of what the critics had to say. The only rebuttal I ever heard in response to the movie's central claim—that the unborn actually felt the pain of abortion—was the so-called "reflex" argument. This was simply the claim that the baby was not recoiling in pain as a result of being dismembered by the surgeon's knife. Instead, it was argued that the baby was simply reacting reflexively from being touched by an unknown object. But the argument fails for one simple reason: if it has fully functioning reflexes, then the baby is a living being. It is not a mere blob of tissue.

Whether it was actively fighting or reflexively reacting, the thing I saw was surely living. And if it was a living being, then how could one escape the conclusion that it was a living human being? Surely, no one could assert that it was a member of another species until its birth.

The criminologist in me also had questions concerning the presumption of innocence: If there is any ambiguity about whether the unborn is human, then should it not be resolved in favor of calling it a human being? In the eyes of the law, is it not better to let ten guilty men go free than to wrongfully punish one innocent man? And if the human being has never committed a crime, then doesn't abortion always kill an innocent human being without due process?

While some have argued that the Constitution includes an "implicit right to privacy," I saw nothing of the sort actually written into the United States Constitution. Instead, I saw specific mention of the "person" who is entitled to both "due process" and "equal protection." The words are there and need not be read into a "living" constitution—ironically, to justify killing.

Eventually, I concluded that it is up to the proponent of abortion to distinguish between an innocent human being and a "person." The burden rests upon those who wish to sentence the unborn to death. They must show "it" is not a person. For years, I've been asking pro-abortion-choicers to draw that distinction, and I've never been satisfied with their answers. Few have even tried to supply an answer based on science and reason. Ironically, since I've become a Christian, I have found that I do not need to rely on religion to make the case for life. Science and reason are enough. Of course, both, like life itself, are gifts from a God who is at once a lover of life and the author of truth.

When one examines my journey from abortion-choice advocate to pro-life activist, there is obvious cause for alarm. How could a man spend ten years in college, earn an M.S. in psychology and a Ph.D. in criminology, and never even think about the central question in the abortion debate? The fact that people were calling me "Dr." before I ever seriously answered the question "Are the unborn human?" is disturbing. It speaks volumes about the lack of intellectual diversity in higher education.

However, there is also good news: Notice that it all began with one person deciding to plant a stone in my shoe. Lisa Chambers did not set out to argue with me until I changed my mind. Had she done so, I would not have listened to her. My heart was not in the right place, and she knew it. Instead, she decided she would simply plant a stone in my shoe by spending about fifteen minutes with me and making sure that I began to think seriously about the central issue in the abortion debate: Are the unborn living human beings? That was all that was needed to create a great awakening in my conscience. I began to fundamentally rethink the issue of abortion.

Please remember this lesson and use it to your advantage. When someone you want to influence is simply not listening, go and find yourself a stone. Slip it into their shoe so that every time they take a step, they will be reminded of it. Let their growing discomfort with their own position cause them to stop and re-evaluate their thinking. You don't have to beat them over the head. You just have to leverage their own weight—the weight of their inner conscience—against them.

As I write these closing words, I am 2,000 miles from home. In three hours, I will speak to 200 students here in Colorado. We'll talk about how to defend life using logic paired with basic scientific evidence. In a few weeks, I'll fly to Pennsylvania to do the same thing. A few weeks later, I'll travel to North Carolina to give that message again. After nineteen years, the stone Lisa Chambers planted in my shoe is still there. As I travel around the country, I still feel its presence with every step I take.

And travel around the country, he did, giving speeches and participating in debates. Mike's most illustrious debate—and one of his proudest accomplishments—was with abortion provider Dr. Willie Parker. To read a transcript of this debate and to read more of Mike's writings on abortion, please read his posthumously published book, Aborting Free Speech. *Mike also wrote persuasively about abortion in Chapters 8 through 11 of his 2013 book,* Letters to a Young Progressive.

CHAPTER 41

Arguments Do Not Have Testicles

June 29, 2012

Recently, a student asked me whether I had a right to speak out on abortion given that I am a man and could never experience pregnancy. I countered by asking him whether arguments have testicles. The question drew laughter from other students who were listening to the exchange. But my point was serious and worth addressing at length.

The idea that men are ineligible to speak out on abortion has at least six flaws, each of which should be understood and articulated by men who desire to speak on the issue. Those argumentative flaws follow in no particular order of importance:

1. **The argument is sexist toward men.** There have been 26 million males aborted in America since *Roe v. Wade*. Men have every right to speak out on behalf of those millions of males who were victims of violence at the hands of women. To accept that men cannot speak up for them because they could never choose to have an abortion would have dangerous implications. Could a woman not speak

up for a young female rape victim because she could never choose to commit a rape? Would they be prohibited from speaking because they were not members of the gender ultimately responsible for carrying out the crime? Surely not. Furthermore, the argument reinforces the dangerous idea that rights belong to groups and not to individuals.

2. **The argument is sexist toward women.** We must also consider the effects of male anti-abortion advocacy on unborn women. An unborn woman has a right to choose simply by virtue of the fact that she is a woman. Or so the argument goes. If a woman is persuaded to let her unborn female child live, then she too can hear the evidence on both sides of the abortion debate. If she dies, she is not at liberty to hear arguments on either side of the issue from either a man or a woman. And she cannot make a decision concerning what to do with her body if she is dismembered in the womb. Ironically, a woman's so-called right to body autonomy, when exercised, defeats another woman's right to bodily autonomy (in roughly one out of every two cases of pregnancy).

3. **The argument defeats *Roe v. Wade*.** Feminists would like to see the two dissenting justices in *Roe v. Wade* silenced because they are men. But the same argument would silence the seven justices who voted in favor of *Roe v. Wade*. They were also men. In other words, if a man's opinion on abortion is invalidated simply by virtue of the fact that he is a man, then *Roe v. Wade* would also be invalidated.

4. **The argument would also apply to other medical procedures.** Women usually decide to let their male offspring

live. When they do, they usually have their male offspring circumcised. As Francis Beckwith points out, a woman can never know what it is like to have a portion of her penis removed. So how can she be allowed to participate in both the abortion and circumcision decision while a man is excluded from the former?

5. **The argument assumes the male pro-life speech is directed toward women**. People simply assume that the pro-life male is trying to control women when he argues against abortion. But oftentimes he is not even speaking to women. He is often motivated by a desire to change the hearts of men. This is because he knows that men often coerce women into abortions by threatening to leave them if they have the baby. Therefore, by entering the debate, the pro-life man may be reducing coercive control over women's bodies. If women are better suited to speak to women, then it stands to reason that men are better suited to speak to men.

6. **The argument also applies to slavery**. No one could reasonably argue that abortion only affects women. A better argument would be that it affects women disproportionately. But that does not mean women are the only ones who can address the issue of abortion. Historically, slavery has affected blacks disproportionately. But it does not lead to the conclusion that non-blacks are disqualified from commenting on a moral issue that clearly spills over to all segments of the human population.

Liberals are constantly trying to reduce the marketplace of ideas by reducing the number of voices that are eligible to participate. They have already silenced 52 million voices with the blade of a sharp knife. We cannot let them do further damage with dull ideas. Sharpening arguments requires vigorous debate. And vigorous debate requires acceptance of the idea that arguments are not gendered. Neither is the right to speak on matters of profound moral consequence.

CHAPTER 42

How Obama Earned My Doctorate

July 20, 2012

This also appears in the book Life and How to Live It *(2023).*

Back in 1989, I decided to pursue a Ph.D. in criminology. I was nearing the end of my master's program in psychology. I had a teaching assistantship that paid a mere $345 per month. I knew that I could not live on $345 per month for the minimum of three years I would need to finish my doctorate. I also knew that my parents would not be able to extend the same financial support they had so graciously extended while I was working on my master's degree. So I devised a plan to start a new business with just a $1,000 initial investment.

My grandfather had passed away in December of 1988. In the late spring of 1989, my grandmother mailed me a check for $1,000 that had been part of a life insurance policy payout issued upon my grandfather's death. In the late summer of 1989, I met a graduate student by the name of Shannon Ruscoe. He had been playing tennis with my roommate, Harry Wilson, the day I met him. I was sitting in my living room playing a song by James

Taylor when Shannon started singing along. After just a few minutes of listening to Shannon sing, I knew my life would never be the same again.

I called Shannon later that fall and asked if he wanted to get together and rehearse a few songs. We did. Within a few weeks, we were hanging out at keg parties in places like Starkville's College Station apartment complex. After a few beers, I would go to my car and get my 12-string. As our repertoire increased, so did Shannon's confidence as a singer.

After a few months of getting to know Shannon, I laid out a plan. I found a beautiful Alvarez six-string with a cedar top and black jacaranda back and sides. I realized I could buy the guitar and install a Martin thin-line pickup under the bridge for just $700. With the remaining $300, I told Shannon that, for just $30 per night, we could rent a PA system from our friend Jim Beaty, the owner of Backstage Music in Starkville. The idea was that after playing free ten times, we could start to earn a living as musicians.

First, we had to find a place to play. Fortunately, a Kappa Sigma named Mike worked as a manager at J.C. Garcia's—a Mexican restaurant/bar that featured acoustic acts, including the legendary Jeff Cummings and Jeffrey Rupp. We went to see him with an offer, telling Mike we would play free of charge on a Tuesday night, but only on one condition: if they sold $2,000 worth of liquor, they would have to hire us the next week for 10 percent of the liquor sales, or $200.

Mike laughed. J.C.'s had never sold $2,000 worth of liquor on a Tuesday night, which was generally their slowest night of the week. Naturally, he felt he had nothing to lose. So we booked our first gig at a real restaurant in a real college town.

I called all of my old friends at the Sigma Chi house and told them to show up at J.C.'s the following Tuesday night. Shannon told all the girls at the Chi Omega house where he worked as a "houseboy" in his spare time. As a result of our marketing, we packed the place out. J.C.'s sold over $2,000 in liquor that night, and we were invited to come back the next week.

Playing free at keg parties also paid off. By May of 1990, we were getting hired to play private parties. At one of those parties, we met the manager of the Bully III, a restaurant/bar near downtown Starkville. His name was David Lee Odom. He upped our salary to $250 per night, plus free dinner and free beer. By the time I graduated, I had played in that bar over one hundred times. It was there that I met other musicians and eventually had a chance to play all over the state and region. As a businessman and friend, Dave Odom changed our lives forever.

After Shannon moved to Nashville in 1991, I decided it was time to rely on the government for financial support. I'm just kidding. I simply went out and found another great singer named Anne Ford. We would play together until 1993. Our act was so successful that in April of 1993, my last full month of college, we played a whopping twenty-two gigs in just thirty days.

As a result of my business venture, I was able to graduate with a Ph.D. without taking out a single student loan. And it *was* a business venture. I was not just a guitarist. I booked most of our gigs, handled equipment purchases, and did a modest bit of accounting.

The irony is that, back in those days, I was a Democrat with socialist leanings. I voted for Dukakis and Clinton as the "lesser of two evils"—all the while complaining about the lack of a far-left alternative. Shortly thereafter, I would get involved in a two-year relationship with the daughter of the head of the socialist party of Ecuador. I simply failed to reconcile the discrepancies between my theoretical view of the world and my real-world experiences. Eventually, I grew out of my childish socialist mindset and realized that capitalism had allowed me to utilize my God-given talents to earn a living that government could never provide.

Although he never again played professionally, Mike retained an abiding love of music. He had eight lovely guitars when he passed.

While I was clearing out his house, I found original recordings of him playing with Shannon and Anne, along with pictures and flyers from that time, and I put together several slide show videos, which I shared on my YouTube account:

Fleetwood Mac's "Songbird" performed by Mike and Anne.
https://www.youtube.com/watch?v=jqPrBB7Dg7 Q&ab_channel=DaveAdams

Neil Young's "Heart of Gold" performed by Mike and Shannon.
https://www.youtube.com/watch?v=aP5d1-NCA6I& ab_channel=DaveAdams

Chapter 43

When Students Cheat, Liberals Retreat

September 13, 2012

The best argument against liberalism is that it doesn't work. That should be obvious to any teacher who has to deal with student cheating. Even some sociology teachers are beginning to learn this, although they are not aware that they are learning it. Like rats in a Skinner box, their behavior is being modified by reality even when they lack the intellectual capacity to recognize it. It warms my heart to see old liberals changing their ways, even if mindlessly. So I have written a column about it, which I am hoping will someday be reprinted by the *New York Times*.

Liberals are reticent to address the issue of student cheating because it reminds them of the fallen nature of man. Utopia requires cooperation, and evidence that people tend to cheat undermines the view that they are inclined to cooperate. So liberals would prefer to ignore evidence of cheating in order to preserve a vision of what "society" ought to be and could be if only they were given the means (read: more of our money) to re-engineer it.

But evidence of student cheating has become too widespread to ignore. So the liberals in my department have started circulating articles on the subject coming from reputable sources like the *New York Times* (sarcasm = off). Some of these articles and some of the faculty reactions to them have focused on what they describe as "a culture of cheating." Accordingly, some liberal faculty members have started talking about what needs to be done about it. Others have started acting on it. This should be causing cognitive dissonance for several reasons:

1. **Merit is irrelevant**. Sociology students are frequently fed the liberal line that people do not succeed in America on the basis of their own merits. The old "it isn't what you know, it's who you know" maxim is more than just a cultural adage. It seeps into the college curriculum in sociology classes that focus on Marxian conflict theories. Students are routinely taught that wealth, power, and privilege are the keys to success. This tends to denigrate the importance of knowledge. It should go without saying that people are less inclined to rely on their own achievements if their efforts are thus devalued. The connection of such notions to acceptance of cheating is fairly obvious. If we teach people that they cannot succeed through legitimate efforts, we will soon see them pursue success through illegitimate means. As always, liberals fail to understand that ideas have consequences. And bad ideas can have very bad consequences.

2. **Ethnocentrism is unacceptable**. Sociologists like to teach others that it is wrong to judge other cultures by the standards of one's own culture. Such judgments are

called "ethnocentric." This concept has slowly crept into mainstream liberal thinking. That is unfortunate because promoting anti-ethnocentrism is problematic for at least two reasons: 1. It tends to undermine the idea that one's actions (including cheating) can be considered objectively wrong. 2. It renders efforts to condemn a "culture of cheating" hypocritical. Remember that we aren't supposed to judge other cultures!

3. **Punishment is ineffective**. Sociologists routinely teach the liberal idea that punishment is ineffective and the corresponding idea that "society" has an obligation to rehabilitate criminals. Then, in their own syllabi, they warn students that cheating will be punished. Claiming to be shocked when their threats are ignored, they send students through the campus penal system, not through rehabilitation. And the liberal campus penal system can be quite punitive and dismissive of due process. No attorneys, no tape recorders, no note taking, no soup…oops! I mean, no due process for you!

In a nutshell, sociology, like modern liberalism, teaches that we can't get by on our own merits, we should not judge other cultures, and punishment does not work. When students cheat, however, the sociologist urges advancement through one's own merits, condemnation of the culture of cheating, and punishment of the transgressor.

It is little wonder that many students are intellectually lost and morally confused. They make the mistake of taking their sociology professors seriously, which means buying into contradictory liberal ideas. So my advice is twofold: First, don't cheat in college because it is objectively wrong to do so. Second, don't cheat yourself by choosing a major populated by hypocrites who cannot abide by the consequences of their own ideas.

Mike also wrote:

Ideas have consequences. The ideas we express have specific consequences in the course of human history. They may either produce life, or they may produce death among those who hear them.

Chapter 44

Unlearning Liberty

October 23, 2012

Despite their feigned interest in tolerance, college campuses are among the most punitive and stifling environments in the country. Students are routinely punished for "offenses" ranging from penning mild satire to holding the wrong opinions on important social and political issues. One book, *Unlearning Liberty* by Greg Lukianoff, documents these abuses better than any other that has been written since I joined the campus culture wars over a decade ago. Greg is able to document these things well and for a simple reason: he has been the president of the Foundation for Individual Rights in Education (FIRE) for the last seven years.

The stories Greg tells in his new book are so disturbing it will be difficult for some to believe that they are all real and all come from American universities. *Unlearning Liberty* at times sounds like an account from some faraway land that never valued the kinds of freedoms our Constitution guarantees. For example:

- A student is punished for racial insensitivity for publicly reading a book that condemns the KKK.

- Students are required to lobby before legislatures for political bills they disagree with in order to graduate from a public university.
- A student senate passes a Sedition Act to punish other students for criticizing them at, of all places, a public university governed by the First Amendment and funded by their tuition dollars.

However strange these stories seem, they deserve our undivided attention. The reason is simple: when these students graduate, their anti-liberty mindset is unleashed on the larger society.

Indeed, after a generation of unlearning liberty, these things will begin to seem normal if not addressed soon. FIRE co-founder Alan Charles Kors said it best when he stated that "a nation that does not educate in liberty will not long preserve it and will not even know when it is lost."

For over a decade, I have been trying to explain that the campus free speech war transcends politics and religion. It is a threat to everyone. That is why I am glad that a book echoing my arguments—but in far greater depth and with much greater eloquence—was written by someone who disagrees with me on a broad range of issues. Greg Lukianoff is an atheist, a Democrat, a supporter of same-sex marriage, and a supporter of abortion rights. We have worked together for years as allies in the free speech wars because we both recognize that liberty is a sacred process, not a pre-ordained result.

We also understand that true commitment to liberty is measured by the conduct of our institutions of higher learning and not by their statements about their conduct. For example, Harvard University claims that "curtailment of free speech undercuts the intellectual freedom that defines (Harvard's) purpose."

In reality, it fires even presidents who refuse to bow down to the gods of political correctness and gender sensitivity.

Harvard and other private universities claim to be free from the technical requirement that they conform to the dictates of the First Amendment. That much is true. But they are not free from the moral requirement that they must always be honest about the true state of the marketplace of ideas in their classrooms and across their campuses.

Truth be known, Harvard has a long record of suppressing free speech among students, faculty, and, more recently, non-conforming administrators. Given that reality, they should refrain from telling prospective students that "the free exchange of ideas is vital for our primary function of discovering and disseminating ideas."

To the extent that administrators make these patently false claims, they fraudulently induce students into taking on debt, often in the realm of six digits. All this in order to join a marketplace of ideas that barely exists in an age of administratively mandated and supervised political correctness.

The best and most accurate measure of the depth of our constitutional crisis in higher education can be seen in the campus speech codes of our public university campuses. These codes are a measure of not just the censoriousness of our public administrators but also their audacity. The fact that they knowingly enforce them—even with no prospect of winning in court—shows us two things:

1. They know that even when they lose in individual cases, the presence of the often multiply layered speech codes will help maintain orthodoxy by chilling speech that is not politically correct.

2. Due to qualified immunity, they will never have to pay personal damages and the general public—the same people they seek to censor—will have to foot the bill for the litigation.

The problem is not just at Harvard and Yale. It is at other universities—even ones located in conservative areas of the nation. For example, Texas A&M has a speech code that prohibits violating the "right" to "respect for personal feelings" and protects "freedom from indignity of any type."

Of course, many of the smaller liberal arts colleges are even worse. Davidson College bans "inquiries about dating." So you can't ask someone on a date at Davidson without violating the speech code. Even if you could, you would not be able to ask your date to go see *Guys and Dolls*. Use of the word "doll" is considered sexual harassment.

The University of Iowa does the best job of combining the speech code and the sexual harassment policy into a powerful weapon people can use to destroy just about anyone they don't like. Sexual harassment is when "somebody says or does something sexually related that you don't want them to say or do, regardless of who it is." Did you get that, folks? If you are a student at Iowa and the girl you like has sex with someone else and you get jealous, then guess what? You've been sexually harassed!

Because the speech code issue is so important and because this book is so important, I will review it in several installments. In the meantime, order a copy now. Learn about the American values students are unlearning on campuses all across America today.

This shows, once again, that Mike was for free speech for all, not just for fellow conservatives, and he was happy to "reach across the aisle" to this end. He used Unlearning Liberty *as a text in his class "CRM 395 – THE FIRST AMENDMENT AND CRIME."*

On October 17, 2023, while this book was being written, Greg Lukianoff and Rikki Schlott published The Canceling of the American Mind, *which includes six pages of favorable coverage of Mike and his predicament at UNCW.*

For more book recommendations, see Chapter 7, "An Anti-Communist Reading List."

Chapter 45

Stand For Life

January 14, 2013

A former student recently emailed that she was disappointed that I had gotten so heavily involved with the student pro-life movement in recent years. She said she could remember a time when I had a love for defending free speech rights. Her email was somewhat unfair as I am still defending First Amendment rights (did she read my last column?) *["Every Idea Is an Incitement," January 4, 2013, which specifically refers to the First Amendment.]* Also, I have been involved in pro-life advocacy since I became a columnist in 2002. In fact, my very first published column was on the topic of abortion. *[Mike merges both in his last book,* Aborting Free Speech, *published posthumously in 2023.]*

In the event my former student is reading this expression of anti-abortion advocacy, I would like to enumerate the reasons why she—a pro-lifer herself—should have been involved in the student pro-life movement when she was in college. The following are also reasons why all pro-life students should be actively pro-life:

1. **The societal diminution of all human life.** The pro-abortion choice movement has produced a general devaluing of human life that can only be corrected by a strong pro-life movement among students. How many of you were shocked by the acquittal of Casey Anthony? I was certainly angry, but I was not shocked. She wanted to party and to date without being weighed down by the responsibility of motherhood. I believe she killed her little girl in order to live a life of convenience. The evidence clearly points toward her unmitigated guilt. But tens of millions of women have done the same thing since *Roe v. Wade*. No wonder the Anthony jury seemed bored throughout most of the proceedings. No wonder she walked despite the evidence. Her kind of guilt is commonplace.

2. **The proximity of the threat.** The culture war is raging in America. There are battlefields everywhere but none as large or contentious as the university campus. This is where the immensely profitable non-profits make a lot of their money off abortion. They are marketing their services to your fellow students. Therefore, simply by virtue of where you are, you can make a greater difference if you are willing to cut against the current.

3. **Momentum.** A May 2009 Gallup poll found 51 percent of Americans call themselves pro-life. Gallup began asking that question in 1995, and this was the first time a majority of Americans identified themselves as pro-life. Pew Research Center did a survey around the same time showing that only 46 percent believed abortion should be legal in all or most cases. That was down from 54 percent the

previous year. Therefore, I would urge pro-lifers to become activists because they would be joining a winning team. In so doing, they could help accelerate these positive trends.

4. **State and individual neutrality.** The state cannot be neutral on abortion. It either a) recognizes that the unborn are human and have a right to life or b) permits killing them. Since our government has taken the public policy position that the unborn are not afforded the same rights as toddlers—including the right to be free from dismemberment—you need to take a public policy position too. That means becoming an activist, not being a pacifist in the midst of a war on the unborn.

5. **Propaganda and passivity.** Pro-choice arguments are so bad that they cannot survive scrutiny. They must be confined to soliloquy rather than subjected to debate. For example, the "back-alley abortion" argument suggests that we must make killing children safe or else adults might be killed in the process. Abortion-choice advocates warn that "thousands" would be killed in back alleys if abortion were once again illegal. This is the way they justify legalizing the murder of millions. The logic is twisted, and the facts are wrong. The Centers for Disease Control reported that only thirty-nine women died from illegal abortions in 1972, the year before *Roe v. Wade*. Put simply, propaganda is activism. And it is only effective when repeated endlessly in the presence of the passive. So we must all be active in combatting this deadly information.

6. **Men's liberation.** Men tend to be more supportive of abortion than women. That is why it is more accurate to call

the so-called abortion rights movement a men's liberation movement—as opposed to a woman's liberation movement. Abortion liberates men by allowing them to sleep around without fear of consequences. It frees men from fatherhood and allows them to exploit women. So we need more male activists. Next time someone says, "men have never had abortions, so they should not be commenting on it," say this: "women have never played in the NFL, so they should not be sportscasters."

7. **Underlying causes.** People will tell you that you should never become an activist seeking to make abortion unacceptable or, heaven forbid, illegal. Instead, they say you should focus on underlying causes. Rape has underlying causes. Should we make it legal and instead try to treat its underlying causes? Come to think of it, spousal abuse has underlying causes too. We would never elect a politician who ran on a platform of making it legal for a man to beat his spouse. But we routinely elect politicians who run on a platform of saying it should remain legal for a woman to kill her baby. As you young people would say, "that's messed up." Indeed, it is. That's why we need activists.

Reading this column, you may have noticed that all of my observations to this point have been brilliant. I'll have more brilliant observations in my next book, *Up from Humility*. But the brilliant observations in this column have not been mine. In fact, each and every one of them was stolen from a new book called *Stand for Life* by John Ensor and Scott Klusendorf.

I highly recommend John and Scott's new book. You can pick it up on Amazon for less than the price of two tall skinny lattes or a single ticket to the late show. By the time you are finished reading, you'll be ready to take your first steps as an activist fighting for the right of the unborn to take their first steps.

Stand for Life is more than just aptly titled. It's a real lifesaver (and I mean that literally). Of course, that's just my humble opinion.

For more book recommendations, see Chapter 7, "An Anti-Communist Reading List."

Chapter 46

The Enemy Within

May 7, 2013

Most people who read my weekly column at Townhall.com remember how I got into the business of criticizing higher education. It began with a controversy that started in the wake of 9/11 when an anti-American student sent me an email blaming the U.S. for the attack on the World Trade Center. When I sent an email response calling her ideas "bigoted" and "unintelligent" and "immature," her mother, a college administrator, spearheaded an effort to have my email account searched in order to find evidence to charge me with "libel" and bring me before the campus judiciary. *[This episode is covered in detail in Mike's first book,* Welcome to the Ivory Tower of Babel *(2004)]*

Of course, there was no need for such a controversy to have occurred. I was simply expressing core political beliefs shared by most Americans. Nonetheless, the Marxist administrator/mother simply could not understand how anyone could criticize the idea—a truism in her view—that America was evil and deserved to be attacked. This view has long been common on American college campuses.

About a year after that controversy, a close friend of mine decided to change careers and enroll in a master's program. At her first social gathering among fellow graduate students, one of her new professors casually mentioned the fact that he used to be a member of the Weather Underground. It was the first time I heard about the group that would become so widely known during the 2008 presidential race. The fact that the professor so casually revealed his affiliation with a domestic terrorist organization was intriguing. Was he merely unashamed, or was it actually a badge of honor?

Academic indifference toward anti-American terrorism was at the forefront of the biggest story I have covered in my career of critiquing higher education. The story revolved around Julio Pino, an associate professor of history at Kent State University. In 2006, Pino was connected with a terrorist website called the "global war" blog. Professors at Kent State previously knew about the connection and did nothing. Pino's activities eventually became nationally known—but only after bloggers brought him to my attention by sending me links to his writings.

When I first saw the links, I was shocked. Under a pseudonym, Pino had posted bomb making instructions. With them, he also posted exhortations to use the bombs to murder American troops. After reading the posts, I needed specific evidence proving that Pino was indeed the person who was responsible for writing them. The Kent State student newspaper had already published Pino's writings praising Palestinian suicide bombers. I hoped and strongly suspected that he had been careless enough to tell other professors about his other blog writings.

Thankfully, Pino had indeed told his boss, John Jameson, that he was writing for the terrorist website. When Jameson admitted it to a local reporter, we had our man. I ran a column exposing

Pino. Drudge soon picked up the story and, before long, I got an invitation to go on *Fox News* to confront Pino on air. Kent State administrators just hid under their desks and waited for the storm to pass. But it did not.

After the feds learned of Pino, I was asked to meet with them and share other information I had gathered. While Pino was under FBI surveillance, Jameson foolishly allowed him to take leave for a couple of weeks of travel during the middle of the semester. Pino's destination was the Middle East, of course.

Jameson was eventually fired from his department chairman position for authorizing Pino's trip to the Middle East while he was being investigated for possible connections to terrorist organizations. But he was only fired because people outside of the campus community were outraged. The Kent State community never seems to have grasped the problem. These days, there are lots of pro-terrorism professors teaching in America. It's what they do when no one else will hire them.

Of course, Pino is still teaching and drawing a salary off of frustrated Ohio taxpayers. Equally frustrating is the fact Bill Ayers is now drawing a healthy pension off the backs of Illinois taxpayers. After being acquitted on a technicality, the unrepentant domestic terrorist has had an easy life. He transitioned smoothly from the Weather Underground to the University of Illinois-Chicago faculty all the way to the inner circle of a young politician named Barack Obama.

Last weekend, while I was starting to work on this column, Ayers visited Kent State to give a speech that outraged many Ohio citizens. When a reporter covering the speech asked Ayers whether he could be compared to the Boston Marathon bombers, he feigned outrage. He claimed that he and his comrades only targeted property whereas the Boston bombers targeted people.

In reality, the Weather Underground did kill people, including several of their own members who died assembling a pipe bomb in New York City. The bomb was similar to the ones used in the recent Boston attacks.

Kent State's decision to invite Ayers to speak shows that these radical thugs are more than just forgiven for their past deeds. They are celebrated for their enduring commitment to violence against their fellow countrymen. It is a systemic culture of anti-Americanism that attracts the likes of Ayers and Pino and provides a taxpayer-supported platform for their public commentaries.

The rhetoric of the radical American terrorists of yesterday and the radical Islamic terrorists of today is difficult to distinguish. It all revolves around a burning hatred of America and a desire to see its downfall.

The enemy is deep inside the gates.

Julio Pino was eventually fired, and Mike wrote about that in 2018 in "The Tenured Enemy in Our Midst," which is not included in this book.

Chapter 47

An Embarrassment to Higher Education

August 16, 2013

Dear Edward:

I want to take the time to thank you for writing and telling me that I should be fired from my position as a tenured professor because I am "the biggest embarrassment to higher education in America." I also want to thank you for responding when I asked you exactly how you arrived at that conclusion. Your response, "because you insist that marriage requires one man and one woman," was both helpful and concise.

While I respect your right to conclude that I am the biggest embarrassment to higher education in America, I think you're wrong. In fact, I don't even think I'm the biggest embarrassment to higher education in the state of North Carolina. But since you're a liberal and you support "choice"—provided we're talking about dismembering children and not school vouchers for those who weren't dismembered—I want to give you some options. In fact, I'm going to describe the antics of ten professors, official campus groups, and invited campus speakers in North Carolina and let you decide which constitutes the biggest embarrassment to higher education.

1. In the early spring semester of 2013, a women's studies professor and a psychology professor at Western Carolina University co-sponsored a panel on bondage and S&M. The purpose of the panel was to teach college students how to inflict pain on themselves and others for sexual pleasure. When you called me the biggest embarrassment in higher education, you must not have known about their bondage panel. Maybe you were tied up that evening and couldn't make it.

2. At UNC-Chapel Hill, there is a feminist professor who believes that women can lead happy lives without men. That's nothing new. But what's different is that she thinks women can form lifelong domestic partnerships with dogs and that those relationships will actually be fulfilling enough to replace marital relationships with men. I can't make this stuff up, Ed. I don't drop acid. Well, at least not since the late 1980s. But I promise this story is real and not an LSD flashback.

3. At Duke University, feminists hired a "sex worker" (read: prostitute) to speak as part of an event called the Sex Workers Art Show. After his speech, the male prostitute pulled down his pants, got down on his knees, and inserted a burning sparkler into his rectum. While it burned, he sang a verse of "The Star-Spangled Banner." I believe that stripping incident was almost as embarrassing as the other one involving the Duke lacrosse team.

4. A porn star was once paid to give a speech at UNC-Greensboro. The topic was "safe sodomy." After her speech, the feminist pornographer sold autographed butt plugs to students in attendance. I'm not sure whether the ink could contribute to rectal cancer. I'm no health expert. But I do know it was pretty darned embarrassing when the media picked up on the story.

5. A few years ago, at UNC-Chapel Hill, a feminist group built a large vibrator museum in the middle of the campus quad as a part of their "orgasm awareness week." I think that was probably the climax of the semester, academically speaking. But they certainly weren't too embarrassed to display a vibrator that was made out of wood back in the 1920s. Keep your batteries charged, Ed. We're about halfway done.

6. A feminist administrator at UNC-Wilmington (UNCW) sponsored a pro-abortion event. During the event, they sold T-shirts saying "I had an abortion" to students who… well, had abortions. That's right, Ed. The students were encouraged to boast about the fact that they had killed their own children. That's how the UNC system is preserving the future of our great Tarheel State.

7. The following semester, that same UNCW administrator sponsored a workshop teaching students how to appreciate their orgasms. I learned art appreciation in college. Today, college kids are taught orgasm appreciation. I will let you decide whether that's an embarrassment to higher ed., Ed.

8. A few years ago, a UNCW English professor posted nude pictures of underaged girls as a part of an "art exhibit" in the university library. The provost then ordered the nude

pictures to be moved away from the library and into the university union. This decision was made after several pedophiles had previously been caught downloading child pornography in the university library just a few yards away from the location of the display. The English professor was incensed, so she asked the faculty senate to censure the provost for violating her "academic freedom." The faculty senate sided with the feminist professor. The provost was later pressured to leave the university.

9. A different feminist professor at UNCW accused a male professor of putting tear gas in her office. She was later caught putting her mail in a microwave oven. She did this because she thought people were trying to poison her with anthrax and that the oven would neutralize the toxins. She was not placed on leave for psychiatric reasons. Instead, she was designated as the university's official "counterterrorism" expert.

10. And then there is Mike Adams. He thinks marriage is between a man and a woman.

So those are the choices, Ed. You can simply write back and tell me which of these professors, groups, or guest speakers has caused "the biggest embarrassment to higher education"—either in North Carolina or in America altogether. Or you can just concede that our system of "hire education" is the real embarrassment because it has been hijacked by radical feminism. And please pardon any puns—especially those that take the form of ms-spelled words.

I've had people tell me this is their favorite—or, at least, this is the first to come to mind.

Chapter 48

Teaching to the Ten

January 14, 2014

This also appears in the book Life and How to Live It *(2023)*.

Dear CRM 381 students:

Welcome back! I just wanted to write and let you know that the syllabus is up and running on the departmental webpage. I have been instructed to direct you to the link rather than distribute individual copies. The university needs to save money on paper so the LGBTQIA office can continue to offer orgasm awareness seminars and so the women's resource center can continue to promote abortion.

In addition to going over the syllabus on day one, I plan to introduce each one of you to my somewhat informal teaching philosophy. In a nutshell, that philosophy can be summarized in the phrase "twenty-seventy-ten."

When it comes to students, there are at least three distinct groups. They follow in order from the least pleasant to the most pleasant among you.

1. The Tweeny Twenty.
2. The Sagacious Seventy.
3. The Tenacious Ten.

The first group, the Tweeny Twenty, derives its name from its character and its proportions. This is the group of students who, as the name implies, are woefully immature to almost preadolescent proportions. Fortunately, they are only a minority—about 20 percent of the student population.

The Tweeny Twenty somehow managed to get out of high school without having even a vague sense of what they want to accomplish in life. But they are able to go to college for a few years to explore their options because a) anyone can get into college these days and b) anyone can get a government-backed loan to help pay for college these days. And so they go. What else is there to do?

Having no clue what they are doing in college, they behave as clueless individuals do. They come and go from class as they please—arriving late and leaving early. They dress inappropriately as if they are coming from a bar or are heading to the beach. In short, they come to college for social reasons. To party. To meet a spouse. Or maybe to meet a "connection" or someone who will "hook them up" with a job upon graduation.

I will do everything within my ability to drive these people out of the classroom before the drop date. That is my sincere promise to the other 80 percent of you.

The second group, the Sagacious Seventy, also derives its name from its character and its proportions. This is the group of students who, as the name implies, are shrewder and more goal-oriented than the Tweeny Twenty. Fortunately—I only say "fortunately" because they are fairly well behaved and manageable—they are about 70 percent of the student population.

Having some clue of what they are doing in college, they behave as rational individuals. They come to class pretty regularly and go through the motions in order to get their course credit. They have calculated that having a degree is better than not having a degree and that the amount they pay in student loans will be exceeded by the salary increase that accompanies having a college degree. Of course, many of these students have miscalculated and will never pay off their loans, but that is another issue to be explored at a later date.

In short, these students come to college to get credentialed. They know that employers want to see an applicant's degree because that means they had the stick-to-it-ness to set a goal and follow through. They also know that it doesn't require much work to get their expensive degree, so they divert study time toward work time. They take a part-time job in order to keep their student loans down even if this means turning in sub-par work. They know their professors have come to expect sub-par work. Like most of our students, they are intelligent and keenly self-interested. They do the cost-benefit analysis and make a reasonable decision in a difficult situation that is becoming more difficult as college becomes more expensive.

The last group, the Tenacious Ten, also derives its name from its character and its proportions. This is the group of students who, as the name implies, are highly determined and persistent and cannot easily be distracted from their goals. Unfortunately, they are only about 10 percent of the student population.

The Tenacious Ten may well have good genes. I don't know for sure. But I do know that they usually have good parents who taught them good life lessons. Also, more than likely, they had good counselors in their schools or in the churches. And so they are focused and ready from day one.

In short, the Tenacious Ten are here because they desire specific knowledge that will help them attain a specific goal. As a result, they have an intrinsic appreciation of the material I plan to teach throughout the semester. So there is no need to threaten or cajole or manipulate them into performing at expected levels. They just do it because they come to college having already gotten into the habit of doing it on their own.

This message is just my way of reminding you that when I talk about "our" class, I am not talking about all thirty of you. I am talking to about three of you—those who constitute the Tenacious Ten percent. You are the only reason I am still teaching. I look forward to finding out who you are. I don't suspect it will take very long to identify you.

I hope this message finds you well. If you are in the Tweeny Twenty, I hope it scares the hell out of you—so much so that you drop the course. Otherwise, I will see you in class on Monday.

Mike had commented multiple times about the decline in the quality of incoming students since he wrote this in 2014. If I were able to ask him for an update, I wonder: Would the Tweeny Twenty now be the Dirty Thirty? Or perhaps even the Forlorn Forty?

Despite his growing frustration with the decline in student quality, I know that he never lost his love for "Teaching to the Ten." For example, in 2019, he posted the following:

After a great evening in "Trials of the Century," I return home with the satisfaction of knowing that I was born to do what I do for a living. Nothing is as satisfying as knowing your life is not wasted by not following your calling.

Mike certainly followed his calling, and his life was well lived indeed.

We do not have any video of Mike teaching at UNCW, but here is a short video of Mike teaching at Summit in Colorado in the summer:

https://www.youtube.com/watch?v=xtKG-tT0Y2c&ab_channel=TonyEvans

Chapter 49

Defining Life

January 23, 2014

Sometimes, people approach me and say that they are personally pro-life but pro-choice as a matter of public policy. In other words, they oppose abortion because they believe it is murder but wouldn't want to force their view on others who might disagree. Over Independence Day weekend, a young man from Boulder approached me and expressed a similar view but with a slightly different twist. Our constructive exchange inspired the present column.

It is very easy to correct someone who thinks that abortion is murder but is reticent to "impose" that view on others. The proper thing to do is to help him by restating his position in this manner: "So let me get this straight. You would never support abortion because you could never kill a baby. But you would never want to stop someone else from killing a baby. Does that accurately reflect your position?" As soon as he sees the flaw in his argument, the proponent is forced to re-evaluate his position.

But the young man from Boulder offered up a slight variation of that argument. Instead of saying that he did not want to impose his general beliefs about abortion on others, he noted that there was disagreement over the issue of when life begins. He then asserted that he did not want to impose his precise definition of life on others. His exact words were as follows: "I believe life begins at conception, but others may have a different definition of life. They might believe it begins at birth. So for them, abortion would not be taking a life."

It is true that there is a lack of *absolute* consensus on the definition of life. But an absence of consensus does not imply an absence of truth. When the shape of the Earth was in dispute, the Earth still had a shape. Furthermore, while not absolute, there is a remarkable degree of consensus on the definition of life. The leading texts in the science of embryology have arrived at a broad consensus that life does indeed begin at conception.

So what if some people disagree concerning the precise point at which life begins—or what if they simply don't know the answer? What are we to do with the existence of some lack of consensus (or lack of knowledge) on the matter? The best answer is to be found by examining our society's disdain for the legal defense of mistake of law.

Our objection to the "ignorance of the law" defense is based upon the principle that subjectivity tends to water down the moral authority of the law. To say that the illegality of murder or rape hinges on whether we are aware of its illegality is to invite relativism. The law of gravity is not contingent upon our perceptions. We did not remain suspended in the air before we learned about gravity in grammar school. We were bound all by the law of gravity even before we were aware of its existence. Similarly, we are bound to moral laws regardless of our perceptions of them.

The more obvious objection to the "ignorance of the law" defense is that it would invite fraud. People who murder and rape will also feign ignorance in order to escape liability. This requires no further elaboration.

To tolerate subjectivity in defining life and its onset would cheapen life itself. It would also invite the murder of teens at the hands of those who assert that life begins in the twenties. Tolerance is not always admirable. In fact, it is often unworkable.

Scott Klusendorf sums the issue up nicely, noting that "the science of embryology establishes that from the earliest stages of development, each of us is a distinct, living, and whole human being. True, we have yet to mature, but the kind of thing we are is clear. This is settled science. Of course, there remains a philosophical debate on how we should value humans in their earliest stages of development, but let us not confuse the value question with the empirical."

Most people know when life begins. The issue is not the value we place on the views of dissenters. The issue has always been the value we place on life itself.

Life was always on Mike's mind. People mainly think of him as a political writer, but it is his musings on life that stick with me the most. For example:

Never take the bus from the museum complex to Monticello. Walk the trail. This is generalizable life advice. Never take a bus when you can walk a trail.

Resentment is like cancer. It will eat you up inside until it consumes your soul. But it is worse than cancer. It can also consume everyone around you.

I believe in a God of second chances. Otherwise, I would not be writing anything at all or speaking anywhere about anything.

I caught up with an old friend tonight. We've been friends since 1972. This is the first time in a decade that one of our phone conversations was over in less than two hours. My advice is simple: hang on to your old friends and make time for them, regardless of what life is throwing at you. When you talk with old friends, you realize that your present troubles are often meaningless. Keep focused on an eternal perspective. Never let it go.

Chapter 50

Standing at the Summit

March 27, 2014

Today, I write with some good news some of you may have already heard. On March 20, in Greenville, North Carolina, a federal jury unanimously sided with me in my claims that the University of North Carolina–Wilmington (UNCW) violated federal law in a 2006 promotion decision. Specifically, the jury found that my First Amendment protected speech was a "substantial or motivating factor" in the defendants' decision not to promote me to full professor. They also found that defendants could not prove they would have made the same decision in the absence of my speech activity. The case now moves to the judge to determine relief. *[This case is covered in detail in Chapter 54 through Chapter 59.]*

This has been a long seven-year legal battle, and I am exhausted. Accordingly, many have suggested that I take a long vacation. And so I am. In fact, between early May and late August, I'll be taking a fourteen-week vacation in Manitou Springs, Colorado. Well, it isn't exactly a vacation. It's the place I've spent the last five summers. It's almost become my second home.

I go to Manitou every summer because that is where Summit Ministries is located. The ministry was established in 1962. They first invited me to speak there in 2008. Not long afterward, they decided to have me stay all summer and teach in every session. (They offer seven two-week sessions over the course of the summer.) It is always refreshing to go there in the summer after spending my fall and spring at a secular university. The place keeps me grounded and rekindles my spirits.

Since 1962, tens of thousands have similarly benefitted from the Summit experience. To date, more than 35,000 families have enrolled their sixteen- to twenty-one-year-old sons and daughters in the Summit Ministries' twelve-day experience. There, they are mentored by Christian leaders in academia, public policy, and business and prepared to be courageous leaders who stand strong in a culture that tries to break them and cause them to abandon their faith.

Don't just take my word for it. Summit has won the endorsement of Christian leaders such as Eric Metaxas, James Dobson, Josh McDowell, and the late Charles Colson. Chuck called Summit the "gold standard" for training students in the Christian worldview. I certainly agree. That's why I always tell concerned parents to look into the summer Summit programs.

When faced with the choice of sending kids to a secular public university that charges $10,000 a year and a Christian university that charges $30,000 a year, people will often pick the latter. They probably figure it's worth an extra $20,000 a year to guard their children's souls. That kind of thinking is flawed for two reasons: First, many of these universities aren't really Christian anymore. Second, there are other remedies that cost less than $20,000 a year. In fact, you can send your college-age kid to Summit for $1195. If you register before April 1, you can send them for $995.

Summit has a long track record of preparing young adults to stand strong against hostile worldviews and become courageous leaders at a time when our nation needs them desperately. That atmosphere has done nothing but strengthen me as I have fought against the UNC system over the last seven years. Please check out their website today. This could be the summer that changes your life trajectory, or that of a loved one, forever.

I'll be there all summer, not just resting but also teaching with my good friends Frank Turek, Scott Klusendorf, Sean McDowell, John Stonestreet, and, of course, Summit President Jeff Myers. *[Six years later, four of those five men would speak at Mike's memorial service.]*

Of course, I'll also be doing a little rafting and climbing to the top of Pikes Peak. I hope to see you at the top. And thank you all so much for your prayers and support. They have helped me make it through another year and to end it with an incredible victory. We serve a mighty God indeed. It is a lesson we must pass on to future generations.

Mike also once wrote:

If you want to destroy a great nation, then just undermine the gratitude of its young citizens. Tell them the nation in which they live isn't special. Tell them that for a generation. Then, your work is done. They will pass it on to future generations.

Please also see Chapter 31, "Mike's Peak," for more about Summit Ministries.

Chapter 51

Do Something

April 21, 2014

American culture is in trouble. It is impossible to watch television for long without concluding that we are all living in one big reality TV show that is defining deviancy down one embarrassing episode at a time. Unfortunately, the church isn't doing much to fight against the cultural current. By trying to be "relevant," the church is simply getting pulled into the undertow. Consequently, most churches are slowly drowning in the shallow water of our declining culture.

So how do we turn the tide and begin to have a meaningful church experience that also influences the culture in a meaningful way? The answer is that we must learn to deal with relativistic thinking in a proactive fashion. Take, for example, the issue of abortion.

No one wants to confront a woman who has had an abortion and tell her that she has just committed a profoundly evil act by taking an innocent life. So the natural impulse is to simply pretend that no evil act has transpired. Indeed, this is what most pastors do. They don't condemn abortion. Nor do they praise it. They just ignore it. In this way, the taking of innocent life becomes just another morally neutral choice in a society that is becoming increasingly incapable of making moral distinctions between alternative courses of action.

This trend must be reversed. As long as the church refuses to push away from relativism, the culture will push the church toward it. More innocent children will die as result.

So what specifically is to be done on an issue like abortion? I believe the answer is to get churches actively involved in preventing abortions from happening in the first place. The best way to do that is to provide direct financial support to women who are considering abortion—and to make the availability of that support known to them well in advance of their decision. *[Mike elaborates on this in Chapter 80, "Life Lines."]*

If your church is doing nothing on the issue of abortion, please take the time to meet with your pastor. Ask him to prayerfully consider starting a specific ministry aimed at reducing abortions within the church and in the broader community.

By actively collecting tithes that will be directed toward paying the expenses (medical and otherwise) of women in crisis pregnancy situations, two important things will be accomplished:

1. The church will implicitly communicate that abortion is wrong by acknowledging that it is a thing to be avoided. But it will do so without slapping a scarlet "A" on the garments of church members who have had negative experiences with abortion. This will satisfy the more conservative members of the congregation who want the church to do something instead of remaining neutral on the abortion issue.

2. The church will also appease those who argue that we need compassionate approaches to the abortion issue rather than focusing on legislative and judicial restrictions. This approach will satisfy the more liberal members of the congregation who want conservatives to do something charitable that doesn't involve "legislating morality" (as if it were somehow possible to legislate in a morally neutral way).

Of course, there will come a time when people ask questions about why the church takes a stand against abortion, even if it is merely an implicit stance. This is where education, rather than reflexive condemnation, should become the focus of the church. Note that 1 Peter 3:15 calls us to defend the gospel. I believe we should also use apologetics to defend the unborn. In fact, when we do so, we create new opportunities to share the gospel.

My good friend Scott Klusendorf *[as was discussed in Chapter 45, "Stand for Life"]* provides the best example I've seen of how we can defend the unborn in a way that draws people to the gospel without harming them by shielding them from uncomfortable truths. He knows how to defend the unborn by relying on science and philosophy rather than simply quoting scripture. That approach helps him share the good news every time he speaks on an otherwise difficult topic. Once they decide to do something to prevent abortion, churches would do well to invite Scott to educate their congregations on why they are weighing in on the matter.

Compassion is good, but pulling drowning kids out of the water isn't enough. At some point, pastors must take a hike upstream and confront the ones who keep throwing our children in the water. Indeed, the true measure of our compassion is our willingness to confront injustice. And injustice toward the unborn can't be confronted by ignoring the central question on the issue, which is a simple one: Are the unborn fully human and made in the image of God?

If God is the creator of life, then He alone has the authority to define it. Cultural definitions are irrelevant. So are the churches that refuse to challenge them.

As Mike once said:

The purpose of the pro-life movement is not to impose guilt over past decisions. It is to impart wisdom over future decisions.

Chapter 52

Hello, Stranger

May 6, 2014

Controversy has once again hit the campus of UNC-Wilmington. This time, it's not my fault. The controversy is actually the fault of a student. His crime is simple: He decided to behave like a feminist behaves every day on campuses all across America. Unfortunately for him, he chose to do so without the proper genitalia and without the approval of the UNCW Women's Resource Center.

I was introduced to the controversy shortly after a student of mine finished taking her final exam of the semester. After she had left my 2:00 p.m. exam, she came into my 3:30 class and, as discreetly as possible, told me that a male student had just walked up to her and asked if she wanted to have sex with him. It took me a few minutes to figure out that she wasn't joking. So I asked her to give me more information as we walked out into the hall to look for the offending student.

Apparently, the young man had been working his way through the building, asking every female student he saw if she would like to have sex with him. Some just walked away, but some wanted an explanation for the wildly inappropriate request. When pressed, he simply told them he hadn't had sex all semester and didn't want to go home for the summer until he had. One woman reacted a little more strongly to his indecent proposal. She started to cry and went upstairs looking for help from someone in the psychology department. That's when things got interesting.

Fortunately, the visibly shaken student found a concerned psychology professor who went downstairs with her, found the male student, and told him to knock it off. The propositioning student became incensed and told the professor he needed to get over his hang-ups about sex. The student's argument was pretty simple: Asking someone to have sex is no different than asking them to engage in any other recreational activity, such as playing basketball.

Of course, that argument was rejected, and the UNCW police were called in to apprehend the student. Fortunately, the psychology building is in walking distance from Dunkin' Donuts, so the police made the trek in less than an hour. Upon arrival, they scoured the building in search of their suspect.

But what crime did the desperately horny student commit? Did he sexually harass these women in a traditional sense? No, this was a case of creating a hostile environment in the workplace. Had he done this in a bar, rather than on campus, there would be no controversy. In other words, the venue made a difference.

Of course, there is another important variable to consider. If he were a female student, his conduct would have been seen in a very different light. In order to assess the possible role that gender played in the incident, please consider the following:

- Every year when they put on *The Vagina Monologues*, UNCW feminists send out an email that begins with the line "Greetings vagina lovers." And they use the university email system to send this to everyone. Feminists at another women's center advertised *The Vagina Monologues* by purchasing a six-foot vagina costume. They later took turns walking around campus dressed as a giant sex organ.
- Feminists at the UNCW Women's Center once advertised *The Vagina Monologues* with a large sign saying "p***ies unite." It was posted outside a campus diner where faculty and staff often took their children to eat. Note that those responsible for making the profane sign were professors, not students.
- Feminists at the UNCW Women's Center sold "p***y pops" made out of candy and shaped to resemble female genitalia. Some feminist professors walked around the lobby of Kenan Auditorium licking the candy-coated genitals in front of students.
- Feminists at the UNCW Women's Center have set up tables showing people how to put condoms on cucumbers. But this isn't nearly as bad as the feminist students at UNC-CH who actually built a vibrator museum and erected it (cough) in the middle of campus.
- Feminists at the UNCW Women's Center posted pictures of nude women—some of them under-aged—in the lobby of Randall Library as part of an "art" exhibit.

- Feminists at the UNCW Women's Center sold "I had an abortion" T-shirts on campus so students could let strangers know they had killed their own children and were proud of it.

All of these incidents are a reflection of a consistent philosophy promoted by feminists here at UNCW. That philosophy is made up of two core principles: 1) Women have a right to act as vulgar as they want in public because the rules of ordinary decency and civility don't apply to them. 2) The key to personal fulfillment is to have sex with as many people as possible and to view any restrictions on sexual liberty as forms of patriarchal oppression.

So what was the crime of the male student who was publicly asking for casual sex with female students who were total strangers? His crime was simply that he accepted feminist arguments and behaved in a manner that is consistent with feminist philosophy. But he did so without the proper genitalia.

Some who were near the propositioning male student said they overheard him saying he had a premonition he was going get to a "yes" from one of his targets. This talk of "premonitions" caused some to speculate that he was mentally unstable.

However, if accused of a specific crime, the offending student should not plead insanity. His chances of acquittal would be better if he had a sex change.

Mike was always looking for the humor in situations:

Waitress: My name is Heidi if you need me.
Response: What is your name if I don't need you?

Person in Starbucks: Every time I see you, you're in Starbucks. Do you live here?
Response: Every time you see me in Starbucks, you're also in Starbucks. Do we live together?

Friend: I agree with you most of the time. Not sure what to make of that.
Mike: I will tell you exactly what to make of it. It means some of the time you are wrong.

Follower: The end is near. Buy now and save ten dollars on my book about Bible prophecy.
Me: If the end is near, why do I need to save ten bucks?

CHAPTER 53

Hands Up, Don't Abort

August 22, 2014

I have a tendency to crash protests even though no one invited me. It happened when I donned a burka back in 2003, disguising myself as an Iraqi woman in order to infiltrate a campus protest against the War in Iraq. It happened again in 2009 when I joined a protest against myself at UMASS-Amherst. *[This story is told on page 199 of the book* Life and How to Live It.*]* It happened yet again last Saturday night when I went to Ferguson and protested against the man while holding a sign saying, "Hands Up, Don't Shoot!" I learned a lot that night. So today I'm writing a column to share it with my readers.

I only spoke with a few protestors in Ferguson. And I only asked them a few questions. But the responses were still revealing. In fact, they revealed two undeniable truths that some readers could have gleaned from extensive media coverage of the protests:

1. Ferguson protestors are bored and in need of a cause. I struck up a conversation with a middle-aged black woman

who brought a longhaired chihuahua to the protest. Her dog seemed to like me. That's how we struck up a conversation. At one point in that conversation, she told me I was making history by participating in the protests. She had been protesting for eight consecutive days. She added that we needed to go back to the protest era of the 1960s. I silently thought it would be nice to go back to a time when people didn't terrorize their own neighbors in the name of civil rights.

Another protestor whom we will call Ron (because that's his name) said that we needed to bring attention to all the hidden injustices taking place in black neighborhoods. He added, "This kind of thing happens every day." When I pressed him on whether unarmed black men were being shot every day, he gave me some clarification. He noted that black men were often pulled over for no reason. In fact, it had once happened to him. Ron was probably in his mid-thirties and had been living in that neighborhood his whole life.

When you talk to these protestors, you get the sense that they are sincerely angry and in need of some way of redressing their grievances. It's just that they have difficulty articulating exactly what those grievances are.

2. Any black civil rights cause must focus on what whites have done to blacks in the past, not on what blacks are doing to other blacks right now.

Ron wasn't able to name any other examples (besides Michael Brown) of unarmed black men being shot in his neighborhood. But he did explain why it was so important.

According to Ron, black people are doing all kinds of bad things to each other on a daily basis. Given that pressure, the black community just can't handle the extra pressure of a white cop shooting a black kid. So the question for Ron is pretty obvious. If you are looking for something to protest, which one will it be: a) the bad things blacks do to each other every day or b) the one shooting of an unarmed innocent black man (by a bad white man) you can point to in a period of about thirty years of living in the neighborhood.

Of course, we all know the answer. It is "b." It's the only option for Ron because it's the only option black culture allows.

Fortunately, there is a solution to this dilemma. If the Ferguson protestors are bored and need a cause—and one that focuses on bad white people—I have one for them. It's called abortion.

Blacks are only 12 percent of the population in America. But 36 percent of the babies aborted are black. That means that of the more than 3000 babies aborted per day in America, over 1000 of them are black. To put things in historical perspective, doctors wearing white masks abort at least 7000 babies in a week. Klansmen wearing white hoods have lynched fewer blacks in the entire history of America.

Given that Planned Parenthood is right there in the hood and that they were born (no pun intended) of the white-dominated eugenics movement, the solution is pretty simple. Stop committing uncivil wrongs against your own people in the name of civil rights. To put it bluntly, stop defecating in your own backyard. Join the pro-life movement instead.

After all, the unborn are disproportionately black, always unarmed, and never guilty. Someone has to protect them from white doctors wielding lethal weapons.

I remember this well. My wife and I took Mike to that protest. We live in another suburb of St. Louis forty minutes away. Mike was passing through town on his way home from Summit, as was his annual routine, and the protests were still going strong one week after the infamous shooting. We went early in the evening because the protests turned violent after dark. We walked into the crowd and hung out for a bit. Mike had no trouble striking up conversations with random people. He seemed genuinely interested in hearing what people had to say.

Chapter 54

This Is Providence

August 27, 2014

Part 1 of 6

March 18, 2010, was one of the worst days of my life. That was the day Judge Malcolm Howard threw my lawsuit against UNCW out of court. Three years after filing suit and a full eight years after I started to criticize universities, including my own, for violating the First Amendment, I lost a bid to go to trial. I also lost all credibility as a free speech advocate. Or so I thought.

That night, I called a friend and explained that all hope was lost and that I would soon have to look for a new job and abandon my work as a free speech advocate. Shortly after that conversation was over, I tried to go to sleep. But I just sat up and stared at the ceiling for eight hours until the alarm rang. I got up and started the next day the way I usually do—by making coffee and reading for about an hour and a half. Right about the time I finished reading, the phone rang. It was one of my ADF attorneys, Joseph Martins.

After telling me how sorry he was that we had lost on the motion for summary judgment, he did something unexpected. He began to tell me that what seemed like defeat really wasn't defeat. In fact, he said what had happened the day before was really providence. I began to think he was losing his mind. In fact, it was good that he wasn't in the room with me. Had he been there, I would have punched him in the nose. And that would have been bad for two reasons. First, he's a lawyer. Second, Joe is much bigger than me.

But Joe took the time to explain himself. He said that we would likely appeal to the Fourth Circuit and win an important First Amendment precedent. After all, the judge's ruling was based on an open question in an important Supreme Court case. No circuit had yet ruled on the specific issue in our case. Indeed, we really were in a good position to establish an important legal precedent. So Joe was optimistic. I just wasn't in the mood for his optimism.

But Joe wasn't done yet. He insisted that there was a chance we could lose in front of the Fourth Circuit. But according to Joe, a loss at the Fourth Circuit would not necessarily be a defeat either. That would mean we would have a chance to appeal to the U.S. Supreme Court. Joe's enthusiasm was palpable when he told me they would probably be inclined to rule in my favor. After all, Joe reasoned, the liberals on the Supreme Court would not likely issue a ruling that might restrict the free speech of college professors. Most college professors are liberals.

Joe was making sense. If I had had a decent night of sleep, I might have been encouraged. But before Joe got off the phone, he assured me again that what we had experienced wasn't defeat. "This is not defeat," he insisted. "This is providence," he added. I hung up and went to work.

I arrived in my office at about 11:00 a.m. to begin preparation for my afternoon classes. Shortly after I arrived, the phone rang. I answered and began speaking to a guy we will call Tim (because that's his name).

Tim told me he was calling from a college in Rhode Island. He specifically asked if I was interested in coming to speak at his college on the first day of May. He said he wanted me to speak on First Amendment issues. I asked him what the honorarium would be (because I am a capitalist). Since the price was right and the cause was just, I agreed to speak.

Before we got off the phone, I asked Tim what college he was calling from. His response stopped me in my tracks. "Providence College" was his answer. I was so taken aback that I asked him again, "What is the name of your college?" He replied, "This is Providence. Providence College in Rhode Island."

For a split second, I thought Joe Martins was playing a trick on me. But he wasn't. Life was about to get very interesting. And chance would play no role in the rest of the story.

To be continued…

Chapter 55

Pharisees and Pharaohs

September 2, 2014

Part 2 of 6

Don't let anyone tell you that our university officials are ignorant of the First Amendment. They are not. In fact, they know all about it. But they are actively trying to destroy it with one convoluted argument at a time. The most extreme example I ever saw occurred in Richmond, Virginia, on January 26, 2011.

The scene was oral arguments before the Fourth Circuit Court of Appeals in the case of Yours Truly v. the Board of Trustees of UNC-Wilmington. Then Associate Attorney General Tom Ziko was arguing on behalf of the state of North Carolina. His argument was that college professors could lose all First Amendment protection for speeches and columns written as private citizens on matters of public concern if they ever mentioned them on an annual evaluation or promotion application.

While he stood there and made that incredible assault on free speech, two Marxist defendants sat right behind him—failing utterly to grasp the implications of the argument. That's okay because Ziko didn't understand the implications of his argument either. However, he was soon forced to understand when Judge Paul Niemeyer asked him to imagine a three-part hypothetical situation.

In the first part, Niemeyer asked Ziko to imagine that a professor seeking a promotion listed on his promotion application the title, location, and date he gave a speech on the topic of abortion. In the second part, Niemeyer asked Ziko to imagine that the voting members of the promotion committee actually sought out and then read a copy of the abortion speech. Finally, Niemeyer asked Ziko to imagine the committee responding by saying, "Since he's much opposed to abortion, we couldn't live with him. We're not going to promote him." Niemeyer concluded the hypothetical with one very simple question: Is that a position you are defending in your argument?

Remarkably, Ziko refused to reject the possibility that university officials could in fact deny a promotion based on their distaste for a political view contained in a speech—moreover, simply for mentioning (on a single line of a promotion application) that the speech happened. That aggressive position cemented our argument that the university was attempting to engage in wholly impermissible viewpoint discrimination.

Unsurprisingly, the panel agreed. Indeed, they published their unanimous opinion less than three months later—thus proving that Joe Martins was right. All had not been lost when the district court previously threw out our case. In fact, we had just set an important First Amendment precedent. We had not suffered defeat. This was Providential—and it was now precedential as well.

Of course, the Fourth Circuit decision also meant that we were headed for a possible trial, which is serious, stressful, and time-consuming business. Accordingly, Judge Malcolm Howard decided that both sides should sit down and try to negotiate a settlement. So both sides sat down in federal court in September of 2011. The so-called mediation turned into an unmitigated disaster.

Two of my attorneys, making hundreds of dollars an hour, flew in from out of state. They left behind their families and their other responsibilities in order to try to work things out with our adversaries. But it was a nasty affair. The other side simply decided to thumb their noses at us and try to intimidate us by refusing to negotiate in good faith. I left the courtroom that day extremely dejected.

Because defendant Cook, UNCW Counsel Scherer, and Associate Attorney General Ziko were the only ones present on the other side, we simply assumed Ziko was responsible for the belligerence. After all, he had been extremely aggressive in oral argument and had earned a bad reputation among some federal judges for his arrogance and his abrasive demeanor. Later on, we would find out that Ziko wasn't the problem at all.

After mediation, the defendants were allowed to file another motion for summary judgment in response to the Fourth Circuit ruling. This time, though it took Judge Howard sixteen months to rule, they would fail. On March 22, 2013, nearly six years after we filed the suit, Judge Howard signaled that we were headed for trial. But it would not happen until after the two sides sat down for another forced mediation. That mediation took place on October 29, 2013—just one day before my forty-ninth birthday.

This time, in mediation, another associate attorney general named Stephanie Brennan joined defendant Cook and UNCW Counsel Scherer. Tom Ziko had retired, and we hoped his absence would make for a more professional mediation. But we were wrong. Even the federal magistrate was visibly stunned by the arrogance of the university.

It had become obvious that the source of the belligerence was not Tom Ziko. It was defendant Cook, who defiantly showed up for court twenty minutes late. It was also obvious that UNCW lacked competent counsel. But after all, Scherer worked for a public university, not a thriving law practice.

After the failed negotiations were over, my attorneys and I walked out of the federal courthouse and headed up Princess Street to have lunch at a little café on Front Street. As we were walking, the belligerent defendant drove right past us. On the back of her Subaru, there was a lone bumper sticker that read "COEXIST."

The irony was not lost on us. Fortunately, the tab for lunch would eventually be picked up by UNC-Wilmington. But that is the subject of the next installment.

To be continued...

Chapter 56

Prayer and Preparation

September 17, 2014

Part 3 of 6

A trial is a thing to be avoided whenever possible. When it becomes impossible to avoid, it consumes you. You lose a measure of control over your life, and you just have to trust your attorneys and follow their orders. In March, my attorneys ordered me to sit down and read my deposition, which was taken back in 2009. They warned me that in my trial, which was scheduled to start on March 17, 2014, opposing counsel might try an old trick on me. They might just ask the same questions from that deposition, simply for the purpose of eliciting an inconsistent statement that could impeach my credibility.

The deposition was 183 pages long. So I printed off a copy and headed down to my favorite bar/restaurant at Wrightsville Beach. With an IPA in one hand and the deposition in the other, I got to work. I spent seven nights memorizing my prior testimony. But for some reason, I just could not shake the anxiety of having to regurgitate the right portions under the pressure of cross-examination. I was riddled with anxiety, so I reached in my pocket and pulled out my cell phone.

I'm not very good with technology. But I do have about fifty of my essential friends and family members stored away in the contacts section of my trusty iPhone. So I just went through the list and called to tell them all how uneasy and, yes, scared I was about the thing I was about to face. I just asked them to pray for me. Prayer was what I needed. The last thing I needed was misplaced confidence in my own ability to prepare and persevere. The trial wasn't about me or any other single individual. It was about much bigger things.

When I finally took the stand on March 18, I was expecting to be examined for about five hours—roughly three on direct and two on cross. I wasn't worried about the direct examination. After I read my deposition seven times, my lead counsel ran me through the direct questions three times in the two days preceding the trial. So when it came time to tell our story, we were prepared. Things went well on direct. In fact, all in all, things went well that whole morning.

After lunch, it was time for cross-examination, which did not go well at all. The university decided to play the race card—and, to a lesser extent, the gender card—from the bottom of the deck. The associate attorney general repeatedly took isolated lines from satirical columns out of context. It was clearly meant to inflame a jury with four blacks, seven women, and only a single white male. It was also unbelievably embarrassing for me to endure in the presence of some of my students who had driven up from Wilmington to watch the proceedings.

At the time, I did not know that a couple of the jurors were actually laughing at the snippets from my columns—deeming them to be funny, not offensive. I would later find that out from the students who were watching the trial. But I didn't know it at the time. I was too focused on opposing counsel and on defendants Cook, Levy, and Cordle, who were visibly laughing at me. They weren't laughing because they thought the columns were funny. They were laughing because they thought they had the case won.

It was the first time in seven years that I would agree with the defendants. I thought they had the case won too. I had let opposing counsel lead me too far without pushing back. At the end of the examination, I scored some crucial points, but I thought it was too little, too late. I was so convinced of this that I apologized to my attorneys on the way out of the courtroom.

Somehow, some way, I fell asleep that evening. But I woke up at 3:00 a.m. hearing voices of condemnation. They were not audible voices. It was just my conscience speaking to me. I was wide awake and full of regret over filing the lawsuit. I was full of regret over every word I had ever written criticizing the university. I was sure that the end of my career was near.

Sitting there and staring at the ceiling, the subject I thought about most was Abigail. She was the little girl who was born in January 2007 in Vietnam. I was supposed to adopt her and bring her to America. But circumstances beyond my control put an end to the adoption. She had just turned seven before the trial began, and I did not know where she was. I did not know if someone else adopted her. Maybe she was living in an orphanage somewhere in Vietnam. All I knew was that Abigail was better off wherever she was. She was better off not having a complete failure for a father.

When the alarm rang at seven, I got up, got dressed, and prepared to face the inevitable conclusion. At least I no longer had to testify. It was now time for my opponents to take the stand. Each defendant placed a hand on the Bible and swore to tell the truth, the whole truth, and nothing but the truth.

Oddly, no one opted for a secular affirmation.

To be continued...

Chapter 57

Pride and Perjury

September 24, 2014

Part 4 of 6

Defendant Kimberly Cook is not your ordinary sociologist. Before she even opens her mouth, she comes across as an attractive and confident person. When she starts to talk, it doesn't take long to realize that she is also much brighter than the average Ph.D. in the social sciences. Add to the equation the fact that she has a terrific sense of humor and an overflow of personal charm. In other words, she was a potentially damaging witness.

We called defendant Cook, and then the state had a chance to call her. Afterward, we were able cross-examine her on the issues raised by the state. It was during that cross-examination that the defense case would suffer three severe setbacks.

We began by asking defendant Cook what she meant when she wrote a letter to me describing the "negative effects" my service was having on the department. On the stand, she said that she was referring to the fact that my "activities outside of the department left more work for other members of the department to do." My attorneys then flashed on the screen a portion of her sworn deposition from 2009 saying that "negative effects" referred to the "universal concern regarding the personal attacks that have been waged against members of the department in the columns written by Dr. Adams on Townhall."

Strike one. We had now established that a) Cook admitted under oath in deposition that the content of my columns was a factor in the decision to deny my promotion and b) she now denied it under oath in front of the jury. When asked which of her contradictory statements should be considered true, Cook answered, "They're both true."

It was a classically postmodern response. It was also a turning point in the trial.

We continued by asking defendant Cook about the Golden Seahawk service award I won back in 2005. It was a major service award given to only one member of the university community. Cook claimed under oath that she had never heard of the award until the trial. Within seconds, we flashed another quote on the screen. It was from Cook's 2005 annual evaluation of me in which she was talking specifically about the Golden Seahawk Award.

Strike two. We had now established that Cook knew about an award that was not included in any faculty comments about whether my service accomplishments merited promotion. Cook apparently feigned ignorance of the award to make it look like an oversight rather than active prejudice.

When my attorneys caught her in the contradiction, she replied by saying, "Thanks for reminding me." Perhaps it was meant to be cute, but it wasn't. Thanking an attorney for catching you in a material contradiction under oath is never cute. It's just bizarre.

Next, we turned to a book that I had written and asked defendant Cook whether it was scholarly in nature—specifically whether it was an example of ethnography. She had testified earlier on direct that the book was not an example of ethnography. We then demonstrated, using the 2009 deposition, that she had not seen a copy of the book at the time of the 2006 decision and had "no perception of it."

Strike three. We had now established that Cook was offering negative assessments of my books even though, apparently, she had never read them or even seen copies of them.

In short, defendant Cook seemed to be actively and repeatedly trying to mislead the jury. But we knew the deposition and exhibits frontwards and backwards. As a result, the principal defendant's credibility was decimated. After a one-hour cross, I no longer thought that all hope was lost. Clearly, it was not.

Of course, there was no way to top the drama of the Cook testimony. But there were other witnesses. Defendant Cordle would testify truthfully, although not without coming across as somewhat arrogant, dismissive, and confrontational. And even though she was firm in her criticism of my record, defendant Levy would testify truthfully and with much greater humility. She was an effective witness.

After three full days in court, all that was left were the final arguments. The state would close in the morning with a graduate from Yale law school with an impressive resume.

To be continued...

Chapter 58

To Speak the Truth

September 29, 2014

Part 5 of 6

In our first closing argument, my attorney showed the comments faculty sent to defendant Cook in response to my promotion application. Next, he showed how Cook had altered the comments before putting them in a summary document that she distributed at the meeting. For example:

1. The deletion of positive faculty remarks about my research record.

2. The inclusion of a long anonymous evaluation that contained objectively false statements about my publication record. (To date, no one knows the author's identity. I only have my suspicions about who actually wrote it).

3. The use of ellipses to remove portions of sentences that altered their intended meaning (making them more negative than intended).

Among all of the summary evidence discussed in closing, Cook's handling of the evidence was probably the most powerful. It was a Mark Fuhrman moment with one crucial difference: We actually had direct evidence of tampering.

Next, the state gave its closing argument. Then, in accordance with federal rules, the plaintiff would offer a rebuttal closing argument before the jury would be charged. This time, my attorney would do something different. He would appeal directly to free speech principles, and he would invoke history as well.

He would remind the jury that the Bill of Rights protects unpopular speech—and, yes, even speech we disagree with. He also told them that although we are friends, he does not applaud all of my columns.

He can pick and choose between the speech he likes and the speech he doesn't like. But the government can't do the same thing and use it as a basis for employment decisions. That's what he told the jury while I sat watching intently.

By the time he started to talk about the need for a Bill of Rights and the insufficiency of our Constitution without one, I saw her nodding. Seated in the front row, this one juror was nodding so vigorously that it seemed she might fall off her chair and land on the courtroom floor.

Then, I glanced to the right and saw the defendants. You could see it on their faces. They feared the case was slipping away. And, indeed, it was. We would learn later that it already had.

We had been sitting in the attorney and client waiting room for less than two hours when we heard a knock on the door. We hoped it was lunch. But it wasn't. Instead, the knock came from a U.S. Marshal and was followed by the ominous words, "We have a verdict."

In less than two hours, the jury had eaten lunch, selected a foreperson, and rendered a verdict. My heart was pounding through my chest. After we entered the courtroom and sat down at the table, Judge Howard called in the jury. The Marshal ushered them in one by one. We were almost there.

The first juror that entered the courtroom was the woman who was nodding so vigorously that she almost fell out of her chair. She was now the one carrying the envelope. That meant she was the foreperson and thus led the deliberations. I knew exactly what that meant. I didn't need to hear the verdict.

Of course, the clerk read it anyway. And the words seemed to disappear into thin air just as soon as I heard them. Just to make sure it had really happened, I turned to my attorney and asked, "Does that mean we won?"

"Yes, it means we won. We won." He was smiling from ear to ear.

Next, out of the corner of my eye, I saw a procession of defendants, lawyers, and tech supporters filing slowly out of the courtroom. A few were trying not to trip over their jaws on the way out. They could not believe what had just happened.

In a moment, just the three of us were standing there. We put our arms on each other's shoulders while I just silently repeated the words "Praise God Almighty" over and over again. Then, we headed back to the attorney and client waiting room where we would begin to make calls and celebrate outside the presence of the opposing parties.

When we got to the room, I had to place my hands on the table to brace myself because my knees were shaking so badly. I kept repeating the same three words over and over again while a couple of tears landed on the table below me. Rory took out a computer and started to tweet out the news of the victory.

My hands were shaking so badly I could not type. So I gave my Facebook password to Rory, and he typed my status:

"Adams wins unanimous verdict against all defendants on all counts. Praise God Almighty!"

We composed ourselves and then got in the car and headed to the hotel. I spent the rest of the day answering scores of calls, texts, and emails from family and friends. I slept well that evening, and we all enjoyed a big breakfast in the morning.

When Fox & Friends called later and asked for an interview, I had to decline. I was exhausted and would not physically recover from the trial for over two weeks. I had to go home and get some sleep. I simply could not get up early for another interview.

In addition to that, something I had not anticipated was about to happen later on that night. I would need the sleep even more than I had expected.

To be continued…

Chapter 59

Our People

November 9, 2014

Part 6 of 6

When I awoke on the 22nd of March, I fired up the coffee maker and turned on my iPhone as I prepared to catch up on my reading and my emails. I was less than halfway into my ninety-minute daily reading ritual when I noticed that the phone was "dinging" at a brisker-than-usual pace. For some reason, I was getting a lot of emails on that beautiful Saturday morning. When I finally picked up the phone to check my inbox, I noticed that several dozen emails had the following subject line: God's Not Dead!

When I started to open the emails, I figured out what the subject lines meant. Just the night before, the movie *God's Not Dead* had been released in movie theaters all across the nation. My case, along with several other ADF cases, was mentioned in the movie credits. Specifically, the credit said my case was soon going to trial. Therefore, people were writing to tell me they were praying for me. They did not know that we actually won the jury verdict the day before the movie was released. By the end of the day, I would send the good news to several hundred supporters.

The next few weeks would be spent resting and waiting on the judge to make an announcement on the issue of relief. On April 8, Judge Howard handed me two helpings of good news. First, he ordered the university to immediately promote me to its highest rank of full professor. Next, he ordered the university to give me $50,000 in back pay. Before it was all over, the university would be ordered to increase my salary by nearly $10,000 per year and to pay my attorneys a whopping $710,000 in legal fees. It was a thorough shellacking—an unprecedented victory for free speech over the forces of secular progressive intolerance.

Just three days after the judge ordered my promotion, I headed up to Raleigh to give a speech at Christ Baptist Church. North Carolina Supreme Court Justice Paul Newby and Lieutenant Governor Dan Forest both attend the church, so I knew it would be a friendly audience. I spoke to the group for about an hour and then signed a few books before leaving to blow some of the settlement money on a guitar that I really didn't need.

As I was headed across the church lobby and toward the exit, someone caught up to me and grabbed me by the right arm. When I turned around, I saw that it was an older black man standing about six-foot-four. He looked down at me and said, "I just want to thank you for that thing that you done for our people." His words were simple, but they were profound.

As I stood there facing a man who had lived through segregation, I realized he was telling me that in essence we were both involved in a civil rights struggle. It is a struggle that transcends race and spans generations. Though profound, his words also made me feel uneasy. I've never considered anything I've done to be praiseworthy. I never knew it would be such a long ordeal. I just woke up every day and faced the next decision. My goal each day was just to do the next right thing.

I started to explain this to him, saying "But you don't understand. The Lord knew what He was doing when He put me in that radical department back in 1993 before I converted."

That's when the older black gentleman stuck his finder right in my face and interrupted me saying, "No. The Lord didn't start preparing you in 1993. The Lord been raisin' you up to do that thing ever since you was a little boy." That was all he said before he turned and walked away.

Since that day in April, I've been asked to travel to California and Florida and to many points in between to tell my story. Several times during those speeches, I have had to stop and compose myself after repeating the old black gentleman's words. Every time I think about it, I remember all of those lost years and all the people who lifted me up and carried me through them.

In particular, I think about those years when I was supporting myself as a musician and playing long nights in bars just to pay my tuition as I tried to earn my doctorate. I still remember waking up and sitting in front of the television on Sunday mornings. My body was aching, as I was hungover and trying to recover from playing my regular weekend gigs. My head would be throbbing as I watched Dr. James Kennedy delivering his sermons on the evils of the ACLU and Planned Parenthood. I would just sit there and curse at the screen because I hated him and everything he stood for. Yet I kept watching.

I had no idea that during the time I was cursing Dr. Kennedy, he was busy founding an organization called the Alliance Defense Fund, which is now the Alliance Defending Freedom. They are the ones who stood behind me and represented me for seven long years during this epic struggle against the forces of ingrained institutional intolerance.

So it is fitting that I am completing a series (about a seven-year struggle) as I sit on the back patio of the Hyatt Regency Hotel on a cool November morning in Scottsdale, Arizona. I have come here to share my story at an Ambassador's Summit with those who donate to the ADF. I have also come here to thank the ADF and their supporters for the things they have done for me and for our people.

This series is now over. The battle for the souls of the next generation continues.

Author's Note: Some of the themes discussed in this column were part of a speech I gave at an Alliance Defending Freedom (ADF) event in July. The full speech can be viewed here:

https://www.youtube.com/watch?v=bc3zyOLZ-jA&ab_channel=AllianceDefendingFreedom

Chapter 60

Fifty

October 16, 2014

This month, I turn fifty years old, which is surprising to me. At twenty-five, I never thought I would see thirty. I also never expected this period of life to be the best—but it is by a long shot. Perhaps that is best explained by the fact that, over the years, I have made some very serious mistakes that have taught me some very important lessons.

Among the most important lessons I have learned is that personal happiness is not possible without a concerted effort to focus on two key factors: **gratitude and encouragement.**

If one makes a concerted effort to be grateful for one's blessings, it becomes virtually impossible to be overwhelmed by resentment over life's shortcomings. Resentment and gratitude cannot coexist. You must choose one or the other.

Similarly, if one makes a concerted effort to provide encouragement to other people, then it becomes very difficult to be overwhelmed by your own circumstances. The happiest people are always those who provide encouragement to others rather than seeking it for themselves.

As I approach the half-century mark, I thought it would be a good idea to take some time to express gratitude to the people who have most impacted my life to this point. There are many, but these come to mind immediately. They are listed below, alphabetically by first name.

David McMillen was the first person to tell me that I had the talent to succeed in graduate school. So I took his advice and enrolled in the spring of 1988. That first semester, I took two of Dave's classes. Within one week, I decided that I wanted to become a college professor and to model my style after his by a) always telling people exactly what was on my mind, b) always allowing the opposition to speak, and c) occasionally reminding folks that they need to lighten up. The most important lesson Dave taught me was: "If they can't take a joke, fire-truck them." In other words, don't waste your time on pretentious jerks inclined to take themselves too seriously.

Frank Turek is from New Jersey, which means that he's occasionally, umm, assertive (bless his Yankee heart). Thank goodness that he got really assertive back in 2008 and started to insist that I go speak at a place called Summit Ministries in Colorado. I had never heard of the place. But when Summit founder David Noebel finally called to invite me to speak at a summer conference, I said "yes" just to get Turek to stop hounding me. Thank goodness he did because it changed my life in a big way. Of course, Summit changes a lot of people's lives in a big way. And so does Frank Turek. Over the years, I have learned that there are numerous speakers and apologists who get regular phone calls from Frank. He just calls them to check in and offer encouragement. Whenever I have a problem, Frank Turek is one of two Summit speakers I call. The other one is also on this list. *[For more about him, please see Chapter 66, "Life and How to Live It, Part XII." For more about Summit, please see Chapter 31, "Mike's Peak."]*

Henry Thornton believed in me even after I failed high school English for the fourth year in a row. That was the year I plummeted to a ranking of 734th in my graduating class of 740. Mr. Thornton always offered encouragement and invested much more time in me than I deserved. Later, when he was in his late seventies, my former *[Clear Lake]* high school principal ran across a column I had written. Shortly thereafter, he sent me an email asking if I remembered him. Unbelievably, he was still working in education—as he continues to do even in his eighties. We have talked on the phone a few times in the years since we reconnected. Not long ago, he took the time to write me a long handwritten letter reminding me that no matter how much my students irritated me, each one had a nugget of gold buried somewhere deep within all the garbage. He reminded me that it was my job to find it. He was gracious enough not to remind me how long he had to dig in the dumpster to find something positive in me.

Joe Adams can't go for long without talking about the importance of getting a good education. Usually that takes the form of encouraging people to get a formal education. However, when I was a teenager, he encouraged me in a different way by telling me to read a book a month. I ignored him and instead spent all my time playing sports. However, after I tore my Achilles, I could not run and needed a new hobby. That was when I started to hit the books with the same passion I once put into hitting the jogging trail. Later on, Dad told me I needed to start reading books by people who held views contrary to my own. I took his advice and (while I was still a liberal) read a book called *Illiberal Education* by Dinesh D'Souza. That was how I learned about campus speech codes and ultimately joined the campus free speech movement. Now, I often help college students find lawyers and mount legal challenges against outrageous speech restrictions. The decision to turn on my colleagues in higher education and instead defend these students did not happen overnight. It began when I decided to take a first step and start to question the people I once called my political allies. That never would have happened without my father's encouragement. *[This is detailed in Chapter 4 of the book* Life and How to Live It. *For more about him, please see Chapter 82, "Never Underestimate a Father's Love."]*

Lisa Chambers has always overflowed with positive energy and enthusiasm. You know it when she enters a room. But her method of encouragement isn't always orthodox. Sometimes, she tries to plant a stone in someone's shoe to make him think about something that might not be particularly pleasant. She did that to me back in 1993. The topic was abortion. Without starting an argument, she caused me to give serious consideration to the central question in the abortion debate, which is "what are the unborn?" She's the reason why I talk about the abortion issue so much. Thanks to Lisa Chambers, I now know what "it" is. It is not a blob of tissue. *[The full story is in Chapter 40, "Life Chose Me."]*

Marilyn Adams really is the reason why we won our legal case back in March. The seeds of victory were really planted one day back in 1976. I remember it like it was yesterday. I had broken something expensive while I was horsing around at school in the sixth grade. And then I had tried to conceal it. Later, I was taken off the hook because the damaged property was covered by an insurance policy. But I was absolutely riddled with guilt. So I confessed the crime to my mother when we were out in the backyard picking some vegetables from the garden. As soon as I confessed, my mom stopped what she was doing and looked at me very seriously and said, "God will never punish you for telling the truth. As long as you tell the truth, things will always work out in the end." I wish I could say I've always remembered that lesson. The truth is that I have not. On the occasions I forgot that lesson, I paid a very heavy price. On the occasions my enemies ignored the principle that lesson reflects, they have paid a very heavy price. Recently, they paid to the tune of several hundred thousand dollars. *[For more about her, please see Chapter 11, "Life and How to Live It, Part V."]*

Nell Myers Rester is the only person on this list that I have never met. My maternal grandmother died in 1962. The doctor who was treating her for cancer decided not to prolong her surgery and opted not to remove an organ that was suspect. When her cancer returned, the doctor confessed that he thought he had made a literally deadly judgment error. Nell consoled the doctor rather than blaming him. He was so moved by her selfless compassion that he drove ninety miles to the funeral just to tell her surviving relatives how much she had impacted his life. That funeral was the turning point in my mother's life. But it also affected countless others. I wrote about it back in 2006. Several years later, when I was walking down the street in Washington, D.C., a total stranger recognized me and stopped to thank me for writing about Nell. He said that after he read about her, he decided he needed to go back to church. That was almost a half-century after

Nell died. She died when she was only forty-eight. Her positive influence in people's lives continues to this day. *[For more about her, please see Chapter 11, "Life and How to Live It, Part V."]*

Scott Klusendorf is the best pro-life speaker in the world. I reached out to him in 2011 when I decided to start giving speeches on pro-life apologetics instead of just speaking on pro-life activism. He was always helpful and generous with his time. But then he did something really sneaky. He sent a spy to watch one of my speeches. When the spy's report came back favorable, Scott asked me to start speaking for Life Training Institute (LTI), the organization he founded over a decade ago. He has also asked me to fill in for him on a couple of occasions. My other obligations prevent me from joining the LTI team just yet. But I did get a chance to fill in for Scott when he was ill and had to miss a speech in July of 2013. It was such an honor to have such a great man place his trust in me—and with such an important task. He has truly given me life-changing (and -saving) encouragement. *[See also Chapter 45, "Stand For Life."]*

Virginia Rester was my step-grandmother. Before she died, I would end up being closer to her than any of my biological grandparents. In all honesty, though, she had incredibly bad timing whenever she would call. This was especially true during those lost years of the late 1980s and early 1990s. On many of those occasions, I would be high and drunk and with some loose woman in my apartment. And then the phone would ring. I would pick it up, and it would be Virginia just calling to check up on me and tell me how proud she was of me. I would hear my grandmother's voice and be overwhelmed by the realization that I was living a life that was far beneath my potential. After every conversation, I would be left thinking that if Virginia knew who I really was, she would not be proud of me at all. In fact, she would be ashamed. Looking back on it, I think she probably knew exactly what I was going through and just chose to love me anyway.

You may be busy, but you're not too busy to do two things just as soon as you finish this column. First, you need to make your own list. Second, you need to pick up the phone and call all of the people on your list who are still alive. Let them know exactly how they have encouraged you. In the process, you will be paying them back. Better yet, you'll be encouraging them to keep on encouraging others the way they once encouraged you.

Chapter 61

Fat, Ugly, and Morally Inconsistent

May 15, 2015

Not all pro-choice arguments were created equal. Some are much worse than others. Perhaps the worst is the claim that most pro-lifers aren't consistently pro-life but are "*only* anti-abortion." The assertion impersonates an argument when the pro-choice advocate starts to throw in various causes one must support in order to be "*truly* pro-life." Here is an example taken from a recent email exchange I had with a friend:

> "I get tired of pro-lifers who are really only anti-abortion. If they were truly pro-life, they would adopt minority babies, donate to cancer research, and drop their opposition to national health care. Their concern for children seems to stop at the point of birth."

That argument is flawed because it diverts attention from the central issue in the abortion debate, which is whether the unborn child is one of us and, hence, deserving of basic human rights.

Obviously, whether or not pro-lifers are morally consistent has no bearing on the central issue in the abortion debate. If I and other pro-lifers were to do everything pro-choicers want us to do, would they then concede that the unborn are suddenly transformed into human beings deserving of life? And what if one or more members of the pro-life movement were then to relapse into some form of "inconsistency" (according to the subjective judgment of one or more pro-choicers)? Would they then argue that the unborn are no longer human beings possessing equal rights?

If it means anything, being inconsistent means we are human. It doesn't mean the unborn lose their humanity. So my friend's position is absurd from a logical standpoint. But it is also misleading from a factual standpoint—and I mean that in two ways.

First, every pro-choicer has to answer the following question: If the pro-life movement is merely anti-abortion, why are there two pregnancy centers for every abortion clinic in America?

These pregnancy centers help women who are facing pregnancy. They donate clothes, help with medical expenses, and do everything they can to help women make the right choice—because they really believe the choice isn't morally neutral.

Churches who are not supporting these centers should be ashamed of themselves. But the pro-life movement needn't be ashamed. The movement is focused on helping women make good decisions in the present rather that imposing guilt over past decisions. That hasn't always been the case. But our movement continues to move in a compassionate and helpful direction.

Second, pro-choicers have the burden of answering this question: Where is the empirical evidence showing that your policies really save lives?

For example, big government has been making health care more expensive and therefore less accessible for decades. Obamacare is no exception to the rule. Surely, there is nothing pro-life about driving up health care costs. Put simply, feeling good about yourself for supporting programs that you hope will save lives doesn't make you pro-life. Pro-choicers have the burden of supplying the evidence showing that their causes are really saving lives.

Of course, pro-choicers don't want to get into a numbers battle with pro-lifers. The numbers reveal several years in which the abortion industry killed around 1.5 million babies while 1.5 million couples stood in line waiting to adopt. Their "safe, legal, and rare" mendacity is underscored by the fact that the abortion industry has made billions snatching babies from the hands of willing adoptive parents.

The audacity of pro-choicers who demand that pro-lifers conform to their vision of "moral consistency" can be further amplified by applying their arguments to other issues in our nation's history. For example, imagine the arguments of pro-choicers being applied to the nineteenth-century debate over slavery. (It's easy to do because the same party that supports abortion is the same one that supported slavery). Here is what such a conversation might sound like:

> Democrat: Would you support a national job training program implemented by the federal government and supported by a national sales tax?
>
> Abolitionist: I'm not sure I would support that.
>
> Democrat: Well, then you really aren't pro-voluntary servitude. You're only anti-slavery.

Ultimately, "you're inconsistent" is not an argument at all. It's just a political weapon wielded by those who pretend that they might consider joining your cause if you would only support their programs or take care of their children. It is also a personal attack meant to make the pro-choicer look morally superior.

In the end, smug moral superiority is hardly consistent with the claim that the unborn aren't one of us.

This is one of my favorite articles because the "only anti-abortion" charge is a pet peeve of mine. Every church I have ever attended has been anti-abortion while spending almost all of their time and budgets helping living people.

See also Chapter 80, "Life Lines."

Chapter 62

ESPN: The Enlightened Socialist Progressive Network

May 17, 2015

Watching ESPN is painful these days. What used to be a good sports channel is now a platform for bad pop sociology and "progressive" political commentary. The commentary was in full force recently as I watched a sports commentator try to explain how the riots in Baltimore were a function of socio-economic factors. He had it wrong from the beginning. The cultural disintegration that is happening in Baltimore—and, indeed, all around the country—is not due to a lack of money. It is mainly due to a lack of education—or, to put it more bluntly, willful ignorance.

There is a reason why you hear so many class warfare sermons from television sportscasters: Many sportscasters used to be academically unqualified athletes who had to major in sociology in order to survive academically. When these athletes were in their sociology classes, certain subjects were taboo. Here are five rather obvious examples:

1. **Abortion and race.** Although only 12 percent of the population is black, 37 percent of aborted babies are black. In fact, more blacks are aborted every week than have been lynched in the entire history of the United States of America. The prevalence of abortion has a ripple effect on the black community. It makes it easier for men to have sex without commitment to women and children. This weakens the family, decimates the average household income, and paves the way for big government.

2. **Business ownership and race.** People often talk about buying minority votes with welfare. But the welfare checks don't stay in the hands of blacks for very long. They are soon cashed and spent in businesses in black communities. But members of different minority groups own most of the businesses. So the money quickly leaves the black community. The obvious solution is that blacks need to turn to entrepreneurship rather than government to strengthen their communities.

3. **Crime.** Blacks are far more likely to be victims of crime than whites. But focusing on the occasional white-on-black crime diverts attention from the fact that about 80 percent of all crime is intraracial. In other words, about four out of five crimes committed by a black citizen are committed against another black citizen. Of the remaining 20 percent of crimes that are interracial, there are far more black-on-white crimes than white-on-black crimes. This is despite the fact that whites vastly outnumber blacks in the general population.

   The prevalence of serious crime in the black community has serious economic consequences. Putting men in prison means taking them out of the workforce. When men aren't paying the bills, big government steps in to become the family provider.

4. **Dependency**. By wildly exaggerating the extent of white cop on black citizen crime, reporters and academics make black citizens unduly distrustful of the police. This means that black citizens are more likely to tolerate crime as it infiltrates their communities. This is why drug dealers and drug-related gangs are able to operate in plain sight in many housing projects and in other poor black residential areas. In neighborhoods where drug dependency increases, lawful employment decreases. When this happens, big government fills the void. Thus, a community's drug dependency is a major predictor of its government dependency.

5. **Fatherlessness**. Just about every negative social outcome is directly and strongly related to fatherlessness. Whether you are talking about unemployment, illiteracy, crime, or drug dependency, the absence of a father is a principal driving factor. Before big government started subsidizing illegitimacy, most black kids were raised in two parent households. Now, broken homes are the rule in the black community, not the exception. This explains why blacks keep falling further behind other minorities.

By contrast, in the Asian community where illegitimacy is the exception, rather than the rule, crime is lower, educational attainment is higher, and business, not government, is seen as the road to success.

It is sad to see unemployed black men marching in the streets of Baltimore with signs reading, "Racism is the problem, revolution is the answer." It is also disappointing to see black sportscasters sitting on national television giving lectures based on nineteenth-century Marxist ideology rather than twenty-first-century economic reality.

Imagine if college athletes studied legitimate academic disciplines like economics. Later, they could seek employment as educated sportscasters performing a legitimate public service. Instead of legitimizing the mobs, they could teach the masses the obvious: Ignorance is the problem, and basic economic education is the answer.

Mike was always a big sports fan. In school, he played football, baseball, and especially soccer. I remember him and Dad watching basketball games and boxing matches. In his travels, Mike would try to catch an MLB game and buy a cap for his extensive collection.

Every year, he would pass through St. Louis to see me on his way back home from Colorado, but one year, we decided to meet up in Kansas City instead because my adult son was living there at the time. While we were there, he said, "Hey, let's go to a Royals game," since they just happened to be at home. So we just went up to the ticket window, and he bought tickets for the four of us. That's a memory I'll always cherish.

CHAPTER 63

Don't Blame Simpson Release on "Broken System"

July 24, 2015

I have been teaching criminology at the university level for twenty-four years. If I had a dollar for every time I heard the term "broken" to describe our criminal justice system, I would be so wealthy I would not have to have to teach anymore. Of course, with the news that O.J. Simpson will be released on parole, I am hearing another barrage of declarations that the system is "broken." These self-proclaimed experts don't know the facts of the Simpson case. If they did, they would not blame Simpson's release on the "system." They would blame it on Los Angeles District Attorney Gil Garcetti.

I understand the anger over Simpson's release. I watched the parole hearing and was appalled by the jocular demeanor of my former sports hero turned criminal. Furthermore, when I heard the board explain that their reasons for releasing Simpson included his "lack of prior criminal convictions," it made me angry. It raised old memories of the profound miscarriage of justice that occurred in 1995. There was much blame to go around for those casually acquainted with the case. Some possible targets included:

The defense attorneys. Simpson's attorneys played the race card from the bottom of the deck. What was perhaps worse was their decision to lie about the definition of reasonable doubt—telling jurors that the law required them to acquit if only one piece of prosecution evidence was called into question.

The judge. In addition to losing control of the courtroom, Ito allowed the false definition of reasonable doubt to be given by Johnnie Cochran to the jurors without correction. If nothing else, it is the judge's job to make sure the law is applied correctly while lawyers argue facts instead of rewriting instructions for the jury.

The prosecutors. In his interrogation, Simpson admitted he had been cut at exactly the same hour his wife was murdered. Worse still, he provided no explanation for the cut and no consistent alibi for his whereabouts at the time of the murder. But Marcia Clark was so incompetent she declined to introduce the transcript of Simpson's interrogation because he "asserted his innocence" in the interrogation. Newsflash, Marcia: The jury already knew he was asserting his innocence because he pled "not guilty." That's why you had a trial.

The jury. Few, if any, of the Simpson jurors had an IQ above room temperature. One even said that O.J.'s blood at the murder scene was "not an issue" at the trial. Another admitted she just didn't understand the DNA arguments. Yet another said she never read books or magazines. She did say she read the "racing form" but admitted that she "didn't understand it."

We would not be talking about any of this if the first Simpson trial had taken place in Santa Monica instead of downtown Los Angeles. If it had, there would have been no parole hearing for Simpson in regards to armed robbery. In fact, there would have been no robbery. He would still be in prison for two counts of murder in the first degree.

Why did Gil Garcetti move the trial from Santa Monica to downtown Los Angeles? His reasons were numerous but all equally inane. For example, he said it would be more convenient for his prosecutors to drive only fifteen minutes to the downtown courtroom as opposed to forty-five minutes to Santa Monica. Putting convenience over jury composition is a losing strategy.

Garcetti also asserted that the Los Angeles courtroom was bigger and would better accommodate the media. But what kind of fool would rather lose a case in front of a large group of reporters as opposed to winning it in front of a smaller group?

So why does all of this matter? Because the case was lost as soon as Garcetti fumbled the ball and moved the trial, which assured that a highly educated, emotionally detached jury would be replaced with an uneducated jury seeking revenge for Rodney King.

Educated Santa Monica jurors would not have bought the lie that "if the glove doesn't fit, you must acquit." Having not been deceived or even remotely inclined to believe such nonsense, they would not have needed Judge Ito to re-educate them. Nor would they have needed the transcript of the interrogation, as they would have had the education to comprehend the DNA tests that proved Simpson's blood was at the murder scene. Intelligent people know what it means when the blood of three people is found at a murder scene and only one of them walked away alive.

Understanding why Gil Garcetti made such bad decisions requires an understanding of the climate he created during his tenure at the Los Angeles District Attorney's Office. Years ago, one of his calendar attorneys by the name of Ceballos criticized the department for knowingly relying upon evidence obtained from warrants based on affidavits secured through perjured testimony. Rather than addressing the problem, Garcetti demoted Ceballos for talking about it. Ceballos then sued Garcetti in a case that went all the way to the Supreme Court.

Gil Garcetti won a narrow five-to-four ruling when the Supreme Court ruled on *Garcetti v. Ceballos* in 2006. The legal ruling was shocking to defenders of the First Amendment. It said that public employees had no right to comment on matters of public concern (including police perjury and prosecutorial use of illegally obtained evidence) if it was part of their "official duties." That is how Garcetti legally insulated district attorneys from internal criticism. So the only remedy for the likes of Gil Garcetti is external—voting them out of office.

The fact that voters did not fire Garcetti after the Simpson verdict does not mean our democratic system is "broken"—any more than occasional outrageous acquittals mean the justice system is "broken." The fact that many "citizens" avoid voting—sometimes in order to avoid jury service—suggests something else is broken.

Perhaps it's our view of civil responsibility.

Mike was planning to write a book called Seven Trials: How Famous Cases Reflect and Shape American Culture. *I assume this would have been based on his "Trials of the Century" class, which included*

the Simpson case, a topic he also briefly discussed in his "Introduction to Criminal Justice" class.

One of the things I admired about Mike was that he prepared meticulously for everything. In his extensive library, I found many books that he used for preparing his classes, especially on the Till and Simpson cases. It seemed as if he owned every book on those cases!

Chapter 64

Get Out of My Class and Leave America

August 28, 2015

This also appears in the book Life and How to Live It *(2023).*

Author's Note: The following column comprises excerpts taken from my first lectures on the first day of classes this semester at UNC-Wilmington. I reproduced these remarks with the hope that they would be useful to other professors teaching at public universities all across America. Feel free to use this material if you already have tenure.

Welcome back to class, students! I am Mike Adams, your criminology professor here at UNC-Wilmington. Before we get started with the course, I need to address an issue that is causing problems here at UNCW and in higher education all across the country. I am talking about the growing minority of students who believe they have a right to be free from being offended. If we don't reverse this dangerous trend in our society, there will soon be a majority of young people who will need to walk around in plastic bubble suits to protect them in the event that they come into contact with a dissenting viewpoint. That mentality is unworthy of an American.

Let's get something straight right now. You have no right to be unoffended. You have a right to be offended with regularity. It is the price you pay for living in a free society. If you don't understand that, you are confused and dangerously so. In part, I blame your high school teachers for failing to teach you basic civics before you got your diploma. Most of you went to public high schools, which are a disaster. Don't tell me that offended you. I went to a public high school.

Of course, your high school might not be the problem. It is entirely possible that the main reason why so many of you are confused about free speech is that piece of paper hanging on the wall right over there. Please turn your attention to that ridiculous document that is framed and hanging by the door. In fact, take a few minutes to read it before you leave class today. It is our campus speech code. It specifically says that there is a requirement that everyone must only engage in discourse that is "respectful." That assertion is as ludicrous as it is illegal. I plan to have that thing ripped down from every classroom on campus before I retire.

One of my grandfathers served in World War I. My stepgrandfather served in World War II. My sixth great-grandfather enlisted in the American Revolution when he was only thirteen. These great men did not fight so we could simply relinquish our rights to the enemy within our borders. That enemy is the Marxists who run our public universities. If you are a Marxist and I just offended you, well, that's tough. I guess they don't make communists like they used to.

Of course, this ban on "disrespectful" speech is really only illusory. The university that created these speech restrictions then turns around and sponsors plays like *The Vagina Monologues*, which is loaded with profanity, including the c-word—the most offensive and disrespectful word a person could ever possibly apply to a woman. It is pure, unadulterated hypocrisy.

So the university position can be roughly summarized as follows: Public university administrators have a First Amendment right to use disrespectful profanity, but public university students do not. This turns the First Amendment on its head. The university has its free speech analysis completely backwards. And that's why they need to be sued.

Before we go, let us take a few minutes to look at the last page of your syllabus where I explain the importance of coming to class on time, turning off your cell phone, and refraining from talking during lectures. In that section, I explain that each of you has God-given talents and that your Creator endowed you with a purpose in life that is thwarted when you develop these bad habits.

Unbelievably, a student once complained to the department chairwoman that my mention of God and a Creator was a violation of separation of church and state. Let me be as clear as I possibly can: If any of you actually think that my decision to paraphrase the Declaration of Independence in the course syllabus is unconstitutional, then you suffer from a severe intellectual hernia.

Indeed, it takes hard work to become stupid enough to think that the Declaration of Independence is unconstitutional. If you agree with the student who made that complaint, then you are probably just an anti-religious zealot. Therefore, I am going to ask you to do exactly three things and do them in the exact order that I specify.

First, get out of my class. You can fill out the drop slip over at James Hall. Just tell them you don't believe in true diversity, and you want to be surrounded by people who agree with your twisted interpretation of the Constitution simply because they are the kind of people who will protect you from having your beliefs challenged or your feelings hurt.

Second, withdraw from the university. If you find that you are actually relieved because you will no longer be in a class where your beliefs might be challenged, then you aren't ready for college. Go get a job building houses so you can work with some illegal aliens who will help you gain a better appreciation of what this country has to offer.

Finally, if this doesn't work, then I would simply ask you to get the hell out of the country. The ever-growing thin-skinned minority you have joined is simply ruining life in this once-great nation. Please move to some place like Cuba where you can enjoy the company of communists and get excellent health care. Just hop on a leaky boat and start paddling your way toward utopia. You will not be missed.

Thank you for your time. I'll see most of you when classes resume on Monday.

This was included in Townhall's "Year in Review: The 15 Most Popular Stories of 2015." Mike said it surpassed one million shares on Facebook.

It is tragic that Mike's enemies did not realize that Mike was also fighting for THEIR freedom of speech, not just his. If you are only fighting for your speech, then you are not truly fighting for freedom

of speech—as Mike was. Here are some other Mike Adams quotes related to freedom of speech:

The Constitution only protects offensive speech. If it only protected inoffensive speech, then it would be useless. That which is not offensive is not in need of protection.

Our Constitution protects offensive speech. It doesn't protect offended individuals.

Censorship is bullying.

If my columns make you feel uncomfortable, the solution is for you to stop reading, not for me to stop writing.

I'm so old, I can remember when Democrats supported free speech.

I recoil whenever I hear people use terms like "homophobe," "Islamophobe," or "xenophobe." If someone disagrees with you on same-sex marriage, foreign policy, or immigration, it does not mean they are driven by an irrational fear. It just means they have a contrary opinion. Characterizing dissent as mental illness is a dangerous step in the direction of totalitarianism.

A UNCW feminist claims I should not be allowed to speak at UNCW because my past speech has made people at UNCW mad. Imagine a country where people are only allowed to speak if they have never made someone mad. Imagine further a country where people merely have to pretend to be angry in order to permanently silence people with opposing views.

This was written years ago. Today, we no longer have to imagine. Sadly, as usual, his prediction came true—and he became one of those who were permanently silenced.

Chapter 65

Stuck on Hating Whitey

September 4, 2015

Recently, after spending three months in Colorado *[at Summit Ministries]*, I returned to North Carolina to a large list of errands. The first of these errands was replacing a lost passport, which meant I had to go to the post office in downtown Wilmington. I rarely go downtown, largely because the area is infested with drugs and crime. Unsurprisingly, before I left the downtown area, I passed a crime scene. Judging by the number of police cars, I could tell it was a murder.

In addition to the things I knew, there were some things I merely suspected when I happened upon that crime scene. For example, I suspected that both the perpetrator and the victim were young black males between the ages of fifteen and twenty-five. I'm not Sherlock Holmes. You don't need to be a detective to know that black-on-black violence is rampant in downtown Wilmington.

It should go without saying that I was unsurprised when I watched the evening news and learned that the victim was a young black male and that a young black male suspect was already in custody. But the following statement made by Police

Chief Ralph Evangelous did surprise me: "Where is the outcry in our community? God forbid it would be an officer involved in this situation—we'd have a protest."

The immediate reaction of most people reading this statement will be to laud the police chief for having the courage to state this usually unspoken truth: **that the everyday black-on-black murder provokes far less outrage than the occasional white cop on black citizen murder.**

The fact that many will see such a simple statement of such an obvious truth as somehow courageous says something very bad about our society. It takes little to be seen as courageous in a society plagued by cowardice. That epidemic of cowardice has a lot to do with the climate of intimidation created by today's so-called civil rights leaders.

After the chief made his statement, it took only forty-eight hours for a black civil rights leader named Sonya Patrick to go to the press with this demand: "Stereotyping the black community the way he did… I think he owes us an apology."

Of course, this is what civil rights leaders do. They are there to constantly remind us of what "we" owe "them." They are also there to remind us of the dangers of racial stereotyping. Unfortunately, most civil rights leaders have become walking stereotypes and are wholly oblivious to their role in reinforcing negative beliefs about the black community.

As anyone can plainly read, the white police chief went out of his way to place the word "our" before "community." In so doing, he was trying to evenly spread across racial lines any blame for apathy toward black-on-black crime. Indeed, I have met many white liberals who are willing to protest when a white cop kills a black suspect but remain mute on the issue of black-on-black crime.

Ironically, by protesting this obviously racially neutral statement, Patrick simply demonstrates that the chief was correct. Indeed, the assertion that the everyday black-on-black murder far less outrages many black civil rights leaders than the occasional white cop on black murder actually understates the case. In reality, many black civil rights leaders care more about white-on-black criticism than black-on-black murder.

Nor does it seem to matter whether blacks are actually being criticized. Perception of criticism is sufficient justification for outrage because perception trumps reality. It's a worldview issue. It's also an ethical issue because it undermines the credibility of those with legitimate civil rights claims.

Unfortunately, the credibility of the current black civil rights movement is suffering at the hands of two sets of imposters. The first are those who parade in the streets wearing assless chaps and doing pelvic thrusts in front of giant inflatable penises. The fact that these gay pride protesters dare to call themselves civil rights activists is an insult to blacks who once marched in the streets while being attacked by cops wielding fire hoses and unleashing attack dogs.

The second set of imposters is made up of those black activists who are dedicated to tearing down whites rather than lifting up blacks. Unfortunately, they are now the rule rather than the exception.

The product of the new anti-white civil rights movement is a sort of drive-by activism that harms many innocent people in the process. Our white police chief is just the latest casualty. The next is the victim of real racism who simply will not be taken seriously.

In the end, Ralph Evangelous was both correct and prescient. And so was Aesop.

CHAPTER 66

Life and How to Live It, Part XII

September 15, 2015

This also appears in the book Life and How to Live It *(2023).*

One afternoon in early August, I got off a plane in Gulfport, Mississippi, with my friend J. Warner "Jim" Wallace. We were scheduled to speak at a church up in Hattiesburg with our other friend Frank Turek. We had about three hours to make the one-hour drive, so we had plenty of time.

As we headed up U.S. 49 to Hattiesburg, we passed a number of small towns in South Mississippi where many of my relatives were born and raised. My parents met in Gulfport back in 1952, and most of my mother's side of the family was spread across the southern portion of Mississippi. I felt sorry for Jim because he had to listen to stories about my childhood memories of visiting many of those relatives in the Magnolia State.

As we approached the exit for Wiggins, Mississippi, I told Jim about the time in the summer of 1973 when I visited my mother's uncle Wiley Trellis "Bud" Myers in nearby Brooklyn, Mississippi. Uncle Bud offered to introduce me to his friend

Dizzy Dean, who lived just a few miles south of him in Wiggins. "Come back and stay with me a little longer next summer and I'll take you down and let you meet ole Dizz," he promised me. But unfortunately, the old St. Louis Cardinals Hall of Famer died in the summer of 1974 just before I made it back to Mississippi.

I told Jim, who is a retired LAPD cold case homicide detective, that Dizzy Dean was buried somewhere nearby. He took out his cell phone and started to search for the location of the grave. When I asked him what he was doing, he said we were going to find the gravesite. "Today, you're finally going to get to pay a visit to ole Dizz," Jim assured me.

After about forty-five minutes of searching (only to find the wrong graveyard), we got back on the highway. As fate would have it, the next rest stop was named after Dizzy Dean. We figured someone there would know where ole Dizz was buried. Sure enough, an attendant dictated the directions while my ace detective/friend Jim wrote them down. We were off to the races again. We still had time to make it to Hattiesburg after paying our respects to an old baseball legend.

Thankfully, we found Dizzy's grave in a little cemetery just yards off Highway 49 in Bond, Mississippi. There was a large headstone with a smaller plaque just a few feet in front of it. The plaque had a St. Louis Cardinals logo on it, and it also acknowledged Dizzy's membership in the Baseball Hall of Fame.

When I looked down, I noticed a baseball sitting in between the plaque and gravestone. I saw that someone had written on it, so I picked it up to see what it said. It was a short note written by a grown man thanking Dizzy for playing catch with him during the summers when he was just a boy. After staying only a few minutes, we got back in the car and headed toward Hattiesburg.

When we drove off, Jim said, "Well, it looks like you finally got to meet ole Dizz." He also reflected on how a man could rise to such greatness and be known around the world just to end up resting in such a little cemetery in the middle of nowhere in South Mississippi. Jim concluded by saying that it just shows how fleeting this life really is. I agreed wholeheartedly.

When we arrived at the church, we had just enough time to grab a bite to eat before heading to the auditorium. As I was passing through the lobby, a woman came up to me and told me she had driven several hours from somewhere in Alabama just to hear us speak. She explained that her son had just seen Frank and Jim and me speak a few weeks before at Summit Ministries in Colorado. She said the experience had a big impact on him, so she wanted to hear what we had to say.

Another woman approached me and said that her son Nathan had told her to say "Hello" to me. I could not remember his face, but she told me I had a big impact on his life. He, too, was once a student at Summit Ministries.

As I entered the church auditorium, a man walked up to me and introduced himself as the provost of a college in South Mississippi. He said we had corresponded several times many years before. He said he had been trying to fight the good fight as a conservative Christian in higher education. He thanked me for writing about that struggle for so many years.

After Frank spoke to the 650 church members who were in attendance at our Fearless Faith seminar, I had a chance to speak for an hour. When I finished speaking, a man came up to me and said he had just become the university attorney at a school not far from where we were speaking. He told me he had been reading my work on campus free speech for years. Then, he told me he was actively working with the Foundation for Individual Rights in Education to eliminate the many unconstitutional policies at his university.

As I was walking out of the auditorium, I could not help but think about all the fleeting relationships I had established over the years as a speaker and a writer. I have met so many thousands of people and forgotten most of them over time. But strangely, through the wonders of an internet column, many of these relationships were being sustained. And good things were still coming out of them.

Just as I reentered the lobby, I heard someone call my name. When I turned around, I saw it was one of my old college roommates whom I had lived with in the summer of 1988. Standing next to him was one of my old college friends who was now his wife. I had no idea they were married, as I had lost track of both of them over twenty years ago. He said he had been reading my column for over a decade and was enjoying my exploits. We stood there and launched into almost an hour of conversation—just sharing updates on old friends from the Sigma Chi days at Mississippi State.

That night, I thought long and hard about the effect years of travel was having on my life. It had caused me to lose track of many old friends. But it also caused me to meet many new ones. In the end, I realized that it really isn't up to me anyway. It's just what I am called to do.

After my plane landed the next day in my summer home of Colorado, I drove from the airport in Colorado Springs to Summit Ministries in Manitou. Later, when I sat down at dinner, one of the students sat down next to me and asked me what goals I would need to accomplish before I died in order to conclude that I had lived a full life. I told him I really didn't have any. I've accomplished enough in my life. Although I am healthier than I have ever been and plan to live many years, I told him I could die tomorrow and be fulfilled. And I really meant it.

The student was surprised by my answer and just looked at me and asked, "So what do you plan to do for the rest of your life?" My answer was simple: "Just exactly what I am doing now."

The writing and the speeches are great. But the hikes up the sides of mountains talking about life with students and close friends are really more than enough for me. They are about so much more than enjoying God's creation. They are about trying to produce a ripple effect from meaningful relationships with people who care about important things.

I guess there was a time when I thought life was a struggle to make it into the Hall of Fame. Now I know that it's more like a game of catch on a warm summer afternoon.

"I could die tomorrow and be fulfilled." It is a great consolation to me to know that Mike felt that way. And he had good reason to—Mike accomplished more during his 55 years than I or most other people could in 110 years. I will be forever grateful for what he taught me, and so many others, about life and how to live it.

CHAPTER 67

You Are Not Alone

January 17, 2016

Over the last several months, the supportive emails and calls I have received have greatly outnumbered the hate mails, which usually come from feminists who hate males. The influx of support can be attributed largely to a viral column I wrote last semester called "Get Out of My Class and Leave America" *[Chapter 64]*. After it ran, people called my office voicing support for over forty straight days. I say "straight" days based on the safe assumption that none of these callers were gay activists.

As much as I appreciate the support, it is based on the fiction that I am some sort of fearless conservative crusader standing alone against a rising tide of liberal tyranny on a secular college campus. The following correspondence from one of my readers illustrates the misconception:

> *Dr. Adams, I just want to thank you for the stand you have taken. Over the years, you've taken this stand alone and never wavered in your courage or in your faithfulness. I applaud you, sir.*

As much as I appreciate the sentiment, that reader never would have sent his email if he had seen me on September 10, 2012. It was the night before the eleventh anniversary of 9/11. It was also five and one-half years into a federal First Amendment lawsuit that was consuming my existence *[Chapter 54 through Chapter 59]*. My legal team had won an important ruling in the Fourth Circuit seventeen months earlier. However, we were still waiting on the judge to rule on a motion that would determine whether the case would go to trial. Unfortunately, the judge had been sitting on the motion for almost a year. The waiting was excruciating.

Like many times during that period, I woke up in the middle of the night because I was overwhelmed with anxiety over the case. I don't pray as often as I should, and I certainly am not the kneel-and-pray-at-the-edge-of-the-bed type. However, on those nights when I was unable to sleep, I had no choice.

On that particular September morning, when I was kneeling by the bed, something interrupted the normal prayer process. It was this feeling of uncontrollable anger. It was so strong that I suddenly stopped praying and started confronting God with questions. "Why have you left me alone to fight against these godless secularists?" "Why have you abandoned me after I have come to faith and taken a stand?" "Why have you left me weary and without the energy to go on?"

My tirade had started out as a series of questions. Within a few minutes I found myself shouting the questions at the top of my lungs. By the time I was done, I was no longer asking questions. I was screaming profanities into thin air. I'm not sure how long it lasted, but by the time I was done, I had simply collapsed in the middle of that dark bedroom.

When the alarm went off, I was still lying on the floor where I had cursed myself into a state of unconsciousness. I had shouted for so long that I lost my voice, which would not come back for three whole days. The liberals were ecstatic.

After I picked myself up off the floor, I made a cup of coffee and assumed my position in the leather chair in my sunroom. I tried to start my daily ritual of reading, but I could not. I had this feeling that I had just blown it—that my tirade meant that now I really was alone and doomed. So I decided to check my email, which included the inboxes on my social media accounts.

When I logged on to my Facebook account, I had a single message sent from a woman I met working at Summit Ministries several years earlier. The message was a literal godsend. I have copied her words below, and not a single one has been altered:

> *Hey Mike! So, this is really random, but tonight I was talking with the Father and He put you on my heart to be praying for. Sometimes He shows me pictures or gives me specific words also, and He gave me some for you. First, I saw you kneeling and it looked like you were all alone in a dark place somewhere. But then He let me see that picture zoomed out, and I realized you weren't alone or lost in darkness, you were inside His heart. Then I heard Him say that you have a very special place inside His heart. In addition, I pray specifically against any weariness or abandonment in your life and that you speak out His abundance, joy, comfort, and encouragement! You are not alone!!*

This is one email message I responded to. It came at the best possible time, and she needed to know. I also wish I had the time to respond to all of the encouraging emails I have received over the last few months. Unfortunately, time will not allow it.

Suffice it to say that the encouraging emails I get from people should not be viewed as a response to courage on my behalf. I see them as the only reason I have been able to keep going in spite of my own personal weaknesses and my frequent lapses of faith. I am thankful for each of them even though I may never have responded.

Regardless, I thought it would be good to run this column for any of my readers who are presently in a dark place. The picture will eventually zoom out. Then, you will see that you weren't really alone or abandoned in the darkness.

This is so hard for me to read. Why couldn't Mike remember this? Why didn't I call him?

Mike also once posted this:
The next time you feel like firing off a nasty email, pause for a second. Think of someone who does his job well, and fire off an email giving him encouragement. Then, go about your business.

Chapter 68

Dead Things Don't Grow

February 21, 2016

Many who hold the pro-choice position subscribe to a postmodern worldview. They are not arguing that we can kill the unborn because a woman's right to choose trumps the right to life of the unborn. They are arguing that ambiguity on the question of when life begins supplies adequate justification for abortion on demand. The argument from ambiguity was central to former ACLU president Nadine Strossen's presentation when I debated her recently on the campus of Oregon State University (OSU).

I was pleased that Nadine's opening argument relied heavily on the claim that we cannot know when life begins. This played into the strategy I had chosen prior to the onset of the debate. Nadine did two other things I had hoped she would do in her opening statement: 1) argue that *Roe v. Wade* was a moderate decision that balanced the competing interests of the individual and the state and 2) argue that the *Roe* decision was necessary to stop the deaths of women who were dying as a result of unsafe abortions. In my own opening argument, which followed hers, I tried to establish two things:

1. **There is clear consensus in the science of embryology that life begins at conception**. Scientifically speaking, the unborn are distinct, living, whole human beings actively involved in the process of developing themselves from within from the very point of conception.

2. **There is no difference between the adults we are today and the unborn humans we once were that would justify killing us at an earlier stage of development**. In other words, there is no essential difference between a "human" and a "person." Furthermore, any effort to justify abortion with philosophical distinctions among the living would invite systematic human inequality. At the end of the day, our society must choose between human equality and abortion. We simply cannot have both.

After we presented our opening statements, Nadine had an opportunity to offer a rebuttal. In that rebuttal, she challenged my claim that there was an absolute consensus among embryologists that life begins at conception. She quoted a source saying that the question could not be answered conclusively. This was a good tactic for Nadine to employ. She was obviously prepared. Fortunately, I had fully anticipated her move.

In my rebuttal, which followed hers, I drew on the work of Francis Beckwith. As Beckwith has previously written, *Roe v. Wade* concedes that the question of the parameters of a woman's right to abortion is inextricably bound to the question of when life begins. Therefore, if someone is agnostic on the question of when life begins, they are also agnostic on the parameters of a woman's right to choose. I began my rebuttal by establishing this crucial point.

Rather than conceding that there was a legitimate doubt about when life begins, I decided to reassert the point that the matter was settled. I did this by firing off numerous sources. Among them, I included former Planned Parenthood president Alan Guttmacher and Princeton philosopher Peter Singer. I wanted to establish the fact that many honest pro-choice advocates conceded the point. In fact, they have done so for decades.

Fortunately, OSU Socratic Club debates are structured in such a way as to allow opponents to have an informal half-hour exchange following the opening statements and rebuttals. During that exchange, Nadine came across as cordial and well informed. She also impressed me as sincerely interested in my views on a number of issues related to the debate topic. She was a worthy and articulate opponent.

One downside to Nadine's choice of questions was that they sometimes gave the appearance of trying to divert the issue from the question of the status of the unborn. When Nadine interjected the phrase "potential life" into our discussion, I tried to seize the moment to refocus the debate. I asked her whether by using the phrase "potential life" she meant to deny that the unborn were humans (in a biological sense) or persons (in a philosophical sense). Her answer was "both."

Having established that the unborn have separate DNA and that there is cell division and metabolism from the point of conception, I replied with the following: "But Nadine, dead things don't grow." In fact, I said it twice during the exchange.

That statement ended up being the takeaway line from the entire debate. In fact, nearly everyone who saw the debate and spoke to me afterwards quoted that one line. It was effective because Nadine and I were in danger of getting into a war of quoting texts no one has ever read. But "dead things don't grow" was an unmistakable appeal to common sense that I believe solidified my central thesis and allowed the pro-life position to prevail in the overall exchange.

Therefore, I would like to conclude this column by thanking my friend Jay Watts for supplying me with that line, which I saw in a recent episode of "Life Is Best," a series hosted by my friend Scott Klusendorf. That series may be the best thing Scott has ever done for the pro-life movement—and that is really saying something.

My advice to pro-life debaters who wish to compete (and prevail!) in debates on hostile turf is twofold. First, read everything Francis Beckwith writes on the topic of abortion. Second, watch every video, speech, and debate featuring Scott Klusendorf speaking and teaching on the topic of abortion. *[His book is discussed in Chapter 45, "Stand for Life."]*

Author's Note: The debate discussed in today's column can be accessed on YouTube (see https://ww.youtube.com/watch?v=YdMqmDyOrnw&feature=youtu.be).

Mike would later debate abortion provider Dr. Willie Parker, which is briefly mentioned in Chapter 98, "Two Kinds of Pro-Choice Advocates," and is covered in Aborting Free Speech *(2023).*

Chapter 69

Imagine Heaven

February 25, 2016

For almost a quarter of a century, I have spent my days working with utopians. The utopian is motivated to create heaven on Earth because he is convinced that there is no other option. Put simply, the utopian believes there can be no heaven in the sense that it is described in the Bible because there is no supernatural realm. This commitment to naturalism is a philosophical commitment. It isn't based on science. In fact, it flies in the face of science.

To paraphrase Josh McDowell, we only have three options when it comes to the origin of the universe. First, we can say that it came into being spontaneously—in other words, that it came to be without a cause. Second, we can say that it has always been. Third, we can posit some cause outside the physical universe to explain its existence.

The second option is no longer reasonable. Science has been leading inexorably to the conclusion that the universe is not infinite but instead had a beginning. That evidence has been accumulating for decades. It is therefore wrong to characterize the notion of a timeless physical universe as a scientific position. Once again, it is a philosophical position. However, in light of all the evidence, it is not a reasonable position for someone to hold.

This leaves us with only two options: the universe came to be either with or without a cause. In other words, the universe either came from something or it came from nothing. Reasonable people grasp intuitively that it makes far more sense to say that something came from something than to say that something came from nothing.

Of course, admitting that the universe was caused by something rather than nothing comes with a price. Any cause predating the physical universe must therefore be non-physical in nature. To acknowledge such a cause is to abandon philosophical naturalism and recognize the existence of a supernatural realm. In and of itself, this by no means proves the existence of God. However, it raises the prospect. And that is enough to make the secular utopian nervous. It threatens his self-ordained role as the creator of heaven on Earth.

It is against this backdrop that I initially refused to take seriously the claims of writers like Raymond Moody, who began writing about near-death experiences (NDEs) in the mid-seventies. I read his book *Life After Life* in 1985—but only because I was forced to do so as part of an undergraduate course in psychology. At that time, I was an agnostic and rejected the prospect of all things supernatural.

After a religious conversion—to theism in 1996 *[as told in Chapter 27, "The Shadow Proves the Sunshine"]* and to Christianity in 2000 *[as told in Chapter 97, "Everlasting Life on Death Row"]*—I abandoned the indefensible notion that the cosmos is all there is, all there ever was, and all there ever will be. Such a statement was appealing to me as a humanist in search of cosmic justice. But upon critical examination, I had to go where the evidence led me.

For those of us who have made the transition away from a strict materialist view of the universe, there is no readily apparent need to examine the issue of NDEs. In my post-conversion life, I never had much interest in the topic until I stumbled across a copy of *Imagine Heaven* by John Burke.

Pastor Burke is one of the finest teachers in America. He is also a brilliant writer. I devoured all three of his previous books and, quite frankly, was shocked to see that he was taking on the issue of NDEs. But since I had enjoyed everything he had written previously, I took the plunge and decided to read it.

Having finished reading *Imagine Heaven,* I now realize that I have been seriously mistaken in my decision to ignore the issue of NDEs for over thirty years—ever since taking that psychology course back in 1985. Presently, I can see at least two compelling reasons to examine the issue carefully. The first reason applies to believers. The second applies to skeptics.

1. **Clarifying the issue of life review and judgment**. There are many consistent patterns reported by people who claim to have had NDEs. Among those commonalities is the idea of a life review where people are able to see an overview of everything they did on Earth. Those who have described the life review consistently report some interesting things. Among them is the idea that we are able to see with remarkable clarity the long-term ramifications of our actions. They often report that the things they did on Earth that seemed trivial had a significant domino effect that ended up altering the lives of numerous people. Additionally, many report that the life review

is used to show what really matters to God. These reports consistently claim that our relationships are revealed to be far more important than our individual accomplishments.

Pastor Burke wisely decided to write one chapter on "the life review" and another on "rewards and judgments." The reason both are needed is that people reporting NDEs often say that there is an absence of judgment in the life review. Others assume that this translates into an absence of judgment in the afterlife *per se*. Such a conclusion is unwarranted. Put simply, an absence of evidence is not always evidence of absence. Pastor Burke uses scripture to explain judgment in the afterlife in very specific terms. His references provide crucial guidance on how we should live our lives on Earth and how we should prepare for the afterlife just as we would prepare for retirement. These two chapters alone are worth the price of the book.

2. **Clarifying the nature of consciousness.** Many skeptics are convinced that consciousness can be explained in strictly material terms. I would urge these skeptics to take the time to read *Body and Soul* by J.P. Moreland and Scott Rae. In that comprehensive book, the authors make a compelling philosophical and ethical case for substance dualism, which views human nature in terms of both body and soul. But those who have never seriously doubted that consciousness can be explained in strictly material terms might benefit by first reading *Imagine Heaven*, which Moreland now considers to be the "go-to book" on the subject of NDEs.

Skeptics who read Burke's book will struggle to find naturalist explanations for the cross-cultural similarities in NDEs. They will also struggle to find naturalist explanations for NDE accounts that have been verified by external evidence. I will close this review with one such example, which is not in John Burke's book. It came to me in the form of a firsthand account from my friend Carl who died of a heart attack in 2014 and was later revived by attending physicians.

Carl and I were recently spending time with a mutual friend whose mother is dying from cancer. I was sharing some of the stories from *Imagine Heaven* and urging him to read the book as he prepared for his mother's passing. As we were talking, Carl joined in and shared the specific details of his NDE.

After Carl was pronounced dead and revived, he described his out-of-body experience to the doctor who revived him. As an unbeliever and a skeptic, the doctor began to pepper my friend Carl with questions. Carl responded with an extremely detailed account of what went on while the doctors were reviving him. In fact, he told them everything that happened between the time he was pronounced dead and the time he was revived.

At one point during the account, Carl's doctor stopped him and said, "No, we didn't do that." In other words, he vigorously denied the veracity of one specific aspect of Carl's report of the procedures used to bring him back to life. They argued back and forth for a few minutes until my friend Carl demanded in frustration, "Just go and check the records!"

Carl's doctor retrieved the attending nurse's records, which provided a detailed overview of what the doctors did to bring him back to life. The notes on the clipboard showed that Carl's version of events was correct, and the doctor's version was wrong.

As a reminder to my readers, Carl was dead at the time the disputed events occurred. Yet his account of what happened during those minutes was proved by external evidence to be more accurate than the doctor's recollection. Readers are free to attribute this to luck just as they are free to believe that the universe popped into existence out of nothing.

I know that stories like Carl's are difficult to believe when viewed in isolation. But they are far from isolated. Skeptics owe it to themselves to study the issue and provide honest explanations for these recurrent empirical patterns. In the final analysis, skeptics must decide whether they will follow the evidence or their philosophical presuppositions. They simply cannot do both.

For more book recommendations, see Chapter 7, "An Anti-Communist Reading List."

Chapter 70

Onward Christian Pansies

July 7, 2016

Last week, a young Christian male asked me a pretty direct question. He wanted to know whether I ever worried that my blunt commentary on social media was "turning people away from Christianity." I thought it was an honest question. So I gave him an honest answer. I told him that I believe the problem is just the opposite. In other words, it isn't occasional blunt commentary that turns people away from Christianity. It is the constant displays of Christian cowardice that make people both reticent to join and quick to attack us.

During the year 2000, when I was in the process of my conversion, there was only one prominent pastor I would even listen to on television. His name is Greg Laurie. He was bold without being rude. He was physically fit and casually but sharply dressed, and to top it all off, he rode a motorcycle. He could deliver the gospel in a way that made even gangbangers weep and respond to an altar call in front of thousands at his Harvest Crusades in Anaheim Stadium.

In the fall of 2000, after I actually converted and joined a church, I started to notice something unusual about my pastor. He was a lifelong Republican leading a liberal denomination. But the only time he ever talked about politics or social issues was when he quoted people like Jerry Falwell and Pat Robertson. The blanket statement that always followed those quotes was that he wasn't "that kind of Republican." In fact, he was so afraid of his mostly liberal congregation that he never told them what he actually believed. He only told them that he did not believe what all the other "mean Republicans" like Falwell and Robertson believed. It got old pretty fast. So I left his church and found another.

I wish I could say my next pastor was different. But he was not. He was privately appalled by the concept of same-sex marriage. But every time he broached the subject, you could see him shaking from the pulpit. His voice would tremble as he tried to express his views in coded phrases. Unfortunately, the congregation was too obtuse to know what he was saying. When push came to shove, he failed to take a firm stand on Amendment 1, which was North Carolina's traditional marriage amendment. Clearly, he cowered out of fear of offending the droves of Obama supporters that helped pay his massive mortgage. I could no longer stomach his cowardice. So I left his church in frustration.

A personally anti-abortion pastor led another church I attended briefly. The problem was that his personal anti-abortion stance remained private and did not make its way into his sermons. In fact, he would not allow any discussion of the topic in his church for fear that someone in the congregation might have had an abortion. So he tossed any chance of redemption out the window for the post-abortive congregant. To make matters worse, he adamantly opposed pro-lifers showing pictures of aborted children in the public square. In other words, he was "pro-life" so long as no one ever talked about it inside or outside the church. To make matters even worse, two of the members of his congregation later castigated pro-lifers for showing pictures of abortion on the UNC-Wilmington campus (where I teach). There is an obvious lesson here: If the pastor is a coward, it will always spread through the congregation.

It has taken several tries, but I am happy that I have finally found a pastor and a church that is solidly pro-life and pro-family and not afraid to say it. I'm just sad that in the last sixteen years, I have learned that at least three-quarters of the pastors who actually know what is right still lack the intestinal fortitude to take a stand for what they believe.

Many Christians are fed up with the capitulation of the church and respond in a way that is different from my chosen response. Rather than continuing to try to find a courageous pastor, they simply stop going to church. So this raises an interesting question: *If Christians actually stop going to church because they are tired of pastors refusing to take a stand, is it possible that some people never seriously consider Christianity in the first place for the same reasons?*

I think I got the answer to that question nearly five years ago when I received an email from a troubled reader. Some of my regular readers may remember the story, as I have written about it before. The man had lost his home and job and family and was about to commit suicide. Before he did, someone forwarded one of my columns to him. The column was one of those typical "blunt commentaries" where I was tearing into a corrupt administrator who was intentionally violating the rights of college students. The suicidal reader was captivated by the tone and content of the article and decided to start reading other columns from my archive.

After reading several hundred of my "blunt commentaries," he came across one talking about the New Testament and how to approach reading it. So he sat down and read the New Testament. Instead of killing himself, he converted to Christianity.

I had the pleasure of meeting this fine young man two years ago when I was speaking in Ohio. He is now very happy and living a productive life working in the conservative movement. I'll never forget his explanation for previously refusing to consider Christianity. It is a paraphrase, but he basically told me the following: "For a long time, I would never consider converting because I thought you had to be weak and passive in order to be a Christian."

Let that sink in for a minute. The next time you self-censor, you may be hurting Christianity, not helping it. We need brave young warriors, not spineless "evangelists" who are more concerned about being liked than influencing the culture.

In a nutshell, Jesus was not Mr. Rogers. He had little tolerance for the smug moral superiority of those who grasp the truth but lack the faith and courage necessary to defend it.

The title refers to "Onward Christian Soldiers," an old hymn that we sang in the church of our youth.

Mike also wrote:
It is our job to get up each and every day and tell the truth. The fact that people are not listening does not absolve us of our responsibility. The one who refuses to speak and the one who refuses to listen will be judged alike.

Chapter 71

Silencing Whitey

July 14, 2016

Recently, I have made some pretty charged statements about Black Lives Matter (BLM). In a nutshell, I have argued that the organization is not a pro-black civil rights group. Instead, it is an anti-white anti-free-speech mob. Evidence of my contention isn't very hard to gather. In fact, you have to have your head buried pretty deep in the ground in order to miss it. Consider the following examples:

- In August of 2015, Black Lives Matter protestors overtook a Bernie Sanders event in Seattle. They physically stormed the stage and demanded that they be heard lest they shut the event down altogether. They actually shouted, "Your event will be shut down," as they yelled in the faces of those who were rightfully there speaking. They finally strong-armed the Sanders campaign into relinquishing their First Amendment right to speak—not by using reason but instead by using physical intimidation to take over the stage.

- In the fall of 2015, the Mizzou *[University of Missouri]* "safe space" controversy made national headlines. When journalists tried to film their protest, a now-infamous Black Lives Matter activist/professor asked for some "muscle" to physically intimidate members of the press who were simply seeking to exercise their First Amendment rights on public property. The protestors gleefully complied and strong-armed the reporters.

- In the spring of 2016, pro-lifers at Purdue sponsored an "All Lives Matter" event denouncing the disproportionate abortion of black babies. Black Lives Matter protestors denounced them as racists, shouted them down, and demanded that they apologize—simply for exercising their free speech rights.

- Soon after that, Black Lives Matter thugs stormed the stage while Milo Y-Can't-I-Pronounce-His-Last-Name was giving a speech at DePaul University. One of the protestors actually assaulted Milo—although he did not strike him hard enough to mess up his fabulously moussed and highlighted hairdo. Muscle trumped free speech on that particular occasion. The thugs then rallied to prevent Milo from coming back to campus later. In other words, they went from physical restraint all the way to prior restraint of free speech.

- Earlier this summer, protestors stormed a stage where LGBT activists were trying to hold a vigil for those slain in the Orlando nightclub massacre. Without any sense of irony, the Black Lives Matter spokesperson began lecturing the audience—but only after expressing apprehension over the fact that most people in the audience were white. For the record, the Orlando shooter was not white, although many of his victims were.

As a free speech advocate, I can say without equivocation that I have never witnessed a more consistently censorious group than Black Lives Matter. Disrupting speech is not just a sideshow for them. It is the principal political tactic of the notorious uncivil wrongs group. It is their primary method of drawing attention to their cause because they lack the intellectual fortitude to persuade people to listen based on the content of their arguments.

It is difficult to avoid noticing the common thread when Black Lives Matter charges podiums, assaults speakers, and rips microphones out of speakers' hands. That common thread is not the subject matter of the speeches. It is the skin color of the speakers. The group does not censor its targets because of their political views or their religion. Nor is their targeting based on the speakers' sexual orientation. They select people on the basis of their race in order to accost them for their true crime, which is simply talking while white.

The problem for such racist extremists is that these tactics eventually backfire. By targeting white people with physical assaults and intimidation, they merely reinforce the racist stereotype that blacks are aggressive, assaultive, and violent. It is worth noting that such stereotypes are the alleged causes of black deaths at the hands of white cops in the first place. One might be tempted to say that the group renders itself useless by reinforcing the very notions against which they claim to be fighting.

Of course, to say that Black Lives Matter is useless is an undeserved compliment. They are far worse than useless. By running the police out of black neighborhoods, they are ensuring that black-on-black violence increases. Predictably, as the slaughter of black males increases, the problem of black fatherlessness increases. Consequently, every single negative social indicator skyrockets along with it. They are therefore destroying far more than their own credibility with their tactics. They are destroying their own communities and helping to kill their own neighbors.

Watching this whole sad, pathetic episode in progressive black history makes it abundantly clear that the principal problem in their community is not white racism. It is black culture. That is why it is imperative that we keep black racists from hijacking the national conversation and thereby keeping our attention focused on imaginary problems rather than real ones.

True civil rights leaders have always understood that the remedy for injustice is more speech, not less. That is the reason why Martin Luther King succeeded. It is why Black Lives Matter racists will be nothing more than a sad footnote in the dark history of progressive intolerance.

Only four years later, BLM would be actively involved in the silencing of Mike.

Chapter 72

The Ferguson Effect

July 21, 2016

After two decades of drastic crime reduction, homicides in America's fifty largest cities increased by 17 percent in 2015. Following two decades of employing proactive police techniques whose greatest beneficiaries were residents of poor minority neighborhoods, officers suddenly started to face new obstacles. When working in inner cities, cops found themselves surrounded by jeering crowds whenever they attempted to make an arrest or simply interview citizens.

Predictably, officers then began to retreat from proactive policing techniques. Rather than questioning a suspicious person who appeared to be hiding a gun, they let an armed robbery take place. They began reacting to crimes whose victims were almost always black. Whether they have been proactive or simply reacting, police have been a major presence in black neighborhoods for decades as a result of the persistent and steady breakdown of black families in America.

Much of the demand for a switch from proactive to reactive police techniques came from the press in the wake of the

Ferguson protests of 2014. The media made much of the fact that blacks were more likely than whites to be stopped and questioned by police officers. Lacking in their reports was any mention of disproportionate black involvement in crime, which would have undercut the thesis that blacks were being targeted simply because of their race. In 2012, blacks were responsible for 58 percent of the robberies and 60 percent of the homicides in Missouri. This is despite the fact that blacks are less than 12 percent of the state's total population.

It is also notable that 42 percent of all cop killers whose race has been identified are black. In contrast, little more than a quarter of all homicides by cops involve black victims. This is all relevant evidence in the ongoing public trial of the police. But it has been ruled inadmissible by the ideologically slanted judges among the media elite.

In the wake of their conviction in the court of public opinion, the police retreat from proactive engagement with suspects has had consequences, which have reverberated throughout the nation. For example:

- In Cleveland, homicides for 2015 were up by 90 percent over the previous year.
- In St. Louis, by the end of April 2015, shootings were up by 39 percent, robberies were up by 43 percent, and homicides were up by 25 percent compared to the previous year.
- By the end of May 2015, shootings in Chicago increased by 24 percent, and homicides increased by 17 percent compared to the previous year. The surge continued into 2016 with 100 Chicagoans shot in the first ten days of January.
- Murders in Nashville rose 83 percent in 2015.

- Washington, D.C., ended 2015 with a 54 percent increase in murders.
- Baltimore suffered its bloodiest month since 1972 with forty-five murders in the first thirty days of July 2015. All but two of the murder victims were black.
- Minneapolis saw a 61 percent increase in homicides in 2015.

Meanwhile, Black Lives Matter "civil rights" activists march through the streets of St. Paul chanting "Pigs in a blanket. Fry 'em like bacon." It speaks volumes about the content of their character.

It is no coincidence that cities with large black populations have been hit the hardest by recent crime increases. When black agitators wage a public relations war on the police by hurling wild accusations of racism against white cops, the result is predictable. They simply defend themselves by withdrawing from black communities. This, in turn, leaves black victims of black crime defenseless.

It is telling that the *Washington Post* has started collecting data on police shootings. In the process, they have discovered that 50 percent of police shootings in 2015 were white. Only 26 percent were black. This can hardly be called evidence of bias when one examines black involvement in crime rather than their representation in the general population, which is only 13 percent. Overall blacks were 62 percent of all robbery arrests, 57 percent of all murder arrests, and 45 percent of all assault arrests in the seventy-five largest U.S. counties in 2009. That pattern has been consistent for many years.

Moreover, the vast majority of the 258 black victims of police shootings in 2015 were armed. Those 258 victims were only a fraction of the roughly 6000 blacks who were killed by other blacks in the same year. But black-on-black crime is seldom discussed in polite circles. Social justice warriors are not slaves to political correctness. They are now running the plantation.

In August 2015, a nine-year-old girl was killed in Ferguson when gunfire ripped through her house and then through her body when she was doing her homework on her mother's bed. Yet very few people remember her name. In contrast, they do know the name of Michael Brown—a thug who propelled a movement *[BLM]* by stealing from a black businessman and attempting to wrestle a gun from an innocent white cop he had just assaulted.

It should be readily apparent that today's "civil rights" activists are not really social justice warriors. They are no longer trying to help society or even to advance justice. In fact, it is charitable to say that they ever were. They are simply progressive racists with an agenda that is both anti-social and unjust. Like most progressive causes, it is killing the very people it claims to be saving and sustaining its own life with a potent combination of ignorance and propaganda.

In the end, it produces hypocrisy so rank that it cannot be obscured by the smell of rotting corpses.

Author's Note: The sole source of information for this column is Heather Mac Donald's excellent new book *The War on Cops: How the New Attack on Law and Order Makes Everyone Less Safe.*

For more book recommendations, see Chapter 7, "An Anti-Communist Reading List."

Chapter 73

Fascists & Theocrats

August 4, 2016

Several months ago, I received a scathing rebuke from a gay professor whom we will call Rod—because that is his name. He was angered by my insistence that a Christian musician should not be forced to perform at gay weddings. He asserted that the "cost of doing business" is that you must "accommodate" all segments of the population, regardless of your religious beliefs. In other words, he articulated the belief that every single business has to serve every single customer in order to "accommodate the public"—even if that means attending religious services that violate his conscience.

I did not think much of Rod's statement and simply discarded it without a second thought. The reason for my flippancy is that Professor Rod writes to me quite often. He messages me on social media and emails me repeatedly. For a guy who seems to hate me, he almost seems to like me. So I generally ignore him in the hope he will go away.

Last week, however, Professor Rod sent a message that I simply could not discard. He was writing again in anger—this time over my criticism of the NBA for doing business with communist China while simultaneously boycotting North Carolina. With no sense of irony, he actually stated the following: "As a capitalist, you should know that private businesses cannot be forced to do business with anyone against their will."

It was just so rich that it inspired me to make Professor Rod the subject of my weekly column—although I have omitted his last name and institutional affiliation. (Note: I sometimes omit the names of obscure professors when I am convinced that they are simply trying to pick a fight with me to increase their visibility—or to get promoted to an administrative position in the division of diversity and inclusion).

Professor Rod's remarks are significant when taken together because they show how members of the LGBT movement are often falsely accused of supporting fascism. In fact, I often hear them referred to as "homo fascists"—and I detest the term because it is inaccurate.

Put simply, LGBT activists are not seeking to have the government control all private businesses—as would be the case if they were truly fascistic. In reality, they are only seeking to have the government control all Christian organizations as well as individual Christian entrepreneurs. If you need any evidence of that, just consider the two positions embodied in Professor Rod's two separate communications:

1. Christian musicians (and photographers and florists and bakers) should be forced against their will to "accommodate" all segments of the population.
2. Secular organizations like the NBA should be allowed to decline anyone's business free from government interference—or, as he put it, "force." In other words, secular

businesses and organizations do not have to accommodate anyone.

Professor Rod's remarks demonstrate clearly that he is not a fascist—simply because a true fascist would try to assume control of all businesses, not just religious ones. His remarks are also significant given that the tenured left regularly accuses the Christian right of trying to set up a "theocracy" in America. In case you didn't yet notice, let me state the obvious point that Professor Rod is a theocrat, not a fascist.

A theocrat is a person who advocates a government ruled by or subject to religious authority. It has become increasingly clear the LGBT movement is theocratic in the sense that it seeks to use the government to purge from the public square all religious ideas that run contrary to their own. Of course, the end result of banning all religious opposition to homosexuality is to make secular humanism the default religion of the entire nation.

But setting up an ideal theocracy requires mandatory worship—and that calls for a shift in the tactics of the LGBT movement. For years, they have relied upon various tactics such as political campaign disclosure laws to identify Christian businesses and individuals who contribute to pro-family causes and support traditional marriage ballot measures. The obvious goal of this "transparency" push is to launch boycotts against businesses (and to get them thrown off college campuses in the name of inclusion). Such measures are also meant to prompt shareholders to pressure companies to fire their Christian CEOs—all for the crime of having convictions and the desire to lobby for them in the political arena.

As Professor Rod's remarks demonstrate unequivocally, the movement has now shifted gears and is seeking to force businesses to actively affirm homosexuality. Make no mistake about the fact that churches are their next targets. That is precisely why they went to the courts to achieve the goals they could not accomplish at the ballot box. They are gearing up for a war of "competing constitutional interests." The conflict will test the question of whether religious freedom is trumped by sexual liberty, which has now taken on a religious dimension.

In the end, the theocratic LGBT movement envisions an America where every knee bends, every head bows, and every tongue confesses that homosexuality is good. Thus, the movement has become more like a denomination than a quest for "civil rights." Pretty soon their denomination will have the full backing of the state. Professor Rod said it best when he warned prophetically that, "You will violate the law at your own peril."

Compelled affirmation is truly the mark of a primitive theocracy. In the end, it is one that legalizes rape in the midst of orgiastic proclamations that love has won the day.

Mike was ahead of his time. When I read this in 2016, I thought he was being hyperbolic. I no longer feel that way.

Chapter 74

Ministers of Multiculturalism

August 26, 2016

Recently, a friend sent me a text after returning from church with his family. He had been a member of the congregation for two months and up to that point had been enjoying the sermons immensely. But then something strange happened that Sunday morning. One of the pastors, a young black man, decided to preach on the issue of race and criminal justice. My friend and his wife were so upset with the overtly leftist overtones in the message that they refused to take communion.

After getting the text, I placed a call to my friend to get some additional context. He described the sermon as one that endorsed the basic claims of Black Lives Matter (BLM) without actually mentioning the group by name. I decided to follow up on the call by going to the church website to see if they had an article or blog post on the issue. Sure enough, they did. I read it and found two things that disturbed me enough to urge my friend to consider finding another church. I was also motivated to write a column warning readers about the dangers of similar churches.

The two specific problems I found on the church's website were as follows: 1) The pastor claimed that the targeting of minorities for disparate treatment is an "undisputed fact" in our culture and 2) The pastor described the church as one that aspired to be "multicultural." The first of these two errors is minor. The second one is not. One cannot grasp fully the first error without a proper understanding of the second. Nonetheless, I will start with a critique of the first statement.

The claim that the targeting of minorities for "disparate treatment" within the criminal justice system in an "undisputed fact" suffers from only one flaw—namely that it is demonstrably false. The claim is disputed often, and rightly so. Within the context of police shootings of blacks, which was the specific context of the black pastor's sermon, some basic statistical facts would cause any reasoned observer to reject the claim of disparate treatment.

It is indeed true that blacks are disproportionately victims of police shootings. Although they are only 12 percent of the population, blacks constitute 25 percent of the victims of police shootings. But there is a pretty simple explanation for that: **Blacks commit nearly half of the violent crimes in America.**

In other words, blacks are bringing themselves into contact with the police by committing far more than their fair share of violent criminal acts. It is hardly disparate treatment to say that consequences are attached to the way you treat others. The black pastor may complain about how he "lives in fear" of being shot every time he is pulled over by a white officer. In reality, he has a much greater chance of being a victim of "disparate treatment" by another black man who wishes to kill him—sometimes merely for the "crime" of wearing the wrong color shirt in the wrong part of town.

Given that blacks commit nearly half of the violent crimes in America, one could say that the police are using considerable restraint with black suspects. After all, if only a quarter of the victims of fatal police shootings are black, then they are actually underrepresented as victims of police shootings. To put it another way, given their involvement in violence, we would expect blacks to be shot in greater numbers relative to the overall population.

Furthermore, the data show that blacks do not return the favor by showing a reciprocal level of restraint toward law enforcement officers. Consistent with their overall involvement in violent acts, blacks are responsible for over 40 percent of the cop killings in America. It bears repeating: **Blacks only make up 25 percent of the victims of police shootings but are responsible for over 40 percent of the shootings of police.**

It is now worth turning attention to the overarching question of why the pastor asserts that the targeting of minorities for disparate treatment within the criminal justice system is an "undisputed fact." The answer to that question is pretty simple: **It is because he's the pastor of a "multicultural" church.**

Multiculturalism doesn't mean what you probably think it means. Every church is "multicultural" in the literal sense. Even the relatively homogeneous church of my youth was made up of people from different cultures. There was one black family and one Asian Indian family. There were also dozens of states and several regions represented in our congregation. Even though it was predominantly white, it's not as if people from other cultures were banned. All people were welcomed.

But that is not what "multicultural" means in the present context. When a pastor specifically claims that his church is "multicultural," and he infuses that term into the identity of the church, it means something very different. It means that he is a truth denier and a slave to political correctness. Put simply, multiculturalism has come to mean an acceptance of cultural relativism. And that by necessity involves a rejection of the idea of absolute truth. Try squaring that with John 14:6.

In the final analysis, the multiculturalist does not care whether black men really are the victims of targeting by white cops. The multiculturalist only cares whether blacks perceive that they are victims of "disparate treatment." If they say they are, then his commitment to being "multicultural" obliges him to nod in agreement—or should I say nod in appeasement?

That is the problem with multicultural churches in general. They are not dedicated to using truth to influence culture. They are looking to the culture to define truth. It's not the approach that was used by Jesus of Nazareth. In fact, it's the polar opposite. But being a member of a "multicultural" church does have its advantages. It helps the follower's self-esteem and helps him retain popularity in "the community."

In other words, it helps him claim to follow Jesus without risking cultural crucifixion.

Mike addresses pastoral courage and clarity again in Chapter 86, "Bold About What."

CHAPTER 75

Academic Elites and Ignoble Duchesses

October 26, 2016

Occasionally, I receive email notices that the Upperman African American Center at UNC-Wilmington (UNCW) is sponsoring a "forum" on a hot topic of academic interest. Whenever I receive such notices, I am reminded that their definition of a "forum" is not the same one most people employ. Most people consider a forum to be a place conducive to the open exchange of ideas. But a "forum" at one of our state-sponsored "diversity" centers is meant do one thing and thing only: to reinforce a false narrative of victimhood and oppression that helps advance the so-called progressive political agenda.

One such example was the "forum" that was held at UNCW in the wake of the Ferguson riots in the fall semester of 2014. I actually went to Ferguson and interviewed protestors during the height of the tensions *[also told in Chapter 53, "Hands Up, Don't Abort"]*. Given my firsthand knowledge of the protests, it would have made sense to invite me to participate in the "forum." But no such invitation was forthcoming. Instead, two leftist professors from my department (Sociology and Criminology) were extended invitations.

Although one participant was a part-time instructor without tenure, her inclusion in the forum made sense. She is a lawyer, and she is black. Therefore, she probably had some unique insights to offer. But the other professor's inclusion was more difficult for me to comprehend. She is a middle-aged white woman from Maine—a state that was approximately 98.4 percent white when the professor graduated from college. Given her lack of experience living among black folks, why was she invited? The answer is simple: **ideology.**

In stark contrast to their input, I could have contributed to the event by offering actual evidence from interviews I conducted on the scene at Ferguson during the week of the riots. For example, one young black man I interviewed had been living in Ferguson for twenty-seven years. He claimed that young black men were being secretly murdered and buried by the police on a regular basis in Missouri. He also claimed that the harassment of blacks was routine in Ferguson. When I specifically asked how *he* had been harassed, he claimed he was once pulled over for speeding without probable cause. He was let go without a ticket.

A middle-aged black woman I interviewed had also grown up in Ferguson. She could not recount a single instance of mistreatment at the hands of the police. When I asked her why she was there protesting, she said she just "wanted to be a part of history…just like Martin Luther King." When pressed, she could not identify any specific change in the law that would help lead her people to the Promised Land. She just stood by the CNN bus holding a sign saying, "Hands Up, Don't Shoot"—words we now know Michael Brown never uttered.

After UNCW presented students with such an unbalanced discussion (and called it a forum), I had hoped we were done with the topic of alleged white cop on black citizen violence. But alas, the desired closure was not to be. Last week, UNCW's Upperman African American Center announced that it was bringing in diversity expert Duchess Harris all the way from Macalester College. In case you have not heard of her, Harris is the author of numerous academic masterpieces such as "Your Feminism Ain't Like Ours, Because We Are Raising Quvenzhane." When I heard she was coming to UNCW, I wrote Professor Harris the following short note:

> *Dear Professor Harris:*
>
> *I recently received a notice that you will be traveling to UNC-Wilmington to give a speech on the Black Lives Matter movement on October 17th at 11:00 a.m. Because the speech will occur at a time that conflicts with my office hours, I will be unable to attend. As a professor of criminology, I am curious as to whether you intend to address any of the following questions, which I think are crucial to assessing the legitimacy of the Black Lives Matter movement:*
>
> *1. What percentage of violent crime in America is actually committed by blacks?*
>
> *2. As a percentage, how many victims of police shootings are black?*
>
> *3. Finally, when race of offender is known, what percentage of cop killers are black?*
>
> *I think that addressing these questions is crucial to assessing both the motives and legitimacy of the Black*

Lives Matter movement. Accordingly, I am curious as to whether you would be willing to answer these questions now or whether you will address them in your upcoming talk.

Predictably, Harris did not respond. Had she possessed both the knowledge and the intellectual honesty required to answer, here is what Harris would have been forced to admit:

1. Blacks consistently commit over 40 percent of the violent crimes in America. In the case of homicide, they actually commit more than one-half, despite constituting only 12 percent of the general population.
2. About 25 percent of the victims of police shootings are black.
3. When race of killer is known, over 40 percent of cop killers are black.

In other words, given their disproportionate involvement in crime, blacks are actually underrepresented as victims of police shootings. But there is no reciprocity, as blacks are also disproportionately responsible for the murders of police officers.

In other words, the Black Lives Matter movement is built upon a lie. It is based on a narrative that simply does not comport with the data. Of course, the truth does not matter to academic elites. They are not committed to the facts. They are only committed to their visions.

Duchess Harris recently co-wrote a book aimed at twelve- to seventeen-year-olds teaching them about the history of the Black Lives Matter movement. This book will be used as a tool to indoctrinate school children even before they go off to college.

When they get there, the offices of diversity and inclusion will be ready to give a voice to people like Harris who will reinforce that false historical narrative.

In the end, there are two sets of victims of this kind of indoctrination. There are the taxpayers who must pay for it in the short term. There are also the young people who will buy into the false narrative and devote their lives to protesting causes they really don't understand.

Chapter 76

Choose My Words Carefully

November 12, 2016

Author's Note: The following letter is not to be construed as an attack on the CSU-Bakersfield Black Student Union. They are simply misguided. However, it is to be construed as an attack on Black Lives Matter. They are simply evil.

Dear California State University – Bakersfield Black Student Union:

Recently, I had the opportunity to speak at your beautiful campus, which is located in the southern portion of the San Joaquin Valley. As a fan of Merle Haggard and Buck Owens, I was glad to finally visit the town responsible for producing some great country legends as well as that unmistakable Bakersfield country sound. I am thankful that Dwight Yoakam turned me on to that style of music a couple of decades ago. But that's not why I am writing to you today.

While I was impressed overall with the hospitality of the Bakersfield residents, I was somewhat concerned when I heard of your objections to the title of my speech about abortion. I chose the title "All Lives Matter: Abortion and the Case for Human Equality" for a reason. I believe that philosophical arguments for abortion actually undermine human equality. Your assessment of the propriety of the title of my speech should have been made only after hearing what I had to say. But none of you were present for the speech.

It has also come to my attention that you submitted four recommendations for how my title could be reworded in order to avoid offending Black Lives Matter (BLM). I never imagined that after living in this country for over half a century kids less than half my age would be choosing my words for me. In the process of choosing my own words, I never considered the prospect of offending BLM. Having seen them assault speakers on the basis of race and take to the streets chanting "Pigs in a blanket, fry them like bacon," I could not care less whether I offend them. To be frank, they come across as uneducated racists with little concern for the feelings of others. In fact, many of them appear to be sociopaths.

However, since you took the time to provide me with some recommendations, I thought I would return the favor. Please take the time to read the following recommendations, which I am giving to you to pass on to BLM. These are my modest proposals for how BLM can rename its organization in order to be less offensive to thinking Americans like myself.

1. **Slack Lives Matter**. BLM could not exist as an organization without the help of uneducated social justice warriors (SJWs). These people are so slack that they never check a fact. They go through life not realizing that blacks commit close to half of the violence in America but make up only one-quarter of the victims of police shootings. Nor

do they realize that blacks are responsible for a whopping 42 percent of the shootings of police officers. If you are so slack that you don't check facts, you will end up wasting your life protesting things you don't understand. Living a slack life does matter.

2. **Shacked Lives Matter**. Illegitimacy rates have skyrocketed in recent decades. And this matters more than anything. It matters if a man gets a woman pregnant and decides to shack up with her for a little while and then move on—as opposed to marrying her and actually raising the child. If the child is male, the consequences of the father's absence are particularly severe. Put simply, there is a clear and inverse relationship between time spent interacting with dad and time spent interacting with the police. Presently, there is only one racial group in America for which fatherlessness is the rule rather than the exception. To be specific, the black community is now experiencing a whopping 72 percent illegitimacy rate. This simply must be dealt with now and without relying on the government. In fact, government cannot be part of the solution because it is the root of the problem.

3. **Black Lies Matter**. It is not just the racism that undermines the credibility of BLM. It is also the lies. These lies also affect those who are not on board with BLM. In other words, there has been collateral damage. When propaganda gets out and police are afraid of going into black communities, who do you think suffers? It is not white people. It is black people. The lies drive out the police. The absence of police emboldens the black criminal who is now being supervised by no one. Dad is not around.

The cops are not around. Now he has a free hand to commit crime. Unsurprisingly, his victims are almost always other blacks.

4. **Black Dreams Shattered.** There have been around 5000 black people lynched at the hands of the KKK. That is the grand total throughout American history. In contrast, in this year alone there will be an average of over 7000 black babies aborted per week in America. It is high time that black America identified the real enemy. Hint: It rhymes with Banned Parenthood.

In sum, apologizing to and for BLM will never solve the problems of black Americans. In fact, nothing will get better until that racist organization pulls its head out of its collective ass and starts addressing real problems within its own community. My words may sound harsh, but I have little patience for hypocritical racists. Nor do I have patience for those who defend racists.

Note that in my opening I did not address you by your preferred name "African American Student Union." This is not Africa, and you are not Africans. This is America, and you need to act like Americans. You should know that Americans don't tell other Americans what words to use in order to keep from offending people. You choose your words, and I will choose mine.

If you don't like the words I choose, then do the right thing and respond with better speech, not with censorship. Free speech is the ultimate pro-choice position. And I am always in favor of choice as long as it doesn't harm an innocent human being.

Sincerely,
Mike S. Adams

Chapter 77

The Last Birthday Card

December 4, 2016

A few weeks ago *[October 30]*, I had my fifty-second birthday. You don't get any new privileges when you turn fifty-two. Nonetheless, I still love birthdays. Among the many reasons is that I always get a funny card from my parents who retired in The Woodlands, Texas. As long as I can remember, they have always sent me humorous birthday cards. In fact, I can never remember a time when they sent something serious. It's just a family tradition for which I take the blame. Mom says I was born laughing and that probably accounts for much of the levity in the selection of cards.

When I checked the mail on the day before my birthday this year, there was no card from my parents. It was the first time that had ever happened. However, on Monday when I went back to check the mail, an envelope was there with my parents' return address. But this time, something was different. The envelope was addressed to me in my mother's handwriting instead of my father's. I opened it up, removed the card, and read the following:

Can't look at you
without feeling
a surge of pride.

Can't hear your voice
without smiling.

Can't remember
your growing-up years
without a little tug
at the heartstrings.

Can't let your birthday go by
without reminding you
how very much you're loved.

The writing at the end of the card was also my mother's. The reason was that my father, Joe Adams, could no longer hold a pen to write. He was diagnosed with brain cancer in September. By the end of October, he had lost his capacity to do many things he had done before. By November, he had lost the ability even to feed himself. *[He passed away November 21, which may have been after Mike penned this but before it was published.]*

There is a reason for the change in tone of the fifty-second birthday card I received from my parents. When they picked it out, they knew it would be the last one they would ever send to me together. The time for levity had passed. There were some things they had to say. And I am glad they did. It's the best card I have ever received from them or from anyone else. I will hold onto it and cherish it forever. *[And he did. It is now in my possession.]*

I've been preoccupied these last few months, and I've been writing very little. Indeed, this is one of the shortest columns I have ever written. I know that it comes at a time when people are starting to select cards to send to their loved ones. Maybe some of you reading this come from one of those families with a tradition of sending humorous cards for birthdays and holidays. Maybe you've been doing it as long as you can remember. If you are like most people, you never know which ones you send will be your last.

I hope that readers of this short reflection will do themselves and their loved ones a favor this year. When you select your cards, imagine each one you select will be the last one you send to them. This is especially true for those who have had a rift in their families during this election season. Never forget that politics are temporary, and death is permanent.

Just make sure you say the things that need to be said before it is too late. It's taken me over half a century to understand just how important that is.

This reminds me of something else Mike wrote:
The best advice I can give anyone is to assume that each call with a loved one is the last one we will ever have. Unless we are taking people for granted, it does not matter whether we know which conversation is the last. Think about it.

Chapter 78

How to Kill Everyone on Welfare

January 9, 2017

My pro-choice friends kill me sometimes with their kindness and compassion. In return, I try to kill them with sarcasm. However, a recent comment made to me by a self-proclaimed liberal was so callous it deserves a serious response. I will paraphrase the remark, which is one most pro-lifers have heard at some point in their lives:

> "I would rather have hundreds of my tax dollars used to abort an unwanted child now than have hundreds of thousands used for public assistance later."

In case you did not grasp the obvious, that comment is not an example of liberalism. It is an example of eugenics, plain and simple. Furthermore, it is unbecoming of an educated person to even consider such a justification for the taking of innocent life. If you are not completely appalled by that remark, then you probably did not grasp its ramifications. Hence, it may be time to dissect it with a little thought experiment. So try to imagine the following:

> *Ronald Rump is running for president. Some see him as the reincarnation of Reagan. Others see him as a horse's ass. Regardless, he has developed a reputation for making charged comments on the campaign trail. He drops this bombshell in response to a question about what can be done to reduce the welfare rolls, saying, "I think we should just kill everyone who is on welfare."*

First of all, don't take the thought experiment literally. No presidential candidate of either major party would ever make such a suggestion. But it is a thought experiment. So take a moment to think about what would happen if Ronnie Rump really did make such a statement. Would anyone seriously expect his candidacy to survive? Could anything possibly be more offensive than proposing a reduction in the welfare rolls by the simple expedient of killing everyone who is on welfare?

Actually, there is at least one suggestion that is slightly more offensive. In fact, my "liberal" friend already proffered it. Put simply, killing someone who you merely *suspect* might one day wind up on welfare—and who hasn't done anything wrong yet—is about as offensive as it gets. If you still are not appalled, then rethink the ramifications with the help of another brief thought experiment. Imagine the following:

> *A man suspects his wife is about to leave him. He does not want her to stay because he is having an affair. But he knows that the divorce will be expensive. He will likely be paying alimony for years unless and until his*

future ex-wife remarries. So he hires a hit man to kill her. He succeeds and is later caught and charged with conspiracy to commit murder. He is also charged with murder in the first degree because the conspiracy was actually carried into effect.

Now stop and imagine that you have been called in to serve on the jury. Would you vote to convict if the evidence established guilt? Or would you acquit by nullifying the evidence on the basis of a broad moral claim that the killing was justified for reasons of economic expediency?

I should think that no decent person would vote to nullify the evidence under these circumstances. The man's wife may have been unwanted, but that's not her fault. She may have posed a potential and undetermined financial burden on him, but that's not her fault either. What could possibly be more callous than deliberately forking over money to have her exterminated simply to ease a potential financial burden?

Let me answer the question I just posed. As offensive as nullification of the guilty verdict of the hit-man-hiring husband might be, it pales by comparison to what my "liberal" friend would have us do as a matter of public policy. The husband in the thought experiment seeks to fund a one-time killing. My "liberal" friend seeks to justify the existence of a permanent fund used to repeat the same atrocity hundreds, if not thousands, of times over. There is no evidence that she does not want the funding of financially expedient abortions to continue in perpetuity. Without any sense of irony, she calls it liberalism and tries to justify it on the basis of avoiding perceived potential future financial hardship.

We are living in dark times in America. The pessimism is so great that some of my leftist colleagues have even suggested that another Third Reich could eventually occur here in America. On that point, we agree. We should not dismiss the prospect that such a regime could be established here in America. But the party trying to ban abortions won't ever establish it.

Indeed, if fascism ever comes to America, it will be at the hands of self-appointed utopians who are incapable of grasping their own arguments, unwilling to learn from history, yet utterly convinced they have a monopoly on compassion.

Chapter 79

Professor Hypocrite, Tear Down This Door!

March 23, 2017

One of my conservative friends recently suggested that leftist professors should be prohibited from putting political posters and bumper stickers on their office doors. I strongly disagreed and told him I would defend the leftists if he ever tried to interfere with their political speech. But I wouldn't do it just for reasons of principle. I would do it because I enjoy the wealth of good writing material supplied by my more extreme left-wing colleagues—most of them self-described feminists. A case in point is the recent poster that is making its way onto so many faculty office doors on campuses across America. In case you haven't seen one, here is the exact wording of the poster:

>REFUGEES AND IMMIGRANTS
>WELCOMED HERE
>NO MUSLIM BAN
>NO BORDER WALL

OUR COMMUNITIES STAND TALL
MoveOn.org

It's hard to comprehend so much idiocy crammed into such a small space. So just in case you missed some of the more intellectually herniated nuances, let me break them down for you. In just five lines, the leftist professor sporting this sign manages to call attention to five distinct things about her character, her professionalism, and her worldview. They follow in no particular order of importance:

1. **She really isn't looking to bring refugees and immigrants into her office; she is looking to bring like-minded disciples into her classes.** This poster is just one way of letting students know that a leftist who teaches politicized classes for white middle-class social justice warriors occupies the office. Those are the people she is really trying to attract—not refugees and immigrants. If you doubt the veracity of my claim, then just put it to the test. The next time you see such a poster on a professor's door, go find a homeless immigrant. Then, pay him to ask the professor to let him sleep in her office overnight. She'll probably call the university police and have him deported from the campus "community" in a matter of minutes. *[This strikes me as another example of Mike being prescient. At this writing, we are now seeing self-proclaimed "sanctuary cities" balking when "refugees and immigrants" actually show up.]*

2. **There is no Muslim ban, but the professor is too misinformed to know it (or ms-informed if she is a feminist).** Her assertion that she does not ban Muslims is posted to

remind everyone that she is morally superior to those who do support the Muslim ban. But there is no Muslim ban. Therefore, she is morally superior to no one. She is just an angry zealot protesting things that are probably too complex for her to understand.

3. **She locks her doors instead of adopting an open borders practice in her day-to-day living**. Recently, I tried to do one of these professors a favor by letting her know that there really isn't a ban on Muslims entering America. So I went to her office and knocked on her door. But she hadn't yet arrived at work. After I knocked, I checked the door to her office and noticed it was locked. I also noticed that the walls of her office are made of impenetrable cinder blocks. I don't know how all those refugees and immigrants will find shelter if she keeps locking her doors while she is away. Maybe I'm cynical, but I suspect that she has deadbolt locks on the doors of her house too.

4. **She works in a profession lacking diversity**. The first time I saw one of those silly posters on a professor's door, I decided to do a little research. The poster says that her "communities stand tall." By that, she must mean they are "tolerant" and "inclusive." Yet going to her department webpage revealed a different story. A cursory examination of the page showed that every full professor, tenured associate professor, and untenured assistant professor in her department is white. Furthermore, after searching diligently, I couldn't find a single registered Republican in her department.

5. **She is a mouthpiece for Marxist propaganda**. The MoveOn.org logo on her poster really says it all. Anyone who uses this Soros-funded propaganda website as

a means of staying "informed" is a willfully uneducable Marxist. She could have chosen to criticize regimes that are so oppressive they must build walls to keep citizens inside their own countries against their will. Instead, she criticizes countries that are so desirable they must build walls to keep citizens from other countries out. In other words, she is too blinded by utopian notions of cosmic justice to bridge the gap between economic theory and historical reality.

In a nutshell, these posters perform the valuable public service of alerting impressionable youths as to the whereabouts of uninformed, hypocritical zealots posing as objective educators. When students see them on a door, they should not bother knocking. The lights are off, no one is home, and it's better to just move on.

Elsewhere, Mike has a few more choice words:

This trait of being more in love with consumption than production is one shared by most of my socialist colleagues in academia. They base their lives on the idea of taking "from each according to his ability" and giving "to each according to his need." The problem is that they do a better job of articulating their needs than promoting their abilities. This is, of course, because socialists are generally short on abilities. They seek socialism because they think being guaranteed an average outcome is safer than trying to beat the average in a system based on merit, which is otherwise known as ability.

Chapter 80

Life Lines

April 8, 2017

I get tired of hearing pro-abortion choice advocates claim that pro-lifers are really "only anti-abortion" but not "truly pro-life." The motivation behind such attacks is usually political. Typically, the accuser wants to shame a pro-lifer into supporting some massive social program, which ostensibly helps the "already born." As usual, the pro-abortion choice advocate makes the major error of assuming without evidence that the born are humans worthy of support while the unborn are non-humans and thus lacking intrinsic value. That major scientific and philosophic error is compounded by a factual error: **It ignores the massive investment the pro-life movement is making in crisis pregnancy centers, or CPCs.**

Even during the height of the abortion holocaust in the early 1990s, there were two million couples willing to adopt children here in the United States alone. This easily exceeded the 1.5 to 1.6 million children that were being aborted in America annually. Pro-life couples have long been prepared to save lives and to provide good homes for those babies whose lives were spared.

But it gets even better. As the decade progressed, the willingness of pro-lifers to step up and adopt "unwanted" babies was supplemented by another positive trend: **The CPCs actually began to outnumber the abortion clinics.**

Fully appreciating the importance of this requires knowing something about what CPCs actually do. Contrary to pro-abortion choice propaganda, they are not there to shame women into keeping their babies. In fact, such slander against our CPCs is just the opposite of the truth.

The initial trip to a CPC usually results in a pregnancy test. Often, the pregnant woman cannot yet have an ultrasound because she is not far enough along in the pregnancy. Fortunately, many pregnancy centers are fully equipped with the technology and personnel needed to provide ultrasound testing when a woman returns for a second visit.

Our local Life Line Pregnancy Center here in Wilmington, North Carolina, is one such center. They have an ultrasound machine, and they always have nurses on hand to perform the tests and explain the results. The end result of their work is nothing short of miraculous. At Life Line in Wilmington, 89 percent of the women who seek their help in a crisis pregnancy situation end up choosing life over abortion.

But the help does not end there. Life Line also helps the women get connected to a church that can provide them with additional support. Life Line does not provide direct financial assistance to women facing crisis pregnancy situations. They do so indirectly by plugging women into networks that provide needed resources.

If you take a quick survey of the church websites here in Wilmington, you will see that many of them support Life Line Pregnancy Center. The only question is why *every* church does not support a CPC like Life Line. Imagine the impact if all of them did. By some estimates, there are about 750 churches in the Wilmington area alone.

The decision to support a CPC is not one that should be politicized. When it comes to the work of CPCs, we have a rare issue upon which both conservative and liberal Christians can agree—although they may arrive in the same place for somewhat different reasons.

Consider the following:

1. **Conservative Christians want to eliminate abortion and preserve innocent life.** Obviously, the conservative wants to eventually overturn *Roe v. Wade* and save millions of lives. But that is no impediment to saving some lives in the interim by supporting his local CPC. One can attack abortion in both the community and legal realm simultaneously.

2. **Liberal Christians want to eliminate poverty and preserve a woman's bodily autonomy.** Anyone claiming to be liberal should be on board with helping poor women obtain much needed financial support. Furthermore, those who support the idea of a woman doing what she wants with her body would never want a woman to be forced into having an abortion due to economic hardship. Clearly, supporting a CPC is consistent with basic liberal principles.

At all times, we must remember that abortion only exists in America with the permission of the church. It is past time for congregations with different political views to unify and do something about it. We are all commended to care for women and children. We are also reminded that sin is not just doing something bad—it is also knowing the right thing to do and refusing to do it.

For further reading: See James 1:27 and James 4:17.

James 1:27: Religion that God our Father accepts as pure and faultless is this: to look after orphans and widows in their distress and to keep oneself from being polluted by the world.

James 4:17: If anyone, then, knows the good they ought to do and doesn't do it, it is sin for them.

See also Chapter 61, "Fat, Ugly, and Morally Inconsistent."

Chapter 81

My New Victim-Centered Tuition Proposal

July 6, 2017

Dear UNC President Spellings:

For years, my opposition to UNC diversity initiatives has been a source of controversy across our seventeen-campus system. Many have assumed that my opposition has been a function of personal prejudice or insensitivity to the needs of various "disenfranchised" groups. In reality, it is a function of my belief that people should be judged according to individual character traits, not group stereotypes. However, despite years of opposition to UNC's victim-centered diversity movement, it appears that my side has lost. Accordingly, I write to you today with an offer to join the war against white privilege and ultimately make your long-term vision a reality on each campus in the UNC system.

As you know, we have traditionally promoted diversity by providing a sliding scale for students in terms of admission requirements. The theory was that we could neutralize white privilege by making whites score higher on standardized tests in order to be admitted to one of the UNC schools. Ultimately, we have failed in the goal of making our campuses less white because we have failed to account for overriding economic considerations. My plan will fix that once and for all. It involves two very simple steps.

1. *We need an immediate $10,000 tuition increase for incoming white students.* Obviously, if we are going to include more marginalized groups on our campuses, we need to make room for them. This tuition hike will help accomplish the goal. Critics who say this is racist are wrong. Some whites who are penalized by the hike will have an opportunity to benefit from some of my proposed diversity exemptions, which will help offset the costs of the initial hike.

2. *We need an immediate $2,000 tuition decrease for students who come from marginalized groups in our society.* The money we gain from charging higher tuition to students benefitting from white privilege can be used to fund my proposed tuition cuts for students who promote victim-centered diversity. A list of eligible groups is provided below with justifications for their inclusion on the list.

Women: Critics will point out that our campuses already have more female students than male students. While this is technically true, it ignores our important obligations to the federal government. In recent years, the feds have made it clear that universities will not be the beneficiaries of federal funding unless they continue to promote the myth that there is an epidemic of sexual assault and sexual harassment occurring in America. The more female students we have, the more complaints we will have. Many, or perhaps most, of those complaints will be false. But that is beside the point. Universities are no longer concerned with promoting truth. We are only concerned with identity politics.

Blacks: When it comes to diversity and inclusion, black students matter. We still owe them for slavery. Granted, it has been more than a century and a half since the Civil War. But some white North Carolinians think it is still being fought. The least we can do to repay blacks for the trauma of seeing an occasional Confederate flag is to give them a break on their tuition. This is far better than bringing them in on athletic scholarships and offering them fake classes in African American Studies.

LBGTQIA (and other alphabetically marginalized people): We know that many students decide to experiment sexually while they are in college. A tuition break will just encourage some of them to start experimenting early. If students are allowed to commit to four years of service in the military for help with their college tuition, then there should be a similar benefit to reward those enlisting in the sexual revolution for four years.

Illegal Immigrants: Trump is making these richly diverse people rare. Hence, we must recruit them while we can. In addition to the obvious out-of-state tuition waiver, we need to give them the additional tuition cut. Every college campus in North Carolina should be a sanctuary city.

Muslims: Trump has not actually started banning and deporting Muslims. But most "social science" and humanities professors think that is happening. So we need to start bringing them to campus in order to give these professors someone to protect, which, in turn, will give their lives meaning. If our diversity mission succeeds, many will graduate as atheists, which might actually save them from eventual deportation!

Social Justice Warriors: This is bound to be controversial given that most social justice warriors are bored middle-class white kids. But we need to face the reality that we can't eliminate *all* white people from campus, regardless of how desirable that may be. The very least we can do is to make sure that the dwindling white minority feels as guilty as possible during their tenure in the UNC system. Even if it is only a process of self-flagellation, it will be a worthy goal. Guilt can be a powerful tool for social reform.

It should go without saying that my proposed group exemptions are cumulative in nature. A black woman can earn a $4,000 tuition credit, a black lesbian can earn a $6,000 tuition credit, a black transgendered illegal immigrant can earn $8,000 (provided he becomes a she), and so on. There is no limit to what a student can accomplish so long as he, she, undecided, or other is willing to take a stand against the status quo.

It should also go without saying that there will be no need for oversight in implementing this new system. We will simply defer to student perception and trust that they are precisely who they claim to be. Those who say they are women are women, those who say they are black are black, and so on. Once we have rejected the notion of truth, we'll no longer live in fear of "falsity."

I hope that you will take my plan as seriously as I've always taken your commitment to institutional diversity.

Sincerely,
Mike S. Adams
Professor and Community Disorganizer

Chapter 82

Never Underestimate a Father's Love

August 6, 2017

This also appears in the book Life and How to Live It *(2023).*

I have a lot of conversations with young people who complain of a broken relationship with one or more of their parents. After listening to their concerns, I always take the time to tell them about the last disagreement I had with my father while he was still alive. It's impossible to hear that story without realizing that we don't fully understand our parents until they are gone.

In December of 2013, I went home to The Woodlands, Texas, to see my parents for Christmas. *[This was their final home after they were fully retired. Mike considered moving there as well after he retired.]* I didn't know that it was going to be a rough visit until my dad asked me to go into his office to speak privately. Those private conversations with Dad were infrequent, but they never turned out well. On this occasion, Dad was telling me that they had decided to sell the house and move into a retirement community.

I was not happy to hear the news *[nor was I]*. I loved that house *[so did I]* and hated to see them sell it. But even more than that, I hated to see the beginning of the inevitable march toward the end. The move from the house to the retirement community was just a first step in that march. Next would be the move from the retirement community to the nursing home. And from there, the next move would be from the nursing home to the cemetery. No one wants to get started down that path.

That day, I was bothered by more than just my dad's decision. I was also bothered by his resolve, which I thought crossed the line into belligerence. When he announced his decision, Dad looked me straight in the face and said, "Son, I know this new place will be expensive, but I don't give a damn. I want to live my last years in luxury. I hope I die as soon as I've written my last check emptying my bank account. I certainly don't care about leaving anything to my children."

I was shocked to hear my father say that. It wasn't because I needed any of his money. I started preparing for retirement long before he died *[me too]*, and I am not at all concerned about my finances. It was just the belligerence I could not handle. His tone seemed pointlessly harsh.

I could not make sense of it. Later, I called my brother to share my concern about the way Dad had acted. *[I remember that, and I was also disconcerted.]* But nothing would make sense until my final conversation with my dad, which was three years later.

I will never forget that last coherent conversation with my dad as he was dying of cancer. His weight had dropped down to 120 pounds, and his eyes were sunken in his face as he calmly looked at me and said, "Son, I am not afraid to die. All I want is for someone to take care of my wife."

During that conversation, Dad calmly explained the financial arrangements he had made for Mom in anticipation of his passing. Finally, he directed me to a drawer where I could access all of his passwords and find up-to-date documentation of all his accounts. I was stunned at his methodical preparation and attention to detail.

It wasn't until after my dad died that I learned three very important things about the kind of man he really was. They follow in no particular order of importance:

First, the fact that my dad never bought anything nice for himself was not because he didn't have money. Dad lived modestly all his life because he wanted to make sure he had put something away to care for Mom in case he died first. He also wanted to save enough so that his kids would inherit something after both their parents had passed.

Second, Dad never really moved into a nice all-inclusive retirement home for selfish reasons. In fact, he would have preferred to die in his own home. But he knew there were problems with their health. Instead of burdening us with his worries, he sold off all his real property, his RV, and his truck to consolidate his finances and make things simple for us once he died. He also wanted a community where people would cook and clean for my mom once he was gone—instead of leaving her with a kitchen and a big house to manage.

Finally, Dad wanted to leave us with the impression that he was spending his savings because he did not want us to expect anything from him. That way, we would worry about our future enough to save for ourselves. He didn't care if it would make us angry with him. He was more concerned about loving his sons than being loved in return.

Earthly recognition meant nothing to Dad, but duty meant everything. That's why he was a great man. Yours might be just as great, even though you might not know it until he is gone.

I am grateful Dad gave us one of the best gifts that a father can give: the gift of self-reliance. Mike and I both worked hard and were successful in our respective careers. We were never on food stamps or welfare. We were not socialists. We were not entitled. We accepted personal responsibility for our own lives. And there is another dimension to this in the sense that Dad's own self-reliance led to yet another gift: the gift of not being a burden on his children in his old age. Thank you, Dad. I am determined to follow your good example.

By the way, Mike is focused on Dad in this article, but Mom was totally on board with all this; they worked together. One didn't drag the other out of the house. After Dad passed, she was responsible with her finances until the end and carried on the strategy that she and Dad had begun. Also, I appreciated how they downsized in a stepwise fashion. They were not hoarders. They did not leave a mess behind for us to clean up. Conversely, I imagine we have all dealt with or heard of individuals who failed to get their affairs in order and refused to cooperate with their family, leaving a big mess behind. Literally and figuratively.

Finally, I want to clarify that although Mike wrote about Dad in glowing terms, Mike was not idolizing or glamorizing our father. There is no denying that Dad had his rough edges, and we had our issues with him, but Mike wisely chose to focus on the good because Dad did, in fact, have positive effects on his children—and in the end, that is what is important.

Chapter 83

Letter to an Aging Communist

October 30, 2017

Dear Gary:

It was a pleasure to read your recent letter to the editor in our local newspaper. I had nearly forgotten about you, as I have only seen you once since you retired as professor emeritus of sociology here at UNC by the Sea. You will recall that our last encounter was the day your wife was successfully sued in federal court for violating the First Amendment. Thus, it is no coincidence that you have drawn my attention by writing an article urging young people to violate the First Amendment rights of campus speakers by using techniques of violence and vandalism. I guess it is asking too much to expect an old communist to learn a new trick. Nonetheless, I am going to try by offering a rebuttal to your grossly irresponsible manifesto. Please find my un-italicized responses to your words, which are indented and in italics.

> *Congratulations to the university students who are aggressively confronting ultra-right wing speakers on their*

campuses. Why these people are asked to speak in the first place is beyond me.

Before I proceed, let me call you out for your cowardice. You are careful not to make specific references to the kind of "aggression" you are applauding. But you and I both know you are applauding both the interpersonal violence employed by protestors at Middlebury College and the vandalism displayed by protestors at UC-Berkeley.

> *Through the ages the university has been a citadel for differing ideas, critical thinking, and debating varying points of view. Today the vast majority of lectures at universities span the gamut of political and social ideologies. The very idea that speech is being stifled by these students is absurd. While I support the current student protests, they are not the norm, contrary to what we hear.*

Before I proceed further, let me also comment on your gross intellectual dishonesty. There is simply no one with an IQ above room temperature who believes that there is ideological diversity in terms of who is invited and allowed to speak on our university campuses. The sole controversy is over whether the current lack of ideological diversity is good or bad for higher education. I take the position that it is bad. You take the position that it is good. In that sense, I am both more liberal and tolerant than you are.

> *However, to provide a platform for white supremacists, sexists, homophobes, and others who would divide us violates the integrity of the academy. It should not be the*

> *responsibility of the university to provide a venue for the intolerant to air their vitriol. Let them spew their spiteful positions in other arenas. The divisive views of the far-right wing demean the academic environment and add nothing whatsoever that is in anyway becoming to the educational experience.*

Justice William O. Douglas once said of free speech that it "may indeed best serve its high purpose when it induces a condition of unrest, creates dissatisfaction with conditions as they are, or even stirs people to anger." You, on the other hand, would seek to ban all speech that is "divisive." By mixing together the categories of "white supremacy," "sexism," and "homophobia," you tip your hand as to what you consider "divisive views." You would ban not just the white supremacist but also the person who opposes abortion or same-sex marriage. By "divisive views," you simply mean "ideas that stir Professor Emeritus Gary Faulkner to anger."

Of course, the propensity to ban all views with which you disagree makes intellectual atrophy inevitable. Such atrophy is on full display when you argue that the university should not "provide a venue for the intolerant." Somehow, you seem unable to grasp the self-refuting nature of your claim. By arguing that we should be intolerant of speech that is intolerant, you negate your own right to speak.

> *I trust these motivated students—our daughters and sons—are able to withstand the onslaught from those of the self-righteous left and right, who have been far too quick to wrap themselves around the First Amendment on this matter.*

This is priceless. In your view, the thugs who are inciting violence and vandalizing our campuses are the ones under "onslaught." And the onslaught is coming from both the left and right. And they are acting irrationally by embracing the First Amendment and criticizing those who would riot. This is classically Orwellian. I am surprised that you stopped short of calling the rioters the ministers of peace.

> *Consider that these students see a different reality, one wherein the time-honored and dignified exchange of ideas at the academy is now threatened by an intrusion of spite, division, and bigotry.*

I do not believe these students see a different reality. I believe they are completely detached from reality. And so are you, Gary. The way to bring the "dignified exchange of ideas" is not by rioting in order to silence opposing views. That is called a heckler's veto. If you were possessed of a sufficient understanding of the Bill of Rights—perhaps just enough to pass high school civics—you would understand that.

Gary, for decades, you taught about the need for a Marxist revolution in America. But you lacked the courage to translate your political ideas into reality. Now, in your declining years, you are calling upon young people to incite the kind of violence needed to impose your worldview on those you have failed to persuade.

I would encourage you not to send them into harm's way. Those of us who are staunch defenders of the First Amendment also tend to be staunch defenders of the Second Amendment. And you can bank on the fact that all proceeds from this column will be spent on ammunition.

CHAPTER 84

Cowards in the Academic Trenches

November 16, 2017

The problem with my leftist colleagues really isn't their politics. It is their lack of courage. And it is getting worse. Granted, I have long heard reports of professors abusing students in the classroom. But those reports have drastically increased since the election of 2016. I would like to provide just a few examples before commenting on the effects such cowardly abuse is having on students and on the general campus climate:

- A professor was giving a pro-Black Lives Matter lecture. A student countered the professor by making the rather obvious observation that "all lives matter." Upon hearing it, the professor denounced his student as a racist three times in front of the entire class. Each time she tried to explain herself, the professor shouted "racist!"

- On the first day of class, a professor circulated her syllabus with a clause telling students they were banned from making "disrespectful" remarks during class discussion.

Over the course of the next three and a half months, the professor repeatedly claimed that all white police officers are racists and that simply aspiring to be a police officer is evidence of racism. Students were prevented from rebutting the professor by the selectively enforced ban on "disrespectful speech." She equated denial of racism with racism, which she classified as inherently disrespectful.

- A professor told his freshman students that anyone who voted for Trump is both a racist and a fascist. A teenaged student raised her hand to offer her non-racist and non-fascistic reasons for supporting Trump, albeit reluctantly. The professor shook his fist at her and shouted "shut up!" repeatedly until the student finally gave up.

- A professor hurled profanities about Trump and Pence in a classroom tirade. When a student countered that Pence is a "good man," he was told that he was mentally ill and needed to go to the counseling center to get "professional help" before returning to class. The accusation that the student suffered from mental illness was repeated in front of dozens of students.

It is unsurprising that students learn from their professors. Generally speaking, that is what they are there to do. So it comes as no surprise that the increase in uncivil classroom conduct by professors is being accompanied by an increase in uncivil conduct by students across our campus. Several members of the College Republicans (CR) group recently found that out when they decided to host a speech about free speech by the author of this column. Some of the more troubling incidents surrounding the event include the following:

- An Iraq War veteran and current UNCW student was posting club flyers for weeks when he noticed they were being torn down. After he went to replace them, he started to monitor the bulletin board. In the process, he caught a feminist student in the act of tearing down his flyers. When confronted, she peppered him with an f-bomb-laced tirade. A few professors approached upon hearing all the commotion. They simply stood by and listened while the feminist verbally abused the veteran.

- After the female president of the CR hung flyers advertising the free speech event, they were torn down. She stapled the next bunch of flyers and left a note promising to hang two for every one torn down. A male student left a note calling the female student and her friends "c*nts." Campus feminists were so outraged they marched on Washington, D.C. Just kidding. They didn't care.

- Days before the speech, the same student defaced more flyers. This time, instead of directing the c-word toward the women, he attacked the speaker with defamatory statements. Specifically, he claimed the speaker was sued for divorce after his wife discovered he liked to "f*ck dogs." The self-professed communist and Antifa supporter was reported to the administration for stealing and defacing flyers. Unlike communism itself, his fate is yet to be determined.

- Finally, the speech day arrived. After the speech itself, no leftists tried to ask questions during the Q&A session. This is despite the fact that the humble and awesome speaker assured those in attendance that the First

Amendment equally protects both respectful and disrespectful questions.

- The day after the speech, the students who waived their free speech rights in the Q&A started putting up signs on campus referring to the speaker as a "c*ck." The ringleader previously interned for the Democratic Party. I know you're shocked.

Readers should immediately discern the obvious parallel between the antics of these cowardly professors and their unhinged student followers. The professors shut down dialogue in the classroom and repeatedly insult students who disagree with them. Similarly, leftist students forgo invitations to engage in dialogue with conservatives. Lacking the power to control their fellow students, they refrain from face-to-face attacks and instead attack their fellow students anonymously. This tactic is employed unless, of course, they are actually caught in the act of tearing down their opponents' speech and must therefore resort to in-your-face hysteria.

My Marxist colleagues are not true revolutionaries. They are cowards in a civil war of their own creation. And they are poisoning the academic climate with their toxic and highly contagious intellectual cowardice. Each one of them should be dishonorably discharged for the crime of academic malpractice.

Regrettably, tenure prevents any prospect of justice. Thus, the freedom to perpetuate tyranny prevails.

See also Chapter 4, "The Abolition of Tenure."

Chapter 85

The Buck Stops Here

December 13, 2017

The Colorado court system is gearing up to hear another case involving exemptions from state public accommodations laws. The case raises the novel question of whether artists in the adult film industry in Colorado have a right to refuse to lend their artistic talents to pornographic film productions they deem to be objectionable. The ACLU is arguing that adult film stars bear no such right and that the United States Constitution compels their involuntary servitude. The Colorado Supreme Court will hear oral arguments in Buck v. Costanza in early January.

The case began to unfold when G. Louis Costanza visited Buck Naked Productions in July of 2016 in order to commission the services of CEO George Buck for a proposed film project. The proposed project, called *The Birth of a Notion,* is a silent film depicting the history of the LGBT movement in America. By Costanza's own admission, the script contains multiple graphic scenes depicting sexual conduct between same-sex couples. Based on the film's content, Buck refused to lend his services as an adult film director and actor. This is despite the fact that Buck has directed and acted in numerous adult films depicting sexual conduct between heterosexual couples.

Longstanding Colorado state law prohibits public accommodations, including businesses open to the public, such as Buck Naked Productions, from refusing service based on characteristics like race, religion, or sexual orientation. Thus, Costanza filed a complaint with the Colorado Civil Rights Division contending that Buck Naked Productions violated Colorado's Anti-Discrimination Act. Following an investigation and hearings, the Colorado Civil Rights Commission determined that the film actor and director illegally discriminated against Costanza when he refused him service.

In August of 2017, the Colorado Court of Appeals unanimously affirmed the Commission's order, finding that Buck Naked Productions discriminated because of sexual orientation in violation of state law. The court also concluded that application of Colorado's Anti-Discrimination Act did not infringe on Buck's freedom of speech or on his free exercise of artistic expression. Buck appealed the ruling, and the Colorado Supreme Court will hear oral arguments in January.

In an exclusive interview, Buck responded to charges that homophobia motivated his refusal to lend his services to the gay film production: "It's not that I have anything against gay people. Some of my best friends are gay. I'm just not into that sort of thing. It would seem that Costanza would have better luck if he found adult film stars who were actually gay. They could certainly put on a more convincing performance. Furthermore, there's no shortage of them in Hollywood or right here in Denver where Buck Naked Productions is located."

Sarah Kate Ellis, president and CEO of GLAAD, sees things differently. She stated, "With his naked bigotry, George Buck is attempting to roll back our nation's progress by pushing a twisted 'artistic conscience' exemption into law. The twisted narrative he has masterminded is part of an insidious strategy that has been pushed by homophobic bigots for decades with the goal of unraveling hard-fought non-discrimination protections for the LGBTQ community."

While the Colorado case is just starting to make headlines, a similar case involving wedding photographers is unfolding in Albuquerque. Previously, the New Mexico Supreme Court decided that public accommodation law requires Christian photographers to work at gay weddings even if they have a religious objection to doing so. A pending case will decide whether the photographers will be required to photograph the honeymoon in its entirety after the official ceremony is over.

The ACLU will be representing the gay honeymooners in the New Mexico case. GLAAD will be filing an amicus brief on their behalf. Meanwhile, in Colorado, the Supreme Court will have to decide whether the respondent is wearing new clothes and whether the petitioner will be wearing any.

Author's Note: Many readers will not be Swift enough to comprehend this column. Others will consider it to be a satirical masterpiece.

Mike's regular readers enjoyed his satire and looked forward to it. His adversaries chose to be offended by it and tried to silence it. As Mike once said: "If a conservative doesn't like a talk show host, he switches channels. Liberals demand that those they don't like be shut down."

By the way, "Costanza" and "Buck Naked" are references to Seinfeld, one of Mike's favorite TV shows—specifically, "The Outing" (Season 4, Episode 17), which originally aired on February 11, 1993.

Chapter 86

Bold About What

January 25, 2018

Every now and then, I visit other churches in order to see what kinds of traditions they observe and what kinds of issues they tackle in their weekly worship services. Last weekend, I visited a non-denominational church. As I write this column on a Thursday morning, I am on my fourth day of trying to figure out what the pastor actually said, if anything. To be frank, I suspect that the pastor is still trying to figure out what he actually said, if anything.

The thesis of the sermon, which was given to a church heavily populated with college students, seems to have been that Christians need to be "bold in their faith." I only inferred that was the pastor's thesis because he said "you need to be bold in your faith" about fifty times. Apparently, this was deeply inspirational to many of those present because I kept hearing people shout back at the pastor with phrases like "tell it," "bring it," and "preach it." Fortunately, none of the congregants actually hurled their undergarments on the stage as the pastor was "bringing it." For a while there, I was worried.

Even though people seemed to be enjoying themselves, I saw the pastor's message as a lost opportunity. Something seemed to be missing to me. So I did what I often do in situations where I think the pastor may have missed the mark. I asked myself what I would have done differently had I been preaching the sermon. Specifically, what would I have said? Here's what I came up with:

Young people, many of you are starting out a new semester in college. Unless this is your first semester, you know you will be attacked for your beliefs. Worse, your professors will actually try to destroy your faith while you are in college. They will do this in a number of predictable ways each semester.

First, your professors will tell you that science and religion are incompatible. They will even go so far as to say that science has disproved the existence of God. To make matters worse, these lectures are most common among professors in departments like education, English, and sociology. In other words, the lectures are usually coming from professors with no expertise in science.

Something unusual happens not long after the professor has pledged his allegiance to science. Inevitably, he will show a willingness to throw science out the window when it is necessary to advance the cause of sexual liberty. The first casualty in this selective war on science is the unborn human. Despite a clear consensus in the science of embryology, which says the unborn is a distinct, living, and whole human being from the point of conception, your professor will insist the embryo is merely an undifferentiated "clump of cells." This is how he justifies the intentional dismemberment of his fellow humans.

The professor's war on science will not end with attacks on the unborn. The next predictable attack will be on the concept of gender. Insisting that the male/female gender binary is somehow antiquated, the professor will throw biology out the window, again in the name of sexual liberty. Even your feminist professors will do this, somehow missing the fact that declaring gender to be a "useless concept" renders their previous research on gender discrimination useless.

Finally, your professors will claim that there is no objective basis for truth or morality. Elevating hypocrisy to a Zen artform, these professors will tell you this after they have handed out the course syllabus outlining their policies on academic dishonesty. In other words, those who insist that nothing is really objectively true or wrong will punish you because it is somehow wrong to be dishonest with them. Thus, they insulate themselves from the consequences of their own worldview. But everyone else is expected to live with the consequences of the professor's bad ideas.

For far too long, we have been ignoring this nonsense. We have been coming to church to hear feel good sermons and to shout "bring it" at a pastor who really isn't bringing anything. It feels good for an hour or so. Then, we return to the cultural battlefield utterly unequipped. But all of that changes today.

We are about to pass around the offering plate. Every single dollar we collect will be used to equip young people to recognize the dangerous ideas that are polluting our culture today. If you are a high school or college student who is at least sixteen years old, I want to ask you to take two weeks out of your summer to train your mind so you can learn exactly why you need to be bold and exactly how to do it in today's culture. Before you commit, take a few minutes to visit the Summit Ministries website to see what we are asking you to do.

I am excited about creating this new opportunity for so many of you. In the past, our pastors have admonished us to "be bold" without giving specifics. The reason such pastors prefer to speak in code when they talk about boldness is because they are simply devoid of boldness. In fact, they are spineless. But there is no room for spineless hypocrisy among those charged with carrying out the Great Commission.

That is all I have for you today. Next week, I am going to begin a new series on defending the unborn from a scientific and philosophical perspective. If you wish to avoid the subject of abortion and instead attend a church dedicated to making congregants feel comfortable by avoiding serious topics altogether, we can help you. We have compiled a comprehensive list of dead churches as well as dead college ministries. Their names and contact information are provided in a pamphlet you can pick up at the welcome desk in the fellowship hall.

I hope you'll join me here next week instead. I intend to bring it.

Mike brought it, all right—every time he spoke or wrote.

Chapter 87

Starkville Pride

March 12, 2018

Most of my conservative friends understand that the current war on so-called offensive speech poses a serious threat to the future of the republic. Many of them understand that it is particularly dangerous because hypocrites posing as classical liberals wage it in a selective manner. Thus, conservatives must be careful that they engage this war in a principled manner. Unfortunately, with their recent efforts to shut down a gay pride parade in my former home of Starkville, Mississippi, some conservatives have demonstrated a disturbing lack of principle. Accordingly, I wish to go on the record in support of Starkville Pride and in opposition to conservative residents who wish to censor them.

Those objecting to the issuance of a parade permit for Starkville Pride have registered at least two objections, both of which are fairly easy to rebut. First, there is the concern that Starkville Pride is seeking an endorsement from the city of Starkville, including actual monetary support for the event. Second, there is the concern that the gay pride parade will involve public exhibitions of lewd behavior.

If Starkville Pride is indeed seeking an endorsement or sponsorship for their parade, this cannot be used as a justification for denying them a permit altogether. Put simply, there are only three things a government can do when it comes to human behavior: it may prohibit, permit, or promote. When that behavior takes the form of assembling to advance a particular viewpoint, the only reasonable option is to permit it. The government has no business prohibiting lawful speech. Nor does the government have any business promoting particular viewpoints. This is simply common sense. That is why we issue things called "permits" instead of "promotes."

The city of Starkville is under no legal or moral obligation to actively promote the Starkville Pride event—unless, of course, they have previously promoted speech that presents a point of view contrary to the one Starkville Pride participants wish to express in their parade. If they have, then they need to contribute an equal amount to the promotion of the present applicants' point of view—and then in the future get out of the promotion and prohibition business altogether.

In a nutshell, Starkville should stick to issuing permits liberally and leave it to the individual groups to raise their own support entirely. This includes security fees for the cost of policing events, which should be low and fixed regardless of the general content and specific viewpoint of the groups seeking permits. None of these so-called promotion concerns are complicated.

But this leaves us with the remaining concern that Starkville Pride parade participants will engage in lewd behavior in a public setting if granted a parade permit. There are only two possibilities here—and neither one justifies the denial of a permit for Starkville Pride in advance of the parade.

The obvious first possibility is that no lewd behavior will be exhibited in the parade. If this possibility comes to pass, then the matter is resolved. No further comment is required here. However, the second possibility raises questions that require a little more discernment—and perhaps a little more restraint.

What should Starkville residents do if the gay pride parade starts to devolve into one of those sad exhibitions we have seen in larger cities all across America? What should they do if men wearing assless chaps start parading up and down the streets doing pelvic thrusts and otherwise simulating sex in a public setting? Two things come to mind:

- First, the citizens of Starkville should use the high concentration of sexually broken people as an opportunity to **minister to the sexually broken**. A woman objecting to the parade was quoted as saying that she did not want to turn Starkville into "sin city." Has she ever considered turning it into "redemption city" by sharing the gospel? Has she heard of the Great Commission? We should not allow a false sense of moral superiority to rob us of an opportunity to minister to those who are hurting themselves by pursuing a lie.

- Secondly, there is a political advantage to be gained from lewd exhibitions when they do occur. While I do support the First Amendment rights of pride groups, I must admit that I am irritated by some of their prideful comparisons. For example, many of their members have the unmitigated gall to compare themselves to the civil rights activists of the 1960s who marched up and down the streets of Mississippi being chased by attack dogs and sprayed with water hoses. To put it bluntly, the man wearing assless chaps and marching in front of an inflatable penis is a hedonistic narcissist—especially if he considers himself to be oppressed in the same way black people were in the 1960s.

If I were simply being pragmatic, I would never want to censor such a lewd individual. I would rather photograph his lewd march and contrast it with the experiences of legitimate civil rights marchers. In fact, I would use the contrasting pictures (the 2018 gay pride parade versus the 1960s civil rights march) to make signs that I would use in counterprotests. But at no point would I censor a lie and thus deprive myself of a more effective means of expressing the truth. We must remember what John Stuart Mill said about censorship. It is wrong when it suppresses the truth. But it is also wrong when it suppresses a greater appreciation of the truth via its collision with falsity.

To the extent that we stay focused on the truth and not censorship, we can better help lead people out of darkness. That is the highest calling of men who are fortunate enough to live in a free society.

Author's Note: Shortly after completing this column, the author attended a re-hearing of the permit issue at Starkville City Hall. The city reversed its ruling and issued the permit. Thanks to the conservative censors, the parade promises to be well attended.

Chapter 88

Liberal Ideology Is an Incapable Guardian

May 21, 2018

The recent shooting at Santa Fe High School, not far from where I grew up, compels me to revisit an issue I expounded upon in my last book, *Letters to a Young Progressive*. Because so many are unnecessarily complicating the discussion of what causes school shootings—and what can be done to stop them—I must take time to weigh in on the issue. The first step in doing so is to remind readers that crime is best viewed as an event that takes place when three conditions are fulfilled:

1. There must be a **motivated offender** to commit the crime.
2. The motivated offender must encounter a **suitable target** for the crime.
3. There must be an absence of **capable guardians** to stop the crime.

This threefold explanation of crime isn't new. It's part of a theory first introduced by Lawrence Cohen and Marcus

Felson in 1979. It is called routine activity theory for a good reason. To put it succinctly, Cohen and Felson wanted the name of the theory to reflect their contention that crime rates are affected by the routine activities of non-criminals and not just the behavior of the criminal. Felson provides numerous examples in his book *Crime and Everyday Life*. First, I will apply the theory to gun violence in general before moving to the more specific issue of school shootings and what we should do about them.

The concept of the **motivated offender** isn't hard to explain. Crimes simply do not occur without motives. In the case of armed robbery, someone might attack a victim motivated by nothing more than a desire to obtain the victim's wallet—so he can spend the victim's cash and use his credit cards.

The concept of the **suitable target** is not much more complicated. Put simply, the armed robber is unlikely to attack a large man wearing an NRA T-shirt. He will select a victim that is less likely to fight back and easier to overcome. The armed robber will consider the victim's size and his body language—in order to gauge both his ability and willingness to fend off an attack. Obviously, he will also consider the likelihood that the potential victim is armed.

Finally, the concept of the **capable guardian** reminds us that other actors beside the victim and perpetrator affect the chances of any crime occurring. It should not surprise anyone that robbers generally seek to pounce upon isolated victims in areas where no eyewitnesses are to be found. Nor should it surprise anyone that this is more likely to take place in a physical location where potential onlookers are unlikely to be armed. The alley is a good place for a mugging. Better still if near a bar district where alcohol is consumed and guns are generally forbidden.

This provides a rather obvious transition into the more specific issue of school shootings and what is to be done about them. Obviously, liberals and conservatives have very different views about which of the three conditions should be the focal point of any response to school shootings. But first, it would be helpful to discuss what they agree about.

Conservatives and liberals may well disagree about the efficacy of arming citizens as a means of making them less **suitable targets** of crime. But to state the obvious, they do agree that arming students as a means of reducing school shootings is not the solution. So that leaves us with only two options. The one you pick depends upon your view of human nature, which is inextricably tied to your political ideology.

Because he has a tendency to view human beings as intrinsically good, the liberal sees reducing the prevalence of **motivated offenders** as the preferred solution. If people are good, then they only become criminals because of "society." Hence, reforming "society" will help reform the criminal. Add to that a penchant for counseling, and a therapeutic model soon emerges. The problem with this approach is that it takes a lot of time and money to cure whole societies and even individual criminals.

Because he has a tendency to view human beings as intrinsically broken, the conservative sees increasing the prevalence of **capable guardians** as the preferred solution. He wants to place armed security guards in public schools. And while he might not favor training and arming schoolteachers, he sees no reason to keep those who are already trained and licensed carriers from having their permits nullified simply because they are on school grounds.

Ultimately, conservatives and liberals must put their ideological differences aside. If there is to be progress, both groups must agree to allow one another to put their ideas into practice within the public school system. Toward that end, there is both good news and bad news.

The good news is that conservatives are not actively opposing liberal efforts to reduce motivated offenders. For example, there is no conservative movement to eliminate school counselors in response to these tragic shootings. Conservatives simply seek to supplement the therapeutic approach with their own ideas.

The bad news is that liberals with have none of it. They generally oppose armed security guards in high schools, and they certainly oppose lifting the ban on concealed carry permits in our public schools. The liberal *Los Angeles Times* recently even opposed metal detectors—and for precisely the same reason: **These are all painful reminders of the conservative view of human nature.**

Instead of metal detectors, the *Los Angeles Times* editors recommended, "Shared parks, clinics, and recreational facilities," adding, "These help to make neighborhoods safer as people engage in community activities together; they also create stronger support for schools."

In short, liberals are more dedicated to preserving naïve visions of human nature than preserving vulnerable children. And that is why we have not seen the last of the shootings.

Mike covered "routine activity theory" in his Introduction to Criminal Justice course, where he listed Crime and Everyday Life *as optional text. He also discusses this in Chapters 15 and 16 of* Letters to a Young Progressive.

Chapter 89

My Preferred Pronouns

June 20, 2018

Last year, I received a strange email from a philosophy professor at Guilford College. Her unsolicited missive asked whether it was true that I think "transgender folk" are "mentally ill." She went on to say that such a view is "an insupportable position" that is "unworthy of a scholar." She concluded her brief sermon by informing me that her "preferred pronouns" are "she, her, and hers." I was so inspired by her that I have decided to change my own email signature to reflect my personal pronouns. But first, I wish to address the substance of the email. It shouldn't take long because there wasn't much there.

Most of us remember a time when it was generally understood that thinking you are something you are not constitutes a mental disorder. In fact, given that the word "disorder" simply means "confusion," all of the following conclusions were universally accepted until recently:

- A man who imagines he is a poached egg suffers from a mental disorder.
- A man who imagines he is a unicorn suffers from a mental disorder.
- A man who imagines he is a child suffers from a mental disorder.
- A man who imagines he is a woman suffers from a mental disorder.

Nowadays, the first three of these scenarios are still considered to be examples of a mental disorder. But the fourth one is now considered to be an expression of sexual diversity. Reviewing the stages in this changing view of the transgendered is instructive. There have been roughly four of them:

1. **Treatment**. Back when we used to treat "transgendered folk" as suffering from gender identity disorder (GID), the goal was simply keeping them from hurting themselves. That is called *compassion*. We would no more want a man to have his genitals surgically removed under the guise that he is a woman than we would want them sewn onto his forehead under the guise that he is a unicorn. This was all before the goal of appearing tolerant in front of others replaced the goal of being compassionate toward others.

2. **Tolerance**. When we removed GID from the Diagnostic and Statistical Manual (DSM), we did so under a false understanding of tolerance. Put simply, tolerance presupposes a moral judgment. But when we abandoned the goal of treatment of those suffering from GID in order to appear "tolerant" by not judging them, we essentially

embraced *cruelty*. When people refuse to help other people who are sick and instead allow them to hurt themselves, it is the very opposite of compassion.

3. **Acceptance**. When our cultural elites began to accept the idea that a he can be a she and vice versa, we crossed a pretty serious line. When people actually accept a delusion, that means they are also suffering from a delusion. Accepting GID is no different than hearing a man declare that he is a poached egg and then coming to believe that he actually is a poached egg. True acceptance and internalization of craziness is properly dubbed as *craziness*.

4. **Mandatory Acceptance**. The idea that a professor with a Ph.D. in philosophy would have the gall to demand that I adopt her delusions in order to be "worthy" to be classified alongside her as a "scholar" shows that the inmates have finally taken over the asylum. It also reveals that intellectual fascism has taken over the academy. This mindset is properly referred to as intellectual *coercion*.

I believe that such academic fascism must be mocked relentlessly. So I have altered my email signature to include my own preferred personal pronouns. From now on, those emailing me at my office will be treated to the following signature:

Mike Adams
Professor of Criminology
Author of *Letters to a Young Progressive*
Contributor to *The Daily Wire*

Preferred Pronouns = He Who Must Be Obeyed, His Majesty, His Royal Humbleness, I AM, and Your Better in All Things.

Hopefully, people will understand my point that professors who list preferred pronouns are simply narcissists. And those who demand special pronouns must think they are God, which definitely constitutes a mental disorder.

To argue otherwise is to adopt an insupportable position that is unworthy of a scholar.

And now for more classic Mike humor:
If you have to choose between a woman who smokes and a woman who has cats, pick the woman who smokes. At least there is a chance she'll quit smoking. The cat thing will only get worse.

A gentlemen's club is always devoid of gentlemen. Sort of like a diversity office is always devoid of diversity.

My mother voted republican until the day she died. After that, she started voting democrat.

My spice rack is nearly empty. Ain't it funny how thyme slips away?

There are two kinds of people in this world: those who dichotomize, those who don't, and those who can't count.

The rain is subsiding. The birds are singing. A small strip of land is emerging in my backyard. Isthmus be my lucky day.

Chapter 90

How to Deal with Transgendered Students

June 29, 2018

I get a lot of emails from unhinged leftists. And I certainly expected to hear from some of them in response to my latest *Daily Wire* column, "My Preferred Pronouns." Being an unselfish person, I like to share my hate mail with readers—and my "hate male" when it is from feminists. Here is what one "woke" *Daily Wire* reader had to say:

> *"You are a real piece of (expletive deleted). Today, you say the transgendered suffer from a mental disorder. Next, you will say that paraplegics suffer from a mental illness. How do you teach transgendered students given your atavistic views on human sexuality?"*

(Author's Note: The term "atavistic" refers to views everyone shared prior to around the midpoint of the Obama presidency.)

Of course, someone has to suffer from a severe intellectual hernia in order to fail to grasp the distinction between a) those who lose use of their limbs through some accident and b) those who cut off appendages voluntarily in order to help their body catch up with their perceived sexual identity. But embedded within the otherwise ludicrous email is a serious question, which I will paraphrase as follows: **What guidelines do you follow when interacting with transgendered students in the classroom?**

I am actually delighted that someone finally asked about my views on how to teach transgendered students. I only adhere to four basic rules when dealing with students who suffer from gender identity disorder, so I will spell them out for my leftist critics:

Always use the student's preferred name. You might call the name of Charlene on the first day of class and be corrected by a voice asking to be called Charlie. Or Patricia might ask to be called Pat. Or the correction could be something less smooth—such as Bruce demanding to be called Caitlyn. Regardless, always show respect for the person by using the name they prefer because it is just that—a preference. There is nothing inherently male or female about a first name. This is a non-issue. Don't make it one.

Avoid using pronouns. Pronouns are different. When Bruce goes from simply asking to be called Caitlyn to demanding to be called "she," you have a potential problem. Calling Bruce "Caitlyn" is simply honoring a preference. In contrast, calling Bruce "she" is telling a lie. In a nutshell, Bruce is now asking you to accommodate his mental disorder by lying and saying he is something he is not. Just as there is good reason to refrain from lying and saying "she," there is also good reason to refrain from saying "he." The reason is that it is completely avoidable.

When my first transgendered student asked to be called by a male name on the first day of class, I had no idea that she would also become my best and most outspoken student in the class. There were numerous times throughout the semester when her comments were so enlightening that I almost responded by saying something like, "Did everyone hear what she just said?" In such cases, when I came to the part of the sentence with the personal pronoun, I simply substituted the student's first name, which is more personal anyway. Professors who make an issue of this by sending around sheets of paper the first day of class asking for each student's preferred pronouns are just being pretentious. This is another non-issue. Learn your student's first names and use them whenever you call on them in class. Issue resolved.

Don't take the bathroom bait. Some people say that North Carolina's HB2 was an "unnecessary law." I agree. Had it not been for the LGBT Chamber of Commerce of Charlotte passing a city ordinance (requiring all private businesses to allow access to any bathroom on the basis of the patron's perceived gender), the state legislature would have had no need to address the issue. Generally speaking, transsexuals have quietly used the bathroom of their choice for years with no problem—that is, until LGBT activists politicized the issue.

When my first "transitioning" student decided she wanted to walk into the men's restroom just as I was walking out, I simply ignored her. It was awkward to be certain. But it wasn't worth calling the bathroom police. If you are ever assaulted in a bathroom by a transsexual, then do what you would do if a normal person outside a bathroom assaulted you: Call the police and/or defend yourself. If not, just go about your business. This is another non-issue. Don't make it one.

Provide an alternate basis for student identity. I cringe every time I hear the phrase "LGBT people" because it implies that those who are outside of the heterosexual norm are somehow defined by their sexuality. As educators, we should have no part of the undignified business of encouraging people to build their identity around their sexuality. We cannot love people by actually encouraging the spiritual evils that victimize them—even when the culture praises us for doing so.

Thus, whenever I see my former student (who is obviously going through radical hormonal therapy to appear male), I do not ask her how her gender identity transition is going. I ask her how her studies are going. I thank her for being such an attentive student. I tell her how much I enjoyed having her in my class. This lets her know that she stands out because of her mind, not because of her membership in a newly contrived class of victims.

This is really all you need to know about how to deal with the transgender issue. Best of all, my advice is free of charge. Because some problems are so simple, they don't require a diversity expert who demands a six-digit salary from our overburdened taxpayers.

Chapter 91

Toxic White Heteronormative Femininity

July 24, 2019

People often ask me what it is like to work with a bunch of Marxists every day—given that I sued them successfully five years ago and have since criticized some of them by name in my opinion columns. People assume that my work environment must be consistently hostile. Actually, there are patterns of variability in the level of collegiality among my coworkers that would make for an interesting sociological lecture. Since I'll never be invited to give a guest lecture in a sociology class, I will tackle them here.

The circumstances leading to my lawsuit were largely the fault of two white heterosexual feminist department chairs who simply could not conduct themselves professionally in a department with even one ideological dissident. The first white heterosexual feminist was an interim department chair. She was so angered by my success as a writer and a speaker that she attacked me in an annual evaluation with considerable enthusiasm and lack of caution. In fact, she directly mentioned my politics, which caused the jury to rule against her in the subsequent jury trial over a viewpoint-based denial of promotion to full professor.

Naturally, that white heterosexual feminist was uncivil during our civil suit. She was also uncivil afterwards, right up to the day of her retirement. She simply never apologized or accepted responsibility for her unlawful conduct. She didn't seem to care. Ultimately, the taxpayer-supported university paid her legal bills.

The story was largely the same with the second white heterosexual feminist department chair. She was a Marxist who hated my politics. Her ideology drove her to the extreme measure of systematically altering email evaluations of my work performance by fellow professors. She later lied about the reasons I was denied promotion. To top it off, she also lied repeatedly when she took the stand during the federal jury trial. The jury figured this out and found her individually liable.

Naturally, that second white heterosexual feminist was also uncivil to me during our civil suit and after the suit was over. She never apologized or accepted responsibility for her unlawful conduct, which cost the university a lot of money and a ton of bad publicity.

I should also add that our white heterosexual feminist chancellor was caught trying to change the criteria of promotion in order to retaliate against me for criticizing her governance of the university. The jury also found her liable in her individual capacity.

Thus, a clear pattern emerges when we look at the demographics of the principal villains who caused the lawsuit to happen. But a very different pattern emerges when we look at those who supported me or were at least civil during the ordeal.

Interestingly, there was only faculty member in the department who openly expressed support for me. He was our only black male faculty member. In addition, there were two others who, while keeping their opinions about the suit to themselves, went out of their way to be warm and civil toward me.

One of those was an instructor who happens to be the only black female teaching in our department. During the seven-and-a-half-year lawsuit, she always greeted me warmly and even went out of her way to stop by the office and see how I was doing. Now, five years after the jury verdict, she still greets me with warm enthusiasm and stops by the office occasionally just to shoot the breeze.

The other happens to have been the only openly gay member of the faculty at the time I filed my suit. This woman is still my favorite coworker. She was warm and friendly throughout the entire legal ordeal. And after the verdict, she continued to be more than just civil. To this day, she stills stops by the office regularly to shoot the breeze or to ask my advice on how to deal with difficult students.

Contrast the civility of these kind colleagues with some of the faculty members we have hired since the lawsuit was initiated. I could name at least three professors who have joined the department since my promotion denial in 2006 who have been openly hostile toward me. I have not sued any of them. Nor have I mentioned them in any of my books, columns, or speeches. In other words, they have no direct reason to dislike me. They just exhibit hatred for ideological reasons and feel no moral obligation to act professionally. And they have exactly three things in common:

1. They are straight.

2. They are white.

3. They are feminists.

This makes for an interesting pattern. Blacks and lesbians have been my best colleagues in the department. But straight white feminists have been my worst. What explains the pattern? It's actually pretty simple.

My sympathetic black and gay colleagues have had the experience of suffering discrimination at some point in their lives. Having had those negative experiences, they simply refused to pile on when I was subjected to discrimination by straight white feminists who espouse a victim-based ideology without ever having been victims themselves.

This distinction between a) being a part of a demographic group that has actually experienced victimization and b) being a part of an ideological group opposed to victimization is important. Those who have not experienced discrimination directly cannot be expected to understand it. Their "knowledge" comes from a worldview, not from the real world. Thus, they are compelled to act based upon visions, not reality.

This helps explain why everything they touch turns out badly. It also explains their condescending need to speak on behalf of real victims by endlessly decrying racism and homophobia.

It's time to start talking about toxic white heteronormative femininity. The white male privilege myth is getting harder and harder to sustain.

Chapter 92

Cultural Appropriation 101

August 2, 2019

It once was the case that only those foolish enough to take a course in sociology risked being accused of "cultural appropriation." Unfortunately, the concept has leaked out into the larger society to the extent that I now get emails from people seeking advice on how to respond to the accusation. The following is an example of an email I received just a few days ago:

> *I don't know if this is appropriate to ask, but what is your response to cultural appropriation? I think it is stupid liberal whining, but how do I address it in a "high road" way? Are there any articles or schools of thought resources I can research? Thanks! Alicia.*

Having found no specific resources, I decided to publish my brief response in column form so that those facing the accusation will be prepared. It is brief, but here is all you need to know the next time you are accused of "appropriating" another culture:

Dear Alicia: The concept of cultural appropriation is like a lot of progressive ideas. It is so ridiculous that all you have to do is ask the proponent of the idea some pointed questions in order to poke a hole in the concept. Let's start with an example.

Several years ago, some fraternity men were accused of cultural appropriation because they decided to throw a Cinco de Mayo party at which they all wore sombreros. The results were predictable. They got drunk, they posted pictures of themselves wearing sombreros all over social media, and then people got offended. That led to the specific accusation of cultural appropriation and subsequent trouble with their school's administration. The question is: What would you do if faced with a similar accusation?

There are two possible responses I would recommend—the first slightly aggressive and the second much more so.

The first option would be to point to the hypocrisy of accusations of cultural appropriation by asking questions about how the accuser also "appropriates" the culture in question.

In the case of the sombrero controversy, the accused could ask his administrative accusers whether they ever eat Mexican food, whether they ever drink Mexican beer, or whether they have ever spoken a word of Spanish. This would force the accuser to either a) lie with no chance of being believed or b) tell the truth and thus face a counterparge of violating the prohibition against "appropriating" Mexican culture.

The second option would be to point to the gross insensitivity of accusations of cultural appropriation by asking questions about how the accuser might also "appropriate" cultures other than the one in question.

Sticking with the example of the sombrero controversy, the accused could also ask his administrative accusers whether they ever eat fried chicken, whether they ever drink Kool-Aid, or whether they have ever spoken a word of urban English, which might include something as mundane as singing the lyrics of a rap song.

This line of questioning would likely offend the accuser. In fact, it would probably force the accuser to indignantly assert that such questions emerge from (and also reinforce) deeply offensive cultural stereotypes. At that point, you will be on the verge of winning the argument. All you have to do is slowly explain the point of your questions, which is simply to illustrate the obvious:

Accusations of cultural appropriation are inherently offensive because they rely upon the accuser's validation of stereotypes of other cultures.

In other words, by saying "you can't do that because that is what _____ people do," the accuser violates a principle he is trying to uphold—namely, that we should avoid denigrating other cultures. Obviously, the reinforcement of caricatures of members of other cultural groups violates that general principle.

But there is an even deeper problem with the concept of appropriation. Taking a coin out of your pocket and reading it can help you to readily understand it. On that coin, you will see three inscriptions: Liberty, In God We Trust, and E Pluribus Unum.

As Dennis Prager has pointed out, these are three core American values that are under assault by the progressive left. From here, it is easy to walk through them and how each is under assault.

We all know that "Liberty" is under assault by the left through the mechanism of socialism. We also know that "In God We Trust" is under assault by the left through the mechanism of secularism. But we sometimes overlook the fact that "E Pluribus Unum," which is translated to "out of many, one," is under assault by the left through the mechanism of multiculturalism.

Put simply, multiculturalism is antithetical to the value of cultural assimilation. It is a dangerous ideology, which says that our society should be composed of different cultural enclaves with different values and norms for behavior. It is the *sine qua non* behind accusations of cultural appropriation. Moreover, it is the very reason why America has devolved into an unprecedented level of tribalism.

In a nutshell, accusations of cultural appropriation are not unifying. To the contrary, they are divisive. They are also deeply un-American.

So thank you for your question, Alicia. I hope this answer helps.

Speaking of socialism, Mike had a few more choice words on that subject over the years:

Capitalism works for you if you work; socialism works for you if you don't work.

Socialism is a philosophy that promotes equality by ensuring that no one has anything. That is why it is only favored by those who are either economically or intellectually bankrupt.

Socialism and moral relativism share at least one thing in common—namely, the tendency to destroy any incentive to rise above mediocrity.

Chapter 93

Bob and the Burning Research Lab

August 19, 2019

Last year, I spoke on the issue of abortion at Calvary Chapel in Chino Hills, California. During the Q&A, I said that I believe we live in a world of trade-offs rather than a world of problems and solutions. Upon seeing the video on YouTube, Bob submitted the following question:

> "We live in a world of trade-offs." Indeed we do. So answer me this. There's a science lab that's burning down, and inside is a 10-year old child, and next to him is a container full of 100 fertilized human embryos. You can save either the embryos or the child, but not both. What value do you put on life? Is it quantity alone? Or is it something else?

This is a common pro-choice hypothetical, which Bob has taken from Ellen Goodman without attribution. As a thought experiment, it tends to intimidate pro-lifers. However, it should not be intimidating at all because it rests on the faulty assumption that our value as humans is contingent upon the intuitive emotional reactions and moral judgments of other humans. Here is the argument in a nutshell:

1. Any human walking into the burning research lab and seeing the ten-year-old would intuitively run to save the child.
2. The fact that the choice would be made intuitively is conclusive evidence that either:
   a. the embryos are not fully human or
   b. if fully human, the embryos are not persons in the same sense as the ten-year-old.

This idea that the choice of saving one human calls into question the humanity of the one not chosen can be easily defeated. I always do it by responding with a *variation of* the hypothetical rather than a *direct answer to* the hypothetical. A typical variation goes something like this:

> There's a science lab that's burning down. Mike happens to be walking by and decides to go inside to see if anyone is in peril. In one corner of the lab, he sees his daughter, Carolyn. In another corner of the lab, he sees Bob, a pro-choice antagonist. Mike can save either Carolyn or Bob, but not both. What does he do?

Obviously, Mike saves Carolyn. The fact that Mike's choice was made intuitively cannot be taken as evidence that Bob is not fully human. Nor is it evidence that Bob is less of a "person" than Carolyn. In fact, the pro-life position does not draw any meaningful distinction between humans and "persons" (because no one can). To do so would suggest that some humans are more valuable than others. And that leads us back to Bob's previous question about human value.

Bob phrases the question improperly when he asks, "What value do you put on life?" Put simply, I do not put value on human life. That is not something I am permitted to do. Humans already have their value at the point of conception. That value is derived from their basic human nature. In other words, their value is based on the kind of thing they are, not the kinds of things they can do. Human beings are not obligated to earn their rights by performing—or by doing anything that would inspire me to "put" value on them.

On one occasion, I used the Mike and Carolyn variation of the lab hypothetical to respond to a young man attending another of my pro-life lectures in California. He objected to the variation, saying, "That's different—a man has a duty to save his own daughter." Actually, my variation reinforces the thesis that the young man had failed utterly to grasp:

Just as our emotions are irrelevant to determinations of human value, our duties are irrelevant to determinations of human value.

Take our charitable decisions as an example. The decision to feed my family and not feed the homeless does not deprive the homeless of their basic human worth. My decisions about which humans to help have no bearing on the inherent value of those not helped.

I believe these are all valid points. But Scott Klusendorf raised the best argument ever leveled against the burning research lab hypothetical. Scott noted that no one would ever enter the lab and destroy the embryos on the way to saving the child. Nor would anyone considering my variation walk over to the other corner of the lab and slit the throat of the pro-choice antagonist. Hence, Goodman's thought experiment is irrelevant to the issue of abortion.

The abortion debate is about the intentional killing of innocent human beings, not the refusal to save them. We cannot let Bob change the subject.

Chapter 94

Victoria's Secret

November 21, 2019

Victoria (last name withheld) is a senior at UNC-Wilmington (UNCW) where I have taught for twenty-six years. She is also an adult who exercised her First Amendment right to criticize me by name in a large online public forum. Unfortunately, some people who read her social media post incorrectly concluded that she had engaged in defamatory speech, which is not protected by the First Amendment. I disagree and write today in defense of her free speech rights. In order to establish appropriate context, I have reprinted her post below:

> *Hey guys, I'm working with an anonymous professor on campus to create a resource where students can anonymously put in negative experiences with professors. Specifically this is in aims to address the racist and sexist remarks commented by professor Mike Adams. If you have any stories from the last two years at the university and would like to help me with this feel free to (direct message) me. Also, If there are any ideas of how to set up this resource,*

> let me know as well. A university that preaches diversity and it's [sic] need for growth should not allow students to feel alienated or uncomfortable.

This post simply expresses an opinion about my speech. In my opinion, it wrongly characterizes my speech—and does so without directly attacking my character. If Victoria had gone further and called *me* a racist and a sexist, she would still be wrong. Even then, she would not be in danger of being sued for defamation because I am a public figure, which means I get attacked often and have less legal recourse when it happens.

But there is an upside to being a public figure. As a public figure, I have a lot of allies. This means that when I am attacked, there are many people who are ready to come to my defense. That is a good thing because the best remedy for bad speech is generally not to be found in lawsuits. The best remedy for bad speech is to be found in better speech.

In the case of Victoria's bad speech, better speech did follow. Within minutes, a student named Brandon responded with the following:

> Lol this has to be a joke. I've felt alienated since freshman year for being a Republican.

Part of the beauty of this remark is that Brandon is Hispanic. He also added a comment specifically denying that I am either sexist or racist. But the fun was just beginning. A student named Rebekah added the following:

> They are just upset that someone is speaking out against them.

Next, a student named Sean added this response:

What would UNCW be without Dr. Adams.

Then, another Hispanic student named Sabrina came to my defense with this comment:

He's my favorite professor.

Indeed, within a span of a few minutes, two women, two Hispanics, and a Democrat had come to my defense. So much for the politicized accusations of racism and sexism!

So what did Victoria do in light of the epic failure of her post? She amended it to include the following:

I appreciate the reactions I have had and have decided my direct mention of a faculty member was inappropriate.

This is an example of the way it is supposed to be. In a free and open marketplace of ideas, there will be many errors. People will say unfair things. But by keeping the marketplace open, such errors can be corrected. Of course, corrections do require some degree of character on behalf of those who make mistakes. And Victoria has shown character here. Two traits of hers are praiseworthy:

Courage. I actually like the fact that Victoria called me out by name. Remember that I was a leftist when I was younger. If I were aware back then of any professors holding the views I hold now, I would have been very tempted to light them up on social media (had it then existed). I'm just not sure I would have had the courage to do it back then.

Humility. This is a character trait I admire in people (as I will explain in my forthcoming book, *Ten Steps to Humility and How I Made It in Seven*). This was a real display of maturity by Victoria.

But let us take a moment to contrast Victoria's behavior with the cowardice of her secret professor and mentor. That professor is hiding in the shadows and trying to target me for my political views. That has been tried before here at UNCW. It ended up with a jury verdict and an order from a judge to pay me over three-quarters of a million dollars in legal fees and back pay. I used the money to buy guns and several expensive guitars. They are prominently displayed in my living room and make great conversation pieces.

Of course, it should go without saying that my view about the desirability of lawsuits changes when the person criticizing me is an employee of the government trying to use the power of government against me. And there is no doubt that this anonymous professor is trying to solicit these secret complaints in order to file formal ones. This will only result in her name being exposed when it winds up on a lawsuit.

In a nutshell, I would strongly caution this anonymous professor to avoid getting her panties in a wad and doing something she will regret. Otherwise, Victoria's Secret will soon be forced to start producing legal briefs.

This column provides more evidence that Mike supports free speech for all, not just his side. Chapter 3, "Of Holt and Hypocrisy," is another example. His adversaries refused to acknowledge this simple but crucial fact.

Chapter 95

Life and How to Live It, Part XIII

December 3, 2019

This also appears in the book Life and How to Live It *(2023).*

My father died just before the holiday season began three years ago. This story concerns an argument we had during one of my Christmas visits to Houston. I thought it would be good for people to hear it before they spend time with their families over Christmas.

I was planning on visiting my parents in The Woodlands, then visiting friends across town in Katy and then in Clear Lake *[where we grew up]* before circling back to see them again prior to going back to North Carolina. But just as I was preparing for the day trip across town to Katy, my dad began lecturing me on my need for a GPS. I told him I did not need one, as I had been to the Katy destination several times before.

For some bizarre reason, my dad just kept on arguing with me. When my mother tried to change the subject, he kept interrupting both of us until my mother begged him to just shut up. She only told him to shut up when he was way out of line—so that usually worked. But not this time. He just kept going.

Finally, in anger, I looked at him and said, "Dad, there is no problem here for you to solve. So stop interrupting me!" Before I realized it, everyone was either yelling or angry. I then told him I did not drive 1,250 miles to put up with his nonsense. I grabbed my bags and stormed out of his house, vowing never to visit my father again.

I spent the night in Katy just as I had already planned to do. The next day, I drove down to Clear Lake as I had also planned to do. After spending the day and the early evening with a friend, I decided to just start the drive back home to North Carolina instead of going back to The Woodlands.

I guess I just did not want to face my father again. I was furious at him for lecturing me and for raising his voice to me after I drove all the way across the country to see him. He was furious at me for telling him I did not need his advice. We both felt hurt, and we both felt disrespected. Nonetheless, for some reason, as I headed up I-45, at just the last second, I decided to miss the I-10 exit to North Carolina and instead drive back up to The Woodlands.

When I walked into the house, my dad was sitting by the fireplace. I sat down next to him and pulled out an iPad and started showing him pictures of our old house in Clear Lake, which I had just taken earlier that day. He never apologized for raising his voice. And I never apologized for storming out of the house. I just met him where he was and started talking in order to break the silence. Later, I found out why Dad had been acting strangely during that visit. A massive tumor had started growing in the middle of his brain.

Had I taken that exit and gone back to North Carolina, things never would have been the same again. Instead, I made peace with him. In fact, I was the last person ever to speak to him. I even delivered a sermon to him on his last Sunday on

Earth as he lay there blind, mute, and dying. He died peacefully, and I have been at peace with it ever since. It was all because I met him where he was and started talking.

If there is someone you love whom you are not at peace with, just swallow your pride and reach out. Chances are the source of your conflict really is not as important as you once thought it was. Perhaps it is just as meaningless as the one between my dad and me. If fact, I'll bet it is.

We are all dying, folks. It is time to meet the people we love where they are and start talking. There is no need to wait until the holidays to start applying this principle. We can start today. We might not have tomorrow.

Mike and I grew up together but were apart during our adult years, having followed different career paths in different parts of the country. Our lives had gone in different directions but would reconverge as we worked together when our parents entered the final chapter of their lives. This is a period when some families become fractured due to conflicts over health care, inheritances, etc. However, this was a period during which Mike and I drew closer. I am proud of him for his patience and attentiveness during this time. I am proud of us for working well together and doing our best under some very adverse conditions at the end of our parents' lives.

I am grateful for the wisdom and insights that Mike left behind, and I am sad that there will be no more of these articles. Here are a few more quotes along these lines:

When my father died, we were at peace. But looking back, I have deep regrets about how I rushed our phone calls because I was working or was simply tired from work. I cannot get those precious moments back. That haunts me from time to time. Work will always be there. Loved ones will not.

The fifth commandment is one that extends beyond death. It is about more than saying "Yes, sir" or "Yes, ma'am" to our parents while they are alive. It is about living a life that honors our parents even after they are gone.

Chapter 96

My New Spread the Wealth Grading Policy

Originally published in 2009; updated December 28, 2019.

This also appears in the book Life and How to Live It *(2023).*

Good afternoon, students! I'm writing you this email to announce that I'm making some changes in the grading policies I announced previously in our course syllabus. As you know, this is an election year, and we again have an opportunity to elect a new president. After seeing several of you with "Bernie 2020" and "Feel the Bern" bumper stickers on your laptops, I thought it would be nice to align our class policies with the policies you seem to be aligning yourself with by supporting an openly socialist candidate.

Previously, I announced that I would use a ten-point grading scale, which means that 90 percent of one hundred is an "A," 80 percent is a "B," 70 percent is a "C," and 60 percent is enough for a passing grade of "D."

The new policy I am announcing today is that those who score above ninety on the first exam will have points deducted and given to students at the bottom of the grade distribution. For example, if a student gets a ninety-nine, I will then deduct nine points and give them to the person with the lowest grade. If a person scores ninety-five, I will then deduct five points and give them to the person with the second lowest grade. If someone scores ninety-three, I will then deduct three points and give them to the next lowest person. And so on.

My point, rather obviously, is that any points above ninety are really not needed since you have an "A" regardless of whether you score ninety or ninety-nine. Nor am I convinced that you need to save those points for a rainy day. Those who are failing need the points.

After our second examination, I intend to take a more complex approach to the practice of grade redistribution. I will not be looking at your second test scores but, instead, at the average of your first two test scores. In the process, I may well decide to start taking some points from students in the "B" range. For example, if someone has an average of eighty-five after two tests, I may take a few points and give them away to someone who is failing or who is in danger of failing. I think this is fair because the person with an eighty-five average is probably unlikely to climb up to an "A" or fall down to a "C." I may be wrong in some individual cases, but, of course, my principal concern is not the individual. I care more about the collective.

By the end of the semester, I will abandon any formal guidelines and just redistribute points in a way that seems just, or fair, to me. I will not rely upon any standards other than my very strong and passionate feelings concerning social justice. In the process, I will not merely seek to eliminate inequality. I will also seek to eliminate the possibility of failure.

I know some are concerned that my system may impact their lives in a very profound way. Grade redistribution will undoubtedly cause some grade point average redistribution. And this, in turn, will mean that some people will not get into the law school or medical school of their choice. Or maybe someday you will be represented by a lawyer—or operated on by a doctor—who is not of the highest quality.

These are all, of course, legitimate long-term concerns. But I believe we need to remain focused on the short term.

This shows how Mike used humor and satire to drive home his points. (Although, in his public life, this would be his downfall because so many of his critics are humorless and do not understand satire.)

By the way, here is what Mike's UNCW department chair wrote in his 1997 annual evaluation:

"Dr. Adams was clearly a gifted and accomplished teacher who was eagerly sought after as an academic advisor. All indications are that he was a productive and talented scholar and a responsible university and departmental citizen."

And in his 2001 annual evaluation:

"Dr. Adams is a skilled, passionate, and dedicated teacher, productive and enthusiastic scholar, and good departmental and university citizen. He continues to demonstrate that he is one of the best instructors in our department and in the university."

Chapter 97

Everlasting Life on Death Row

January 10, 2020

This also appears in the book Life and How to Live It *(2023).*

Every time I get the chance, I use my extended break between semesters to take a road trip through Mississippi, where I was born, and then back to Texas, where I grew up. Visiting friends and family and seeing my old childhood homes gives me a chance to think about where I am going by reflecting on where I have been. This year's road trip just happened to conclude on December 30th, which was the twentieth anniversary of an important milestone in a larger personal journey. It was the day I interviewed Johnny Paul Penry on Texas death row, just a few miles from my parents' house *[in Huntsville, Texas]* and just thirteen days before his scheduled execution.

Johnny Paul Penry was a vicious rapist and killer. His first rape put him in prison, but he was paroled after just two years. While on parole, he committed his second rape, which concluded with his murder of the young victim. He beat her so badly that he burst both of her kidneys. He then finished her off by shoving a pair of scissors into her heart. When he was later convicted and sentenced to die, his lawyers argued that he was mentally retarded [*today termed "intellectually disabled"*] and thus should not be executed per the Eighth Amendment ban on cruel and unusual punishment.

After Penry's case had wound its way through the justice system for twenty years, which included two trips to the Supreme Court, his execution date was reset for the third and what appeared to be final time. My dad had taken a retirement job in the very building where Texas executions took place. Furthermore, our neighbor happened to be the warden. Thus, when I expressed interest in interviewing Penry prior to his scheduled execution, it was not hard for me to make the arrangements.

My goal was pretty simple when I arrived on death row on that second-to-last morning of the twentieth century. I simply wanted to gather important information so I could do a better job of teaching the case to my students. I had been teaching the *Penry v. Lynaugh* ruling (issued by the Supreme Court in 1989) for several years because it addressed some important constitutional and philosophical questions. I had no idea that the interview would affect me so personally.

As I spoke with Penry, we broached the topic of his alleged history of abuse at the hands of his mother. During that portion of the interview, I was convinced of two things. One was that some of his claims were valid. The other was that some of his claims had been manufactured in order to win sympathy in the court of public opinion as well as leniency in a court of law.

Similarly, as we broached the topic of his claims of mental retardation, I was also convinced of two things. One was that there was objective evidence, gathered prior to his criminal career, which demonstrated a clear pattern of at least mild mental retardation. The other was that his claims of mental deficiency had been exaggerated in order to win sympathy in the court of public opinion as well as leniency in a court of law.

After I had gathered all of the information I was seeking, I stood up and placed my hand on the glass in order to do the so-called death row handshake with Penry—just as he placed his hand on the other side of the glass. That was the moment that something surreal happened. Shortly after telling me he was scared of being executed, he recited John 3:16 to me to the best of his limited cognitive ability.

Naturally, I had to ask Penry whether he had actually read the Bible. He indicated that after learning how to read and write on death row, he had read the entire Bible over the course of his many years as a condemned man. After he told me that, I turned and walked away. As I left the prison, I concluded that Penry had read the Bible out of sheer boredom over the course of two decades. But there were clear reasons to doubt that he had any kind of legitimate conversion experience.

As I made the drive back to my parents' house, I was overwhelmed by the emotion of the day. Simply imagining a brutal rape or murder is overwhelming. But the details of Penry's miserable life struck to the core of me as well. To compound things, there is just something sobering about being on death row. Even our dog knew I was upset when I got home. He followed me around and kept sticking his head under my hand to remind me that petting him would put me at ease.

But it was difficult for me to feel at ease knowing that a convicted murderer and rapist with substantial mental limitations had read the Bible, while I had not. After all, I was already a tenured professor. How could I call myself educated having not read the most important book ever put in print? That question led me to make one of the most important decisions I ever made in my life. I was going to go home, buy a copy of the Bible, and read it from cover to cover in the coming year.

I took six breaks and read six apologetic books as I worked my way through the King James Version. When I finished, I became the only conservative Christian in a department full of tenured Marxists. Although the transformation led to a lot of conflict and eventually seven years of litigation in federal court, it was certainly worth it. I had gone there on a mission to help save Johnny Paul Penry from death row. But I ended up being the one who had his death sentence commuted.

This story is for those who consider their own past sins to be an irreversible judgment of death. I have told it before but tell it again because I want people to consider the implications of the fact that God can use even a mentally retarded rapist and murderer for a larger kingdom purpose.

To state the rather obvious point of the column, if Johnny Paul Penry can be used by God, then so can you. So please, don't wallow in self-pity. Know that you are still valuable. And that you are still needed in doing the difficult work of reaching lost souls wherever you may find them.

Elsewhere, Mike added: "It took an additional two years to read four more translations of the Bible (the NRSV, GNT, NIV, and NASB)." *Mike was always thorough!*

Unfortunately, Mike didn't say which six apologetic books he read. However, please see Chapter 7, "An Anti-Communist Reading List," for his favorite recommendations.

Earlier, in Chapter 27, "The Shadow Proves the Sunshine," we learned how Mike's trip to Ecuador broke atheism's hold on him.

Coincidentally, at the same time that Mike was making his way back to God, I was having a spiritual journey of my own. When I left home, I left my church and my God behind. I did not actually become an atheist, as Mike did, but I had the false belief that I could live my own way just fine without God. It took me over two decades to finally admit I was wrong. I was visiting Mike in 2001, and I told him I was having second thoughts about my decision to live without God. He knew just what I needed and took me to Barnes & Noble, where he told me to buy Mere Christianity. *I started reading it on the airplane on the way home, and it deeply resonated with me. Shortly thereafter, I went back to church. Mike did not preach to me, but he was prepared when I was ready—what a great lesson that is!*

CHAPTER 98

Two Kinds of Pro-Choice Advocates

February 21, 2020

I remember once when I was a teenager asking my father "What time is it?" He responded by saying, "There are two kinds of people in this world—those who ask what time it is and those who wear watches." I could not resist the temptation to respond by saying, "No, the two kinds of people are those who oversimplify the world by breaking it into dichotomies and those who don't." Of course, he didn't think that was funny. And now I regret saying it because sometimes things do break down into simple dichotomies. One example is support for elective abortion. As complicated as the issue may seem, there are only two types of people in the pro-choice category: **science deniers** and **opponents of human equality.**

The reason we can break pro-choice advocates into this simple dichotomy is because the pro-life position is really predicated on the veracity to two premises contained in a simple syllogism. This syllogism forces the pro-choice advocate into one of two categories by forcing him to attack either the first or the second premise. For those unfamiliar with the syllogism, which has been popularized by the world's greatest pro-life apologist, Scott Klusendorf, here it is in all of its brilliant simplicity:

> PREMISE 1: It is wrong to intentionally kill an innocent human being.
>
> PREMISE 2: Abortion intentionally kills an innocent human being.
>
> CONCLUSION: Abortion is wrong.

Because it sounds callous to begin an argument by denying the wrongfulness of killing innocent humans, the pro-choice advocate almost always begins an argument by attacking the second premise. A case in point is Dr. Willie Parker whom I debated one year ago today on the campus of UNC-Wilmington. Knowing that Parker tried routinely to deny the humanity of the unborn, I led off my opening argument with a number of quotes demonstrating the broad consensus that the unborn is human. Here are some of the quotes I used:

> Embryologists **Moore and Persaud** state, "A zygote is the beginning of a new human being. Human development begins at fertilization."
>
> Embryologist **T. W. Sadler** says, "The development of a human begins with fertilization, a process by which the sperm from the male and the oocyte from the female unite to give rise to a new organism, the zygote."
>
> Even Planned Parenthood president **Alan Guttmacher** wrote in 1933 that, "This all seems so simple

and evident that it is difficult to picture a time when it wasn't part of the common knowledge."

Philosophy professor **Peter Singer** states, "There is no doubt that from the first moments of its existence, an embryo conceived from human sperm and eggs is a human being."

Philosophy professor **David Boonin** adds, "A human fetus, after all, is simply a human being at a very early stage of his or her development."

And finally, abortionist **Dr. Warren Hern** states, "We have reached a point in this particular technology where there is no possibility of denial of an act of destruction by the operator. It is before one's eyes. The sensations of dismemberment flow through the forceps like an electric current."

Thus, the decision to attack the second premise always backfires. The simple reason is that there is an absolute consensus among embryologists that life begins at conception. Thus, those who attack the second premise can be safely tucked away into the first category of pro-choice advocate, which is:

THE SCIENCE DENIER

Fortunately, the effort to deny science has been undercut in recent years by the development of ultrasound technology. Thus, the science denier appears increasingly ignorant to all but a small minority of the population that has somehow never seen an image of an unborn human via ultrasound. Even a small child can look at the screen and discern that it is a baby that is tucked away in the womb. It is no "undifferentiated blob" or "mass of tissue." Such lies require darkness. Technology has shed light upon them.

Thus, the pro-abortion choice advocate must eventually come to terms with the science and instead attack the first premise. The ways in which he does this are always predictable. In fact, as Stephen Schwarz has pointed out, there are only four ways this is done, which fit neatly into a SLED acronym:

> **Size**: It is permissible to kill the unborn human because it is smaller than the born human.
>
> **Level of Development**: It is permissible to kill the unborn human because it is less developed than the born human.
>
> **Environment**: It is permissible to kill the unborn human because it is located inside the womb, whereas the born human is not.
>
> **Degree of Dependency**: It is permissible to kill the unborn human because it is more dependent on others for survival than the born human.

This is particularly problematic for the pro-choicer who considers himself to be a champion of equality—especially in regard to the "S," "L," and "D" portions of the acronym. If he relies on any of these three criteria, he is asserting that either a) smaller humans are of less value than larger ones, b) less developed humans are of less value than more developed ones, or c) more dependent humans are of less value than less dependent ones.

But even the "E" portion of the acronym poses a problem for the self-professed champion of equality. If the location of the fetus in the womb is problematic, then it must be on the basis of a principle of bodily autonomy. But surely you cannot dismember a human body, which is precisely what abortion does, on a theory of bodily autonomy, can you? Not unless the body that is dismembered is somehow less valuable than the one whose autonomy is preserved.

Thus, no matter which part of the acronym they use, those who attack the first premise of the pro-life syllogism can be safely tucked away into the other category of pro-choice advocate, which is:

THE EQUALITY OPPONENT

My pro-life readers should remember this dichotomy and use it to their advantage the next time they get into a debate with a defender of abortion. Never concede the moral high ground. Just cut to the chase and ask the pro-choicer which one he is: a) a denier of science or b) an opponent of human equality.

There simply is no third option.

For more about the Parker debate, please see Aborting Free Speech (2023). *For more about the question of life at conception, please see Chapter 68, "Dead Things Don't Grow," detailing his debate with Nadine Strossen.*

Chapter 99

The Third Stage of Academic Lunacy

March 8, 2020

After twenty-seven years as a college professor, it finally happened. I was finally compelled to gather my books, computer, and iPhone and walk out of a faculty meeting. I simply could no longer stand being in the presence of academics who have completely lost their minds. I am not writing this brief account of the episode to criticize anyone personally. Instead, I am doing it to illustrate that higher education has now entered a dangerous final stage of decline. We are no longer dealing with lunatics in higher education that demand to be ignored. We are now dealing with lunatics that demand conformity to their lunacy. This requires some elaboration and context.

Recently, a faculty committee in charge of handbook revisions had the simple task of changing the requirements for an administrative position at UNC-Wilmington (UNCW) where I teach. Referring to the applicant in the singular, the handbook stated that "she or he" needed to have certain requirements to be eligible for this position. The committee decided to update the requirements at the behest of another administrator.

The committee's task would have been simple but for the fact that the chair of the handbook revision committee is a women's studies professor. To make matters worse, she has been the subject of informal free-speech-related complaints by students at the university. The complaints have alleged that she penalizes students for making the objectively correct claim that there are two genders, male and female. This is no surprise given that the professor also claims that there is no such thing as absolute truth.

Thus, it should come as no surprise that the radical feminist professor used her position as chair of the handbook revision committee to make unnecessary changes to reject the reality of the gender binary. Specifically, she used the position to remove references to "she or he" and replace those references with "they." She claimed she was doing it because "she or he" was "awkward." Examining the history of the evolution of pronoun use puts the lie to her claim.

Recall that feminists are the ones who first demanded that we stop using "he" and instead use "he or she" to be more "inclusive." Next, they complained that it was sexist to put the "he" before the "she." Henceforth, we started using "she or he" (or sometimes "s/he") to keep the feminists happy. But feminism is incompatible with happiness. So the demands just kept coming. Predictably, they have now taken us across the line from the merely awkward to the objectively incorrect.

The problem I noted in the meeting is that the radical feminist committee chair had placed "they" in sentences specifically referring to singular individuals. Indeed, her grammatical errors were projected on a screen in that meeting for everyone to see. After they were displayed, I turned to the professor sitting next to me and calmly pointed that out. My specific words were as follows: "But 'they' is not grammatically correct."

In other words, I stated the obvious: "they" cannot refer to one person.

The committee chair overheard me saying it, as it was a small meeting room with fewer than two dozen professors. Her defensiveness was predictable. Mustering as much condescension as humanly possible, she smugly stated, "It's okay, Mike. We can explain it to you after the meeting."

The feminist's demeaning condescension was meant to suggest that I am somehow intellectually challenged because I place the rules of grammar above political correctness. I simply refuse to use a plural pronoun to refer to a single individual in an effort to reject the so-called gender binary, which feminists now see as oppression of the gender fluid.

That whole episode might seem like a mundane academic spat, but it is not. It was a watershed moment where I realized that our university has now passed into what I will call the third stage of academic lunacy. We did not get here overnight. We had to pass through two stages first. Here is an overview of what has happened thus far:

1. **Becoming Detached from Reality**. In recent decades, our academics have increasingly embraced postmodernism. It is a worldview that denies that there really is such a thing as objective truth. They say that what we call "truth" is subjective and socially constructed. Obviously, this worldview makes it possible to believe anything, including that men can decide to become women and vice versa.

2. **Demanding Exemption from Consequences**. Academics who wish to deny objective reality (and instead advance obvious untruths) must shield themselves from accountability. Tenure does a lot to isolate them from the prospect

of being challenged. But the postmodernists must also take steps to ensure that like-minded colleagues surround them. That is why they always seem to make their way into important positions such as chairs of hiring committees and university policy committees. This is how the detachment from reality spreads and causes objectively false ideas to become widespread.

3. **Ridiculing Reality.** Once they have achieved critical mass, academics can suppress dissent from their objectively wrong assertions. (Note: Their assertions are not "arguments" because arguments require evidence.) Suppressing dissent involves ridiculing dissenters in public as was done to me in the recent meeting. And it does not have to be done often. The few sane people still left in academia quickly learn that if they are not detached from reality, they should keep their sanity to themselves.

The politicization of language matters in higher education because words matter. When professors stop using them correctly, their credibility is decimated. Moreover, when professors abandon the notion of objective truth altogether, they relinquish the moral authority to downgrade their students on any basis. There can never be any right or wrong answers.

Of course, my references to moral authority assume that morality is an objective reality and not merely a social construction. That is the real basis for the hostility directed toward me. It is also the reason I refuse to tolerate ridicule from objectively inferior minds.

Chapter 100

White Man Can't Breathe

June 2, 2020

Cary Aspinwall is an investigative reporter for *The Dallas Morning News*. She deserves a Pulitzer Prize for an article she wrote last summer that apparently no one in America has read, which is why I am summarizing it here today. It was about a man named Tony Timpa who cried for help more than thirty times as Dallas police officers pinned his neck to the ground. Before he died, Timpa shouted repeatedly, "You're gonna kill me!"

And kill him the police officers did. After Timpa became unconscious, the officers who had him cuffed assumed he was asleep. As the minutes passed, the officers joked about waking him up for school and making him waffles for breakfast.

Body camera footage shows first responders waited at least four minutes after Timpa became unresponsive to begin CPR. Even worse, the police officers pinned his handcuffed arms behind his back for nearly fourteen minutes and zip-tied his legs together. Shortly after he was loaded onto a gurney and put into an ambulance, Timpa was pronounced dead.

This culminated an incident that began when Timpa called 911 from the parking lot of a Dallas porn store. He told a dispatcher he suffered from schizophrenia and depression and was off his prescription medication. Later, police incident reports falsely claimed Timpa's behavior that night was aggressive. In stark contradiction, the police video shows Timpa struggling to breathe and asking the officers to stop pinning him down.

In another contradiction contained in a portion of a custodial death report submitted to the state of Texas in 2016, the department answered "no" to questions about whether Timpa resisted arrest or otherwise behaved aggressively. Indeed, a private security guard had already handcuffed him before police arrived.

Shockingly, footage from the police video shows officers mocking Timpa as he struggled to live. Shortly after one officer ridiculed Timpa's cries for help, an officer observed that he appeared to be "out cold." Nonetheless, they joked that he was merely asleep and tried to wake him, saying, "It's time for school. Wake up!" One officer mockingly said, "I don't want to go to school! Five more minutes, Mom!"

One of the medical responders to the scene falsely claimed, "I was unable to assess the patient due to his combativeness." However, police video footage shows that the responders attempted to take Timpa's blood pressure while he was still conscious, about five minutes before administering a powerful sedative.

Timpa died within twenty minutes of police arriving at the scene. An autopsy ruled Timpa's cause of death sudden cardiac death due to "the toxic effects of cocaine and **the stress associated with physical restraint**." Nonetheless, a criminal case against the police officers that were present never made it to trial.

The three officers—Kevin Mansell, Danny Vasquez, and Dustin Dillard—were indicted by a grand jury in 2017 on charges of misdemeanor deadly conduct. After two days of testimony, the grand jury's indictment stated that the "officers engaged in reckless conduct that placed Timpa in imminent danger of serious bodily injury." However, in March, Dallas County District Attorney John Creuzot dismissed the charges.

The Dallas Police Department's internal affairs investigation resulted in Dillard, Mansell, and Vasquez being disciplined for "conduct discrediting" the department. However, those allegations were later dropped. Vasquez and another officer present at Timpa's death also received written reprimands for "discourtesy" and "unprofessionalism."

Mansell and Vasquez were placed on administrative leave in December 2017. Dillard was also placed on leave in March 2018. But the officers returned to active duty in April after Creuzot dropped the criminal case against them.

The police video shows that Dillard pinned Timpa to the ground with his knee in his back for more than thirteen minutes. When the officers first arrived at the scene, they told Timpa he would be okay. "We're going to get you some help, man," one of the officers told him. But within fifteen minutes, Dillard can be heard saying: "I hope I didn't kill him." Finally, Dillard turned to someone before shutting off his camera and said, "Sorry. We tried."

This is how three police officers presided over the death of Tony Timpa. There were no George Soros funded protests. There were no Antifa riots. He was only thirty-two. And he was only white.

Nonetheless, it is time to reopen this case in the court of public opinion, if not a court of law. Only then will we learn whether current outrage over the death of George Floyd is based upon righteous indignation or political opportunism.

This was Mike's last published column. At the same time, he was working on the manuscript for Aborting Free Speech *(which I published posthumously), but he stopped on July 4.*

Mike loved to write but told me that his increasing depression was making it harder to engage in this endeavor that had always brought him meaning and fulfillment. It was a vicious circle, and he spiraled downward, unbeknownst to me. On July 23, I received the unexpected and unbelievable call that he was gone.

BONUS CHAPTER

The Last Communion

June 6, 2020 (but unpublished)

The year 2018 is one that I will always remember as a year of suffering. For me, it didn't start off that way. But a serious shoulder injury I sustained in April would be a foretelling of how things would be for the rest of the year. I was determined to deal with the pain without resorting to the opioids my doctors had given me when I originally injured the shoulder back in 2006. So I simply headed off to Colorado in May for a few months of rest. But rest never came. In fact, I would not be able to sleep through the night for the next three months. When I finally returned to North Carolina in August, I started physical therapy on my injured shoulder. By September, I was finally able to sleep through the night. But then disaster struck again.

Hurricane Florence did not seem like it would do much damage. But I headed to Charlotte to spend a few days with my friend Frank Turek just to be safe (as if hanging out with the Tureks is ever really "safe"). When I got home, more than just a simple power outage greeted me. I also came home to a flooded garage, crushed fences, and several downed trees. That included a couple of trees that had found their way onto my partially damaged roof.

The next day, I took out an axe and a saw and got to work. Together with a friend wielding a chainsaw, we started to get the trees off the roof and safely to the edge of the lawn for the county workers to haul away. I did not realize that several of the trees had been covered in poison ivy when I began the process of hauling hundreds of branches and pieces of tree trunk.

Over the next few nights, I sat in my house with no power and no running water and covered with weeping lesions. By early October, the weeping lesions would go away, the power would be restored, and the piles of wood in front of the house would gradually subside. But then disaster struck again.

My mother was eighty-two and had been suffering from Parkinson's for several years. So when she wanted to get surgery on her eyes, we tried to talk her out of it. Our failure to do so nearly proved fatal. During the routine surgery, she was not given enough oxygen. She came out of it with symptoms resembling dementia. Thus, a downward spiral in her overall health was set into motion. Just two days before Thanksgiving, she was brought back from the brink of death when her heart rate plummeted during a routine visit for a sore on her ankle.

Several family members went down to Gulfport to see her for what we knew would be her final Thanksgiving. At the end of my sixth bedside visit in three days, I told my mother I had to leave and that I was afraid I would never see her again. We had a good heart-to-heart talk. But when I got up to leave, she stopped me. Although she barely had enough energy to lift her arms, she did so for emphasis as she told me, "God is in control. And one more thing, Mike. God is good. And you remember that. All the time." At the time, I thought they would be her final words to me.

Between Thanksgiving and Christmas, we had to deal with an assisted living home that did not want to readmit my mother after she was discharged from the hospital. To compound things, the insurance people were giving us problems. Even the people at the bank were uncooperative when we tried to move some of mother's money in anticipation of a market downturn. It seemed as if dark spiritual forces were aligned against every move we tried to make.

Through it all, we were not sure how much any of it mattered, as we doubted that Mom would live to see Christmas. But as Christmas approached, she was still hanging on, and we prepared for another visit. She asked only that we buy her a large-print Bible and take her to Christmas Eve services at the Bridge church in D'Iberville, Mississippi, which was established only recently in a church plant led by my aunt.

Somehow, through all of the stress of dealing with finances and medical arrangements, we managed to have a communication breakdown over who would pick my mother up from the nursing home and take her to church on Christmas Eve. My brother and I both arrived at the service fifteen minutes early and asked each other where Mother was. We were horrified when we realized that on top of all of the other mishaps, we might have just caused our dying mother to miss what would undoubtedly be her final church service. In a mad rush, we sped across town to pick up my mother. When we arrived at the nursing home, we slipped on her shoes and put her and her wheelchair in my brother's rental car, hoping to get her there in time—all the while cursing ourselves internally for our lapse of judgment.

But get there, we did. When I opened the door at the back of the sanctuary and wheeled my mother in, the pastor was preaching a sermon that seemed as if it had been written for my mother. Before we took communion and then lit our candles and sang, the pastor spoke eloquently of the symbolism of communion and its relationship to the candle ceremony. As I stood on one side of my mother, holding her hand, my aunt sat on the other side of her and held my mother's hand tightly as she listened intently to the Gospel message. At that moment, I realized that nothing in the world mattered except for that powerful message delivered by a pastor and family friend who had faithfully visited my mother at the hospital over these last difficult weeks.

When the sermon was finished, I waited patiently for the line to subside so I could push my mother to the front of the sanctuary to participate in her final communion. But when the last member of the congregation had taken communion, something unexpected happened. My aunt and my uncle (Mom's youngest brother) had been giving communion to others. They came walking to the back of the sanctuary, knelt down in front of her wheelchair, and extended the bread and the cup. Each spoke to her softly in turn, saying, "The body of Christ given for you … the blood of Christ shed for your sins."

After communion was taken, we passed the candles around and lit them. I placed one in my mother's hand and clasped my hand tightly around hers and held it out so she could see the light. As we sang the closing song, I thought I heard my mother speaking to me. When I leaned over, I realized that she was just singing along. The words I heard her singing were, "Joy to the World."

The year 2018 will always be remembered as a year of suffering. But it will also serve as a reminder that human suffering is not meaningless. It is the mechanism through which we learn to comprehend the beauty of faith and human perseverance.

My mother passed away on January 31st of 2019.

I honestly don't know how this happened, but as the firstborn son, I accept full responsibility for the "communication breakdown."

This article was written after his last published article, and I did not know about it until I found it on his laptop. I am sure he would have eventually published this, but he was already starting to disconnect and shut down. It is heartbreaking because this shows that he still had so many stories to tell.

Afterword

As my meticulous editor, Lauren Green, and I were putting the final touches on this book, I went to bed one night thinking, This is really Mike's book. I hope I am not missing something important that Mike would want in his book. I wish I could just ask him. Like, can you come back for just a minute, just long enough to set me straight? I know that's not the way it works. But the Bible does tell us to ask, right? "You have not because you ask not." So, I'm asking. *That was my prayer before I drifted off to sleep.*

I then had one of those rare dreams that was just too much to be a typical random dream. It went like this…

I was lost in an unfamiliar city. I believe it was Los Angeles… "the angels"… "The City of Angels."

I was surrounded by people, but I was alone (like the song "Sea of Faces"). My car was broken down, and it had been broken into, and the spare tire was broken. In fact, everything was broken. As hard as I tried, I couldn't fix it. Undoubtably, the car was a metaphor for my life in the dream.

I was in despair, and I felt defeated, and I gave up. But then, God's warm, loving, inaudible voice told me something like, "I don't care how broken you are. You would be missed." It was just this indescribable feeling. So I got back into the car, and somehow, I just drove away. I had no idea where I was going or how or why, but I just kept going. And then I woke up, feeling very emotional, missing Mike intensely.

I think he was saying that he doesn't care about all the details and all the data that I am missing. He wants you to know that even if you are broken, you are still worthy. That was his message.

And I think there are a couple of ways to interpret that message. Narrowly interpreted, it is an anti-suicide message. If you are contemplating suicide, don't do it! You will be missed, even if you don't currently believe that you would.

But there is a broader interpretation. God wants you in his kingdom for eternity despite your broken state. If you decline his invitation, you will be missed.

Mike was broken and gave up on life, but he was saved, so God did not give up on him. Now, he has eternal life. That intense dream was Mike's and/or God's way of reaching down and telling me that—and reminding me of what is really important.

Later that day, I came across this. On November 23, 2013, Mike wrote:

It is always better to stop pretending that we are okay when we are not. When we stop worshipping our self-image, we make it easier for another broken person to admit he isn't okay. And then the Holy Spirit moves in and does the things we never thought possible. I'm not okay. I'm broken just like you.

Acknowledgments

I am grateful for Jonathan Garthwaite at Townhall for publishing Mike's articles over the years and for granting permission to reprint them.

I would also like to thank all of Mike's fans and followers who encouraged him over the years and who now encourage me.

Thanks to Mike's fiancée, Marquietta, who assisted greatly in the selection of the columns for this book.

I wish to acknowledge my uncles, Jim Rester and John Rester, for their kindness and support.

Finally, thank you, Mike, for these great articles. As I write this, I am struck by the enormity of my loss because I know you would have written many more had you lived to an old age. But I thank God that you did live long enough to tell us about life and show us how to live it.

Index

A

Abigail 246
Aborting Free Speech 1, 175, 181, 199, 429
abortion 1, 7, 73, 104, 112, 175, 177, 178, 180, 181, 182, 183, 184, 217, 224, 225, 226, 262, 266, 267, 268, 269, 296, 297, 299, 307, 340, 346, 347, 348, 397, 400, 417, 420, 421
Abortion 418
ACLU 257, 296, 366, 368
Adams, Joe (father) 53, 89, 261, 336, 354, 355, 356, 357, 405, 406, 408, 413
Adams, Joe Sr (grandfather) 159
Adams, Marilyn Rester (mother) 28, 51, 53, 75, 81, 178, 262, 335, 336, 356, 357, 405, 431, 432, 434
affirmative action 70, 71, 72, 73
agnostic 59, 60, 97, 99, 176, 297, 301
Alliance Defending Freedom (ADF) 237, 255, 258
Anthony, Casey 200
Appalachian State University (ASU) 171
Aronson, Elliot 99
Aspinwall, Cary 426
assimilation 396
atheism 21, 25, 27, 97, 100, 116, 120, 122, 123
Ayers, Bill 112, 114, 206, 207

B

Baltimore 270, 273, 316
Bannister, Roger 72
Beaty, Jim 164, 187
Beckwith, Francis 184, 297, 299
Bill of Rights 252, 361
Birmingham 112, 113, 159, 160
Black Lives Matter (BLM) 310, 311, 312, 313, 316, 322, 328, 329, 331, 332, 333, 334, 362
bodily autonomy 183, 348, 421
Brennan, Stephanie 242
Bridge Church 432
Brown, Michael 234, 317, 327
Buck Naked 366, 367, 388
Bully III 163, 164, 188
Burke, John 302, 303
Bush, George W. 72

C

Calvary Chapel 397
capable guardians 377, 378, 379
capitalism 29, 31, 130, 167, 169, 189, 396
Carswell, Anne Ford 188, 189
cats 60, 384
censorship 7, 14, 48, 50, 334, 376

Chambers, Lisa 98, 178, 180, 181, 262
Chi Omega 188
Christianity 26, 97, 99, 100, 116, 117
Christmas 60, 90, 354, 405
Clear Lake Baptist Church 57, 178
Clear Lake City 60, 89, 405, 406
Clear Lake High School 87, 261
Clemson University 97
Clinton impeachment 93
COEXIST 243
cognitive dissonance 99, 100, 177, 191
Cohen, Lawrence 377
compelled affirmation 321
Cooke, Bill 164
Cook, Kimberly 242, 243, 246, 248, 249, 250, 251, 252
Costanza 366, 367
Coulter, Ann 27, 114, 124
Crime and Everyday Life 378
CSU-Bakersfield 331
cultural appropriation 393, 394, 395
Cummings, Jeff 164, 187

D

Daily Wire 7, 383, 385
Dallas 426, 427, 428
Davidson College 197
Dean, Dizzy 288
Defoe, Daniel 34
DePaolo, Rosemary 37, 40, 62, 63, 103
DePaul University 311
Dershowitz, Alan 93
Diagnostic and Statistical Manual (DSM) 382
D'Iberville, Mississippi 432
dolphins 101
Dostoevsky, Fyodor 33
Douglas, Justice William O. 360
Dr. Seuss 108
D'Souza, Dinesh 262
due process 192

Duke, Gwen 58
Duke, Jim 57, 61
Duke, Jimmy 57, 59, 60
Duke, Sandy 57, 58
Duke University 209
Dumas, Alexandre 33

E

Ecuador 35, 116, 120, 123, 188, 416
Eighth Amendment 413
encouragement 295
Ensor, John 202
ESPN 270
ethnocentrism 191
eugenics 235, 338

F

Fables of the Reconstruction 53
Fair Tax 76
fascism 319
Faulkner, Gary 84, 167, 358, 360, 361
Felson, Marcus 378
feminist 5, 46, 102, 103, 104, 105, 209, 210, 211, 228, 230, 231, 283, 342, 343, 364, 389, 390, 423, 424
feminists 392
Feminists Say the Darndest Things 2, 12, 94, 105
Ferguson 233, 315, 326, 327
fifth commandment 408
First Amendment 8, 13, 15, 195, 196, 198, 199, 221, 237, 238, 240, 241, 293, 310, 311, 358, 361, 375, 401
Floyd, George 429
Fogelberg, Dan 159
Foley, Red 160
Foundation for Individual Rights in Education (FIRE) 194, 290
Fourth Circuit 238, 240, 241, 242, 293
Freud, Sigmund 97

G

Garthwaite, Jonathan 437
Geisler, Norm 36
Gender Identity Disorder (GID) 382, 386
Gibson Guitars 159, 160, 161, 162
Gibson, Mel 107, 118
God's Not Dead 255
gratitude 52, 223
Green, Lauren 435
Greenville, Mississippi 160
GTO 88
Gulfport 51, 287, 431
Gunderson, Joey 87

H

Haggard, Merle 331
Hamilton, Martha 98
Harvard 195, 196, 197
Hattiesburg 287, 288
heckler's veto 361
Hinson, Sam 87
Holocaust Museum 121
Holt, Wythe 13, 15, 16
Horowitz, David 83
hostile work environment 18
Houston 52, 88, 143, 178, 405
Howard, Malcolm 237, 242, 253, 256
Huntsville, Alabama 13, 14
Huntsville, Texas 412

I

ignorance of the law 218
illegitimacy 333
Illiberal Education 262
Imagine Heaven 300, 301 302, 303, 304
immigrants 343

J

Jameson, John 205
J.C. Garcia's 187
Johnson, Paul 170

K

Katy, Texas 405
Kent State University 113, 114, 205, 207
Klusendorf, Scott 35, 202, 219, 223, 226, 264, 299, 399, 418
Koukl, Greg 35
Kutless 119

L

LaHaye, Tim 78
Lassalle, Ferdinand 168
Laurie, Greg 306
Led Zeppelin 163
Letters to a Young Progressive 1, 181, 377, 383
Lewis, C.S. 20, 26, 35
LGBT 320
liberal 155
liberalism 190
liberals 190
Life and How to Live It 1, 5, 50, 53, 61, 69, 70, 87, 92, 95, 120, 163, 175, 186, 212, 262, 287, 354, 405, 409, 412
life begins 218, 219, 296, 297, 419
Life Line 6, 347, 348
Life Training Institute (LTI) 264
Los Angeles 435
Los Angeles Times 380
Lukianoff, Greg 194, 195, 198

M

Manitou Springs, Colorado 31, 221
Martins, Joe 237, 239, 241
Marxism 168, 191
Marxist 167, 240, 273, 344, 361, 365, 389, 390, 415
Marx, Karl 167, 168, 169, 170
Maxson, Scott 61
McDowell, Josh 32, 59, 222, 300
McMillen, David 99, 260
Mere Christianity 26, 35, 416
Middlebury College 359
Mill, John Stuart 376
Mississippi 287, 289
Mississippi State University 26, 75, 88, 89, 164, 290
Moody, Raymond 301
moral turpitude 18, 19
Moreland, J.P. 36, 303
motivated offender 377, 378
Mr. Rogers 309
multicultural 323, 324, 325, 396
Muslim ban 343
Myers, Jeff 223
Myers, Julia Lee 53
Myers, Wiley Trellis "Bud" 287

N

Nathanson, Dr. Bernard 6, 178
National Association of Scholars 108
near death experiences (NDEs) 301, 302, 304
New Orleans 51
New Testament 59, 78, 80, 81, 309
Niemeyer, Paul 241

O

Obama, Barack 135, 146, 160, 206
Odom, David Lee 163, 165, 188

Olmedo, Mike 87
Oregon State University (OSU) 296
O'Reilly, Bill 74
Owens, Buck 331
Oxford, Mississippi 25

P

Parker, Dr. Willie 181, 299, 418
Penry, Johnny Paul 412, 414, 415
Penry v. Lynaugh 413
Phi Mu 89
Piggly Wiggly 28
Pikes Peak 223
Pino, Julio 106, 113, 205, 206, 207
Planned Parenthood 6, 75, 298
police shootings 323, 324
Pontiac Catalina 28
Prager, Dennis 395
pregnancy center 6, 47, 178, 267, 346, 347
Price, Jammie 171, 172, 173, 174
Providence 178, 237, 238, 239
Purdue 311

R

racism 14, 47, 62, 63, 64, 124, 171, 363
Rand, Ayn 29, 31
rapture 79
refugees 343
rehabilitation 192
R.E.M. 53
Rendon, Del 163, 164, 165, 166
resentment 219, 259
Rester, Jim 437
Rester, John 437
Rester, Nell Myers 50, 51, 52, 53, 263
Rester, Virginia 264
Revelation 79, 81
Rhode Island 239

Rice, Condoleezza 46
Richmond 240
Roe v. Wade 112, 182, 183, 201, 296, 297, 348
routine activity theory 378
Royster, Peter 87
Rump, Ronald 339
Rupp, Jeffrey 164, 187
Ruscoe, Shannon 163, 186, 187, 188, 189

S

Santa Fe High School 377
Schlott, Rikki 198
Second Amendment 361
Seinfeld 368
self-reliance 357
Sermon on the Mount 75
Sexual McCarthyism 93
Sigma Chi 75, 89, 187, 290
Silent Scream 6, 178, 179
Skinner, B.F. 98, 190
slavery 184, 268, 352
SLED 420
socialism 396
socialist 28, 29, 188, 345, 357, 409
social justice warriors 332, 343, 353
sociologist 248
sociology 23, 70, 82, 83, 167, 172, 192, 270
Solzhenitsyn, Aleksandr I. 31
Sowell, Thomas 32
speech codes 196
Starkville 163, 164, 166, 187, 188, 373, 374, 375, 376
stereotyping 285
St. Louis 236
St. Louis Cardinals 288
stripper 55, 56
Strossen, Nadine 296, 297, 298
suicide 100, 205, 308

suitable target 377, 378
Summit Ministries 7, 31, 137, 139, 216, 222, 223, 289, 290, 294, 371
Supreme Court 73, 109, 238, 366, 413
Swift, Jonathan 113
Switchfoot 122
syllogism 417, 421

T

tear gas 42
tenure 17, 18, 19, 20, 22, 23, 92, 365, 424
Texas A&M 197
The Canceling of the American Mind 198
theocracy 320, 321
The Vision of the Anointed 32
The Woodlands 335, 354, 405, 406
Timpa, Tony 426, 427, 428
Tolstoy, Leo 32
topless bars 54
Townhall 7, 204, 437
transgendered students 386
tribalism 396
Turek, Frank 36, 59, 223, 260, 287, 289, 430

U

UC-Berkeley 359
UMASS-Amherst 233
UNC by the Sea 358
UNC-Chapel Hill 209, 210
UNC-Greensboro 210
UNC School of Law 93
UNC-Wilmington (UNCW) 5, 7, 8, 9, 10, 11, 37, 38, 39, 41, 43, 44, 46, 71, 83, 103, 112, 153, 154, 171, 172, 210, 211, 216, 221, 228, 229,

230, 231, 237, 240, 242, 243, 326, 328, 364, 401, 403, 404, 411, 418, 422
United Way 75
University of Alabama 13, 14
University of Georgia School of Law 93
University of Iowa 197
University of Minnesota- Morris (UMM) 66
University of Missouri (Mizzou) 311

Weather Underground 205, 206, 207
Welcome to the Ivory Tower of Babel 2, 5, 11, 12, 204
Western Carolina University 209
white privilege 350
Wilmington 63, 80, 94, 347
Wilson, Harry 186
Women's Resource Center 5, 6, 46, 212, 228, 230
women's studies 423
Wrightsville Beach 244

V

Vietnam 246
viewpoint discrimination 241
voices of condemnation 246

W

Wallace, J. Warner "Jim" 287
Watts, Jay 299

Y

Yoakam, Dwight 331

Z

Ziko, Tom 240, 241, 242
Zobel, Steve 87

www.ingramcontent.com/pod-product-compliance
Lightning Source LLC
LaVergne TN
LVHW041737060526
838201LV00046B/844